GLOBAL PRODUCTION

CW00765975

Global Production Networks

Theorizing Economic Development in an Interconnected World

NEIL M. COE

and

HENRY WAI-CHUNG YEUNG

OXFORD
UNIVERSITY PRESS

OXFORD

UNIVERSITY PRESS

Great Clarendon Street, Oxford, OX2 6DP,
United Kingdom

Oxford University Press is a department of the University of Oxford.
It furthers the University's objective of excellence in research, scholarship,
and education by publishing worldwide. Oxford is a registered trade mark of
Oxford University Press in the UK and in certain other countries

Published in the United States of America by Oxford University Press
198 Madison Avenue, New York, NY 10016, United States of America

British Library Cataloguing in Publication Data
Data available

Library of Congress Control Number: 2014954693

ISBN 978-0-19-870390-7 (Hbk.)
ISBN 978-0-19-870391-4 (Pbk.)

Printed and bound by
CPI Group (UK) Ltd, Croydon, CR0 4YY

Links to third party websites are provided by Oxford in good faith and
for information only. Oxford disclaims any responsibility for the materials
contained in any third party website referenced in this work.

To Peter Dicken—for showing us the way forward.

Preface and Acknowledgements

In this book, we seek to consolidate and develop further a global production network (GPN) perspective for understanding the contemporary global economy and its developmental implications. It is the outcome of a fifteen-year collaborative research journey that both starts and ends in Singapore. In Chapter 1 we chart the intellectual and real-world trends underpinning this journey. Here, by contrast, we want to recap briefly the personal trajectories that have interwoven to create and drive our collective GPN research agenda.

Looking back, the initial catalyst for GPN research can be found in the visit of Peter Dicken (University of Manchester) to the Department of Geography at the National University of Singapore in the second half of 2007. There he was reunited with his former Ph.D. student (Henry Yeung) and was part of a research team—also including Phil Kelly, Lily Kong, and Kris Olds—who were grappling with how best to theorize the vortices of globalization that were already swirling around East and South-East Asia (and were manifest in the ongoing 'Asian' financial crisis at that time). The coalescence of different perspectives proved highly fertile, in particular with regards to tentatively developing a network ontology of the global economy. The tangible result was a collaborative paper in *Global Networks* (Dicken et al. 2001) in which elements of the then highly popular Actor Network Theory were selectively combined with more structural readings to produce a networked and relational understanding of economic globalization. The notion of 'global production networks', as we know it today, was itself born around this time through these intense discussions. Shortly after Peter returned to his base in Manchester, the second of us (Neil Coe) joined the National University of Singapore as a lecturer in 1998, adding an interest in service sector globalization to the ongoing discussions.

GPN research was given 'formal' status with the award of a large Economic and Social Research Council (ESRC) grant to Peter Dicken and Jeff Henderson at the University of Manchester in 2000. With funding to the tune of £330,000, the three-year project, entitled 'Making the Connections: Global Production Networks in Europe and East Asia', enabled both sustained theoretical work and detailed empirical research into three sectors—automobile components, electronics, and retailing—across multiple countries in Western Europe, Central and Eastern Europe, and East Asia. Some 160 interviews were conducted over the course of the project, along with extensive secondary data collection, producing a large real-world dataset with which to test the theoretical foundations of the emergent GPN conceptual framework. Those foundations were literally mapped out on overhead projector transparencies in one of the rooms in the University of Manchester's Mansfield Cooper Building in January 2001, and in 2002 were published in the *Review of International Political Economy* (Henderson et al. 2002). The paper introduced the distinctiveness of the GPN perspective, and contrasted it to prevailing theories at that time, and in particular the global commodity chain (GCC) that was starting to become a significant export from economic sociology.

As importantly as the research itself, the 'Making the Connections' project allowed the formation of a project team that included Peter, Jeff, Henry (as overseas collaborator), Martin Hess, Jennifer Johns, and Neil, who joined the University of Manchester as a geography lecturer in mid-2000, forging and deepening research connections that continue to the present day. In due course, the group attracted the moniker of the 'Manchester School' from one observer (Bathelt 2006). In addition to a series of empirical papers from the project, a second theoretical paper emerged from the ensuing theoretical discussions, resulting in the 2004 *Transactions of the Institute of British Geographers* contribution on strategic coupling and regional development (Coe et al. 2004). The article sought to bridge, analytically, work on global production and the vast literature on new regionalism and clusters, which was dominating debates in economic geography, urban and regional studies, and development studies at that time. Since the project finished, members of the research team have continued to work together, in different combinations and with new collaborators, to deepen and broaden the GPN research agenda, resulting in a number of state-of-the-art reviews and journal special issues (e.g. Hess and Yeung 2006a; Coe et al. 2008a; Yeung 2009a; Coe and Hess 2013; Neilson et al. 2014).

What has been missing up until this point, however, is a book-length treatment and further development of this GPN approach. A monograph was planned as part of the original ESRC project, but for various reasons did not come to fruition. Fortuitously, Neil's move (back) to the National University of Singapore in July 2012 created the conditions to make it possible for this book to be co-written in situ. If ever there was an example of how 'proximity matters', working together in the same department for the first time since 2000 has allowed us to develop the ideas in the book through sustained and intense interaction, including a period writing together during Henry's 2013 sabbatical leave at the School of Geosciences, University of Sydney, Australia. This book looks to consolidate earlier ideas distributed across different journal articles and, more importantly, to engage in a new and ambitious round of theoretical development (GPN 2.0) that seeks to extend significantly the explanatory power of the original heuristic framework (GPN 1.0). In sum, our central aim, after some fifteen years of collaborative GPN research, is to try and initiate a step change in conceptual development that can underpin new rounds of empirical exploration.

The deeply collaborative nature of GPN research means we are inevitably indebted to many friends and collaborators and have many people to thank. We must start with the core members of the 'Manchester School' *c.* 2000–3— namely, Peter Dicken, Jeff Henderson, Martin Hess, and Jennifer Johns. They created an open, supportive, and fertile research environment from within which a new research agenda could emerge. Peter and Martin have continued to be constant interlocutors and co-authors over the subsequent decade, and their insights and knowledge feed into many pages of this book. We thank them for their intellectual generosity; this book could not have been written without them. Our personal debts to Peter Dicken go far beyond the bounds of GPN research, of course, and we hope that he will accept the dedication of this book as a small repayment.

More broadly, we have also benefited hugely from ongoing engagements with a broad community of scholars, both within economic geography and beyond, pursuing global value chain and global production network research of various kinds. We thank (and apologies for any omissions): Yuko Aoyama, Jennifer Bair, Stephanie Barrientos, Harald Bathelt, Gavin Bridge, Peter Buckley, Tim Bunnell, Philip Cooke, Stuart Dawley, Lisa De Propris, Dieter Ernst, James Faulconbridge, Niels Fold, Gary Gereffi, Peter Gibbon, Jim Glassman, Gary Hamilton, Markus Hassler, Jinn-Yuh Hsu, Ray Hudson, Alex Hughes, John Humphrey, Raphael Kaplinsky, Phil Kelly, Roger Lee, Yong-Sook Lee, David Levy, George Lin, Weidong Liu, Peter Lund-Thomsen, Danny MacKinnon, Matthew Mahutga, Fritz Mayer, Will Milberg, Ram Mudambi, Jim Murphy, Khalid Nadvi, Jeffrey Neilson, Kris Olds, Mario Parrilli, Jamie Peck, Nicola Phillips, John Pickles, Stefano Ponte, Jessie Poon, Bill Pritchard, Roberta Rabellotti, Al Rainnie, Andrés Rodríguez-Pose, Hubert Schmitz, Adrian Smith, Tim Sturgeon, Lotte Thomsen, Ted Tschang, Jan Vang Lauridsen, Peter Wad, Kevin Ward, Dennis Wei, Marion Werner, Dariusz Wójcik, Steve Wood, Neil Wrigley, Charlotte Yang, Daniel Yang, and Yu Zhou.

We are deeply grateful for the detailed comments on our draft typescript provided by our four readers—Peter Dicken, Martin Hess, Stefano Ponte, and John Pickles. All four were unfailingly supportive and constructively critical in their comments, which have helped us sharpen and refine our text in very significant ways. All, of course, are absolved of any blame for weaknesses or omissions in the finished product. We also thank the team at Oxford University Press, most notably David Musson and Clare Kennedy, for their unstinting and efficient support of this book from day one. The three anonymous referees for the Press were extremely kind in their comments on our initial typescript proposal. Most importantly, they and David have let us write the book we wanted to write, a freedom that we value very highly. Finally, we would also like to acknowledge that parts of Chapters 3 and 4 are based on our co-authored paper published in *Economic Geography* (91 (2015), Wiley) and parts of Chapters 5 and 6 on another paper published in *Regional Science Policy & Practice* (7 (2015), Wiley).

Closer to home, the Politics, Economies, And Space (aka 'PEAS') research group in the Department of Geography at the National University of Singapore continues to provide a supportive yet challenging testing ground for our research ideas. In particular, we thank Carl Grundy-Warr, Karen Lai, Harvey Neo, James Sidaway, Woon Chih Yuan, Godfrey Yeung, and Zhang Jun (now at the University of Toronto) for stimulating lunchtime debate over the past few years. We also thank our graduate students, past and present, who have helped to 'road test' some of the ideas presented in this book in the field: at Manchester, Costas Antonopoulos, Alexandra Dales, Ross Jones, David Jordhus-Lier, Katie May, Piotr Niewiadomski, Yue Wang, and Jennifer Watts, and, at NUS, Rachel Bok, Chen Rui, Li Na, Lim Kean Fan, Liu Yi, and Aidan Wong. Our home institution, NUS, has generously funded several projects related to our GPN pursuits (R-109-000-148-133; R-109-000-050-112; R-109-000-116-112; R-109-000-173-646; R-109-000-158-646).

As of October 2014, an exciting new phase in our research journey began with the launch of the Global Production Networks Centre at the National University of Singapore (GPN@NUS for short) that we co-direct. This three year NUS-funded initiative brings together a multidisciplinary team of ten researchers (scheduled to reach between fifteen and twenty by mid-2015) with the aim of conducting a comprehensive programme of theoretical development and empirical research on global production networks across Asia. The core team consists of Davin Chor, Kurtulus Gemici, Albert Hu, Soo Yeon Kim, Karen Lai, Jang-Sup Shin, Aidan Wong, and Godfrey Yeung. We are excited about working with them over the next three years and hopefully beyond.

We end by returning to where it all begins—our families. Our children— Laura and Adam, and Kay and Lucas—have literally grown up with GPN research. Quite rightly, however, they have not let our weird ideas bother them, and have provided limitless joy, inspiration, motivation, and distraction along the way. And to our wives, Emma and Weiyu, we can only offer another heartfelt vote of thanks for constantly reminding us, even when we might think otherwise, that three-letter acronyms for global economic transformations reflect just a tiny fraction of what real life has got to offer.

Neil Coe and Henry Yeung
Singapore
September 2014

Contents

List of Figures

List of Tables

Abbreviations

3PL	third party logistics
4PL	fourth party logistics
ANT	actor–network theory
ASEAN	Association of South-East Asian Nations
BOP	bottom of the pyramid
CME	coordinated market economy
CMT	cut, make, trim
CSR	corporate social responsibility
EMS	electronics manufacturing services
EVA	Economic Value Added
FAO	Food and Agriculture Organization of the United Nations
FDI	foreign direct investment
GCC*	global commodity chain
GIN	global innovation network
GMO	genetically modified organism
GPN*	global production network
GVC*	global value chain
HACCP	hazard analysis and critical control point
ICT	information and communications technologies
IT	information technology
IMF	International Monetary Fund
ISO	International Organization for Standardization
LME	liberal market economy
NAFTA	North American Free Trade Agreement
NIDL	New International Division of Labour
OBM	original brand manufacturing
ODM	original design manufacturing
OEM	original equipment manufacturing
QIZ	Qualifying Industrial Zone
R&D	research and development
SoC	system-on-a-chip
TNC	transnational corporation

UNCTAD	United Nations Conference on Trade and Development
VoC	varieties of capitalism
WTO	World Trade Organization

NOTE

* Readers are referred to note 2 in Chapter 1 for further explanation of how these specific acronyms are used in the book.

1

Global Production Networks 2.0

In this book we argue that organizationally fragmented and spatially dispersed production networks constitute a new form of economic structure that increasingly drives the complex global economy and its uneven developmental outcomes. A wide range of terminology and concepts has appeared since the early 1990s to try and capture this emerging phenomenon. From a trade perspective, global exports of intermediate goods now exceed exports of final and capital goods, as more and more parts and components are traded for use in subsequent international production and exports. As Gereffi (2014: 11) notes, 'governments and international organizations are taking notice of this emerging pattern of global trade, which is called a shift from "trade in goods" to "trade in value added", "trade in tasks" and "trade in capabilities"'. From a purchasing firm or 'buyer' perspective, others prefer to use the language of outsourcing to capture the procurement of intermediate inputs from abroad, through either externalized relationships (that is, offshore outsourcing) or intra-firm trade (that is, offshore insourcing from affiliates). From a commodity perspective, advocates of a global commodity chain (GCC) approach focus on the governance processes involved in producing specific services and goods throughout the global economy. In contrast to these perspectives, our approach foregrounds the key *economic actors* involved in these processes and, as such, resonates with growing academic and policy interest in global value chains (GVCs). A 2010 World Bank report on the post-2008 world economy, for instance, claims that, 'given that production processes in many industries have been fragmented and moved around on a global scale, GVCs have become the world economy's backbone and central nervous system' (Cattaneo et al. 2010a: 7). To analysts in many international organizations it seems, global value chains are now recognized as the new long-term structural feature of today's global economy.[1]

In an endeavour to reframe these debates and develop a more dynamic theory of global production, our preference in this book is to refer to the emergence and development of *global production networks* within the global economy. We define a global production network as an organizational arrangement, comprising interconnected economic and non-economic actors, coordinated by a global lead firm, and producing goods or services across multiple geographical locations for worldwide markets. As we shall explain in this chapter, this choice of terminology is not incidental, but rather reflects our commitment to an analytical approach that does justice to the multi-actor and geographically complex contemporary global economy. Our focus is clearly on the *actors* that constitute global production networks, with a lead firm being a central and necessary prerequisite, and on the *multiple locations* that are bound together by the economic relations between those actors. The idea of a global production network goes beyond simple notions of trading tasks and outsourcing to highlight the actor-specific firm coordination and cooperation strategies through which such networks are constructed, managed, and sustained. It also considers the strategic responses of the other corporate and non-corporate actors within the global production network. This central focus on actors also distinguishes global production network (GPN) thinking from those that focus on a particular commodity (for example, GCC research) or the aggregation of different value chains into industries (for example, GVC research).[2] Our central aim in this book is to show how the GPN approach we espouse can provide a powerful framework for explaining patterns of uneven development—both between and within countries—in the contemporary global economy.

In starting our account, this introductory chapter has three objectives. It will introduce the intellectual context in which the GPN framework first appeared in the early 2000s and will distil its basic attributes in relation to cognate approaches. We will also map out the structure and arguments of the book, detailing how we seek to develop an enhanced GPN theory—for which we use 'GPN 2.0' as convenient shorthand—that builds upon, and significantly extends, existing work under this banner. First, however, it is important to establish the key structural forces behind the emergence of global production networks as an organizational phenomenon within the global economy since the early 1990s.

A NEW GLOBAL ECONOMY? TOWARDS AN INTERCONNECTED WORLD OF PRODUCTION

> The goods we buy are the end result of an elaborately choreographed transnational odyssey. These objects are part of an economy whose tendrils reach over further outward, linking, integrating, and transforming both far-flung and nearby places. (Kenney 2004: 1–2)

Kenney's quotation evocatively captures the essence of today's global economy. The ever-deepening spatial and organizational fragmentation of production has produced a global economy that is profoundly different from the one of 1990. Organizational shifts have been accompanied by profound geographic shifts relating to the rise of emerging market transnational corporations (TNCs), and shifts in global patterns of demand towards the Global South, both in terms of burgeoning levels of so-called South–South trade and as a focus for firms from the Global North. These trends have arguably accelerated since the global recession that commenced in 2008, which has also prompted a 'shake out' and consolidation of global production networks in many industries. It is not our aim in this book to map exhaustively these shifting patterns within the global economy.[3] We do, however, need to explain the fundamental conditions and capitalist imperatives that have underpinned the emergence of global production networks as perhaps *the* predominant organizational feature of the world economic system. What follows is necessarily a very brief résumé of what in reality are highly complex and variegated dynamics of industrial and organizational change on a global scale.

During much of the first half of the twentieth century, industrial capitalism was largely nationally bounded in an era of mass production commonly known as Fordism.[4] While there were, of course, international production systems by this time, they tended to be dominated by relatively self-contained multi-domestic structures through which TNCs replicated their home operations abroad. By the late 1970s, the advanced economies of North America and Western Europe had begun to experience a radical transformation in their Fordist production systems towards a more flexible and spatially dispersed mode of economic organization. In their highly influential work *The Second Industrial Divide*, Piore and Sabel (1984) describe this episodic shift in the organization of global capitalism as a move towards 'flexible specialization', manifested in more flexible intra-firm relations, rapid vertical disintegration of production processes, and the emergence of extensive hybrid and non-hierarchical forms of organizing production such as subcontracting and spin-offs. Instead of the extensive intra-firm technical division of labour prevalent in the Fordist production system, a deepened social division of labour was embedded in these new flexible production systems. In *Manufacturing Possibilities*, Herrigel (2010: 186) succinctly characterizes flexible specialization as

> intense and ongoing collaboration between design and manufacture in the context of increasing fragmentation of the division of labor within and across firms. Production units have become smaller, and frequently transformed into separate legal entities. Their relations are continuously recomposed through collaboration and negotiation, rather than market signals or hierarchical directives. Relations among collaborating producers, furthermore, are often governed by an array of extra-firm practices and institutions designed to balance cooperation and competition and facilitate continuous recomposition of roles and capacities. These relations characterize practices within developed and developing contexts as well as those that bridge both milieus.

One of the main impetuses behind this structural shift in Atlantic capitalism during the 1970s was the crisis of Fordism, which related to the challenges of increasing competition at the global scale. The sources of this competitive challenge could be found in the rapid internationalization of domestic production systems and the entry of new competitors from East Asia—first Japan in the 1960s and the 1970s, followed by the four Tiger economies of South Korea, Taiwan, Singapore, and Hong Kong in the 1970s and the 1980s. The adoption of flexible production systems became a capitalist strategy to create and sustain competitive advantage. To Piore and Sabel (1984: 17), flexible specialization was 'a strategy of permanent innovation: accommodation to ceaseless change, rather than an effort to control it. This strategy is based on flexible—multi-use—equipment; skilled workers; and the creation, through politics, of an industrial community that restricts the forms of competition to those favoring innovation'.[5] From the debris of post-Fordist deindustrialization and capitalism's incessant drive for innovation emerged major lead firms, defined by their capacity to exercise product and/or market control, and their expanding global production networks in different 'propulsive' industries such as automobiles, electronics, semiconductors, and machinery.[6]

As their markets and competitors have progressively become more globalized, lead firms in different industries have become driven primarily by three capitalist dynamics: (1) cost, (2) flexibility, and (3) speed.[7] These dynamics can have major and, yet, differentiated consequences for the configuration of their global production networks and economic development in different regional and national economies. In turn, these capitalist drivers need to be 'fixed' in order for specific lead firms to thrive in the post-Fordist global economy; the ensuing reorganization of value activities has led to the emergence of global production networks. Couched in geographical, organizational, and technological terms, these fixes represent distinct but interlinked responses to the three capitalist drivers.

First, the perennial drive towards lowering costs is now an established idiom in almost any economic analysis of industrial competition. As global competition intensified and product life cycles shortened by the 1990s, lead firms became more concerned with *cost drivers*, particularly production costs. With greater maturity in manufacturing technologies, standardization and modularization of products and components, and lower profit margins, manufacturing production could now be outsourced to specialized manufacturers that enjoyed both scale and scope economies and therefore significant cost advantages. Since the 2000s, these specialized manufacturers have grown to a massive scale and become TNCs in their own right. This outsourcing possibility has also enabled lead firms to concentrate on their core competencies and strategic new business areas, and to mitigate the investment risks associated with severe fluctuations in market demand.

In the service sector, similar cost pressures exist in a wide range of producer service industries such as finance, accounting, and software. Supply of non-core services to these industries, ranging from human resources and information and communication technology services to office management and maintenance work, can now be more economically outsourced to specialized service providers in different localities. Overall, this competitive cost pressure results in a *spatial fix* through which lead firms in manufacturing and service industries seek lower-cost suppliers in international markets. National economies suffering from high costs have witnessed the unfolding of the process of deindustrialization, whereas lower-cost economies have gained investment through the emergence of a new international division of labour.[8] This process of spatial fix is best observed in the international relocation of significant proportions of European and American manufacturing activity to East Asian economies since the 1970s.[9] It also constituted a critical precondition for the early success of export-oriented industrialization in these economies during the 1970s and 1980s.

While this spatial fix can alleviate, at least temporarily, the cost problems of global lead firms, it is clearly not a long-term solution to their competitive plight. Two other firm-specific dynamic capabilities—flexibility and speed— have arguably played a much more important role than has been previously understood in the economic development literature.[10] In order to compete more effectively in the post-Fordist global economy, lead firms began to opt for what might be broadly termed an *organizational fix*. Starting in the 1990s, lead firms realized that competitive advantage could be obtained through a more flexible and efficient form of organizing production on a global scale. Reorganization of production networks does not necessarily entail geographical relocation of production, particularly the lead firm's own production facilities. Instead, an organizational fix results primarily from a choice of different business strategies; it is about strategizing around the organizational principles that afford the most competitive advantage.

The strategy of outsourcing to independent suppliers, for example, represents a popular organizational fix through which lead firms are able to increase their production flexibility without incurring the substantial financial and other liabilities associated with continuing existing, or establishing new, manufacturing or service facilities. Lead firms can sell their existing production facilities *in situ* to strategic partners from the same home economy or based elsewhere. The rise of contract manufacturing arrangements between lead firms and their strategic partners can be interpreted as an important organizational fix for these lead firms in several modularized industries such as electronics and machinery.[11] Modularization of key components also substantially lowers the cost of switching parts or production modifications. By making parts interchangeable, modularization promotes shared innovation and technological development because of the potential scale economies to be reaped by firms specializing in producing specific modules rather than the entire product. It encourages lead firms to collaborate with their strategic partners to share expertise and to develop jointly new products and services.

In advanced economies, lead firms have made major attempts to engage in what Herrigel (2010: 22) calls 'industrial recomposition' through which 'reflective and creative industrial actors perpetually recompose the social relations of manufacturing'. His study shows that lead firms in steel, automobiles, and machinery industries in German, Japan, and the United States have recomposed national and sub-national institutions and governance arrangements to respond more effectively to common competitive pressures in these global industries. Some of these recomposition arrangements do not necessarily lead to spatial relocation of production (that is, a spatial fix), but rather reintegration of different supplier–customer relations into new organizational fixes such as lean production and contingent collaboration. Through these different organizational arrangements in the post-Fordist era, production networks have become more internationally oriented and integrated, leading to the emergence of sophisticated global production networks orchestrated by global lead firms. But not all organizational fixes have led to the emergence of global production networks. *In situ* industrial recomposition tends to consolidate production networks within specific industrial districts and regional complexes—well-known examples include Baden-Württemberg (Germany), Silicon Valley (California, USA), and Toyota City (Japan)—creating divergent patterns of value activity configuration. Organizational fixes therefore produce highly differentiated geographies of manufacturing production and service provision that in turn create divergent growth possibilities and developmental trajectories for different regional and national economies—one of the core analytical issues in this book.

The search for low-cost production locations and the creation of organizational economies, however, do not capture fully the nature of capitalist dynamics in an era of globalization. These dynamics have compelled firms to search for new competitive advantages enabled by improvements in transport and communication technologies, a phenomenon described by Harvey (1989) as 'time–space compression'. This temporal acceleration in competitive pressure has substantially increased the demand for quicker *time-to-market* as a critical tool for capturing value from the early stages of the product life cycle and/or winning market share. Time-to-market thus becomes one of the most important competitive pressures that forces global lead firms to reconsider their role in different global production networks. As product life cycles become increasingly short owing to both disruptive technological change (for example, the digital revolution and nanotechnology) and market preferences for product diversity and turnover, time-to-market has emerged as a critical success factor in global competition.[12] To accelerate its time-to-market, a lead firm may engage in a spatial fix by locating its production of goods or services in close proximity to its emergent or realized markets. It may also develop an organizational fix through deeper integration of its various value creation platforms within emergent global production network to accelerate innovation, production, and delivery to market. Production costs now intersect with time-to-market in determining the success, or not, of lead firms.

Apart from organizational flexibility, the adoption of new technological solutions can significantly improve a lead firm's time-to-market capability. This approach can be termed a *technological fix* that points to the critical role of technological innovation in the competitive dynamics of lead firms and other actors in global production networks.[13] Mathews and Cho (2000: 10–11) differentiate three competitive positions based on technological innovation: product innovation, process innovation, and technology diffusion management. They argue that East Asian firms from South Korea, Taiwan, and Singapore, for example, do not necessarily focus on the first two positions— product and process innovation. These competitive positions tend to be taken up by American, European, and Japanese firms that specialize respectively in new product innovation through developing first-mover advantages, and in quality improvements and time enhancements via process technologies. Instead, these East Asian firms take up the third competitive position by leveraging on technological resources embedded in, and diffused through, inter-firm linkages in global production networks and other technological alliances and consortia. In doing so, they are able to compete effectively in high-tech industries such as semiconductors. In the electronics industry, for example, information technology solutions and global electronic platforms have contributed to the successful organization of production networks on a global scale by lead firms. Such a technological fix can be seen in the widespread deployment of digital solutions, such as electronic data interchange with customers and suppliers in both manufacturing and service sectors, internet-based integration of manufacturing processes and enterprise resource planning systems, and the global tracking systems offered by third-party logistics providers.[14]

This technological fix often feeds back into the dynamic organization of global production networks by facilitating the vertical disintegration and the subsequent *vertical specialization* of production in different manufacturing and service industries. Since the 1980s, global lead firms have found it increasingly hard to excel in every aspect of the value chain and instead have preferred to specialize flexibly in segments in which they possess the greatest core competencies. These segments usually encompass research and development (R&D), product design, manufacturing of core products, marketing, distribution, and, in some cases, post-sale services. By the early 1990s, global lead firms in different global production networks and industries had moved towards a business model of increasing specialization in value activities. This trend has been much further accelerated since the late 1990s, particularly in the electronics, automobile, clothing, retailing, and logistics sectors. This specialization entails global lead firms playing a more strategically focused role in the upstream (R&D) and downstream (marketing, distribution, and post-sale services) segments of the value system, leaving much of the manufacturing portion to their international strategic partners and dedicated supply-chain managers.

This process of vertical specialization refers to the multiple specializations of a lead firm in different stages of the same value system. It is vertical because both upstream and downstream specializations can be possible within the same lead firm. It is also different from vertical disintegration, a process not necessarily associated with multiple specializations. While they continue to shed their production activity to specialist manufacturers and strategic partners, global lead firms also accelerate their network-based innovation through engaging with a wide range of knowledge diffusion mechanisms that are increasingly linked to information management systems and the emergence of transnational knowledge communities.[15] The implication of vertical specialization for economic development is highly contingent on the strategies of lead firms and their changing organization of global production networks. As argued by Lüthje (2002: 228; emphasis omitted), 'there may emerge different trajectories of technological learning depending on the position of particular districts or regions within the international division of labor in the production networks of the respective industries'.

In short, global production networks have emerged as the pre-eminent form of integrated 'fix' to the dynamic challenges of cost, speed, and flexibility that underpin competitive success in the contemporary global economy. As an increasingly dominant organizational form, they simultaneously combine elements of the spatial, organizational, and technological fixes described above. If the initial international division of labour established by European colonial powers was primarily based on trade, and the new international division of labour that emerged in the 1960s and 1970s was mostly driven by the establishment of wholly owned subsidiaries by TNCs, the contemporary global division of labour reflects the formation of global production networks across myriad sectors and industries since the 1990s. Control and coordination within this system are enacted not primarily through direct ownership, but by lead firms using complex combinations of subcontracting, alliances, partnerships, and other forms of non-equity relationships.

THE EMERGENCE OF GPN 1.0

These rapid and profound developments within the global economy have posed significant challenges to theorization since the early 1990s. The most productive lines of enquiry within the critical social sciences during that time have shifted the analytical focus from trade between national economies to the tightly coordinated global chains or networks of firms that, as we have just seen, are the key organizational form within the contemporary global economy. In this section we chart and contextualize the emergence of one such approach—the global production networks (GPN) framework that underpins this book. We use the shorthand GPN 1.0 to denote the initial formulation, which emerged in the early-to-mid 2000s and with which we have worked since then. As we shall see in the last part of this introductory chapter, the central aim of this book is to push towards a new version—which we dub GPN 2.0—that seeks to deepen significantly its analytical and explanatory power and move towards a more dynamic theory of global production networks. First, however, it is important to understand the intellectual context from which the GPN 1.0 framework initially emerged and the contributions that it was seeking to make.

Antecedents

While global chain/network theories have roots that can be traced to the 1980s, undoubtedly a key event was the Sixteenth Annual Conference on the Political Economy of the World System, held at Duke University, USA, in April 1992.[16] The edited volume that emerged from the conference and was published in 1994—Gereffi and Korzeniewiecz's *Commodity Chains and Global Capitalism*—launched a genre of sustained research into global commodity chains (GCCs) that continues today.[17] Drawing their initial inspiration from Immanuel Wallerstein's world-system framework (1974)—in which different national economies are sorted in an interconnected order of core, semi-periphery, and periphery—Gereffi and Korzeniewicz contributed in particular the identification of global commodity chains as a new conceptual category for 'understanding the changing spatial organization of production and consumption in the contemporary world-economy' (Gereffi et al. 1994: 2). In an attempt to move beyond the then nation-state centric modes of analyzing the global economy, global commodity chains were defined as 'sets of interorganizational networks clustered around one commodity or product, linking households, enterprises, and states to one another within the world-economy. These networks are situationally specific, socially constructed, and locally integrated, underscoring the social embeddedness of economic organization'. The idea was to forge a meso mode of analysis that could probe 'above and below the level of the nation-state' and reveal the 'macro-micro links between processes that are generally assumed to be discretely contained within global, national, and local units of analysis' (Gereffi et al. 1994: 2).

Each global commodity chain is deemed to have four interrelated dimensions. First, the input–output structure identifies the various products and services that come together in a value-adding sequence to deliver a given economic activity. Second, the territoriality refers to the spatial configuration of the various actors involved, be that in terms of the spatial concentration or the dispersal of the constituent actors and economic activities. Third, each global commodity chain embodies a governance regime reflecting the relations of power and authority within the chain and how they shape the flows of materials, capital, technology, and knowledge therein. Fourth, global commodity chains are also reflective of the wider institutional frameworks that surround them, and particularly state policies and regulations in domains such as trade, investment, and technology.[18] In particular, the third dimension—governance—has provoked a rich furrow of GCC research, building on Gereffi's seminal distinction (1994) between 'producer-driven' and 'buyer-driven' commodity chains. The foundational importance of this distinction is such that we will briefly reiterate it here.

Producer-driven chains are argued to be commonly found in industries where large industrial TNCs play the central role in controlling global production structures—for instance, in capital- and technology-intensive industries such as aircraft, automobile, computer, semiconductor, pharmaceutical, and machinery manufacturing. Power in these chains is exercised through the headquarters operations of leading TNCs, and manifests itself in the ability to exert control over backward linkages to raw material and component suppliers, and forward linkages with distributors and retailers. High levels of profits are secured through the scale and volume of production in combination with the ability to drive technological developments within the production system. Buyer-driven chains, on the other hand, tend to be found in industries where large retailers and brand-name merchandisers are the key actors in establishing and controlling the global production systems of their commodities, usually located in export-oriented countries. This form of global commodity chain is common in labour-intensive consumer-goods sectors, such as clothing, footwear, and toys. Production is usually undertaken using tiered levels of subcontractors that supply finished goods subject to the pricing and product specifications of the powerful buyers. These buyers extract substantial profits from bringing together their design, sales, marketing, and financial expertise with strong brand names and access to large consumer markets in developed countries.

While an impressive body of work has been produced since the initial formulation of the GCC concept, several clear limitations became readily apparent from the late 1990s onwards. First, as already noted, despite the analytical identification of four dimensions, in reality governance structures have dominated research under the GCC banner.[19] A related concern is that the distinction between producer-driven and buyer-driven chains, while useful in highlighting the overall 'drivenness' of particular chains, can serve to obscure significant on-the-ground complexity and variation in terms of the governance arrangements that actually exist within a broader global commodity chain. Second, GCC research suffers from an underdeveloped geographical conceptualization, with the national scale still the dominant 'container' or unit of analysis for global commodity chain activities, and far less attention paid to processes of local and regional economic development within countries, and macro-regional production configurations. Third, this underdeveloped territorial component is also revealed by an inability to delimit the ways in which firm networks link together, and are constitutive of, societies with different social and institutional frameworks. Moreover, there has also been little consideration of firm ownership patterns, and of how firms of different nationalities may adopt varying organizational structures and strategies. Fourth, there are concerns that, while GCC analysis has proved effective at analyzing basic/agricultural commodities, its focus on the commodity rather than the lead actors in the system hampers its ability to explain dynamics of competition within the overlapping multi-product and multi-service worlds of contemporary capitalism. Fifth, and more profoundly, worries have been voiced about the challenge of 'aggregating up' from studies of individual global commodity chains to look at the wider developmental patterns and outcomes in the global economy. As Dussel Peters (2008: 14) has argued, 'most research on global commodity chains approaches the GCC framework as a "methodology" and not a "theory". The result of this is vast quantities of empirical work on particular chains and the experiences of particular firms and regions in them, and relatively little theoretical work attempting to account for these findings in a systematic and integrated way'.[20]

Although GCC work still continues today, some of the limitations noted above have been tackled by the evolution of the GCC approach into the global value chains (GVC) perspective from the early 2000s onwards. At the heart of this initiative—which brings together scholars from economic sociology, development studies, and industry studies—has been an attempt to deepen the theorization of *inter-firm governance*. By intersecting the three supply chain variables of complexity of transactions, the ability to codify transactions, and the capabilities within the supply base, Gereffi et al. (2005) develop a fivefold typology of governance within global value chains. In addition to the pure forms of market and hierarchy, they identify modular, relational, and captive forms of governance that rely on intermediate levels of coordination and control. While highly influential, this typology is still arguably somewhat limiting, and underplays the extent to which governance is also shaped by place-specific institutional conditions and intra- and extra-firm dynamics. However, further work has focused on the different modes and levels of governance operating within global value chains, distinguishing between overall drivenness (buyer or producer driven), different forms of coordination (the five types noted above), and the wider normalization processes that operate along the chain (mobilizing convention theory).[21]

Overall, GVC research increasingly offers welcome recognition of the complexity and dynamism of governance relations within global production systems. Two other significant developments under the rubric of GVCs relate to (1) how sub-national spaces (for example, clusters) plug in to global value chains and with what effect, and (2) how firms and localities can improve their position within global value chains over time. This latter process is commonly known as upgrading.[22] Another undoubted success of GVC research has been its increasing purchase in the policy world, with the terminology being used by a wide range of international development agencies from 2000 onwards.[23] So, while it is hard to find a commonly agreed definition of a global value chain in the key academic articles advocating the approach, UNCTAD's *World Investment Report 2013* offers the following parsimonious definition: 'GVCs are defined by *fragmented* supply chains, with internationally dispersed tasks and activities *coordinated* by a lead firm (a TNC)' (UNCTAD 2013a: 125, table IV.1; emphasis in original).

GCC research and early GVC work were clearly important inspirations for the development of GPN 1.0 in the early 2000s (see Table 1.1). Some of the impulses were similar to those that were driving the shift from GCC to GVC analyses, relating, for example, to the need for more nuanced understandings of governance dynamics and more thorough incorporation of multiple scales of analysis beyond the global and the national. Others were more fundamental, however, and related to concerns about the metaphors and geographical imaginations that underpinned such theories. Accordingly, GPN 1.0 was also influenced by two other theoretical perspectives that were starting to gain considerable traction in the social sciences by the early 2000s. First, and emerging from investigations into the sociology of scientific knowledge, was *actor–network theory* (ANT), an approach that emphasizes how entities in networks are shaped by, and can only be understood through, their relationships to other entities.[24] To be clear, GPN 1.0 does not adopt ANT wholesale. It does not, for example, confer agency upon non-human objects as ANT does, and nor does it do away with more structural notions of power beyond the network that shape the formation and operation of production networks.[25] However, through its conceptualization of social systems as complex networks of power relations with emergent properties, ANT offers important insights into the study of global production networks in theoretical and methodological terms. For instance, the notion of 'following the network' and looking for 'distributed agency' within the system as a whole are important sensibilities to bring to GPN research, as is the insight that networks operate through complex intersections of local and global relationships.

Second, additional insights were derived from work that emphasizes the particularities of what are variously called 'varieties of capitalism', 'national

Table 1.1. Theoretical antecedents to the GPN approach

	Global Commodity/Value Chains (GCC/GVC)	Actor–Network Theory (ANT)	Varieties of Capitalism (VoC)	Global Production Networks (GPNs)
Disciplinary background	Economic Sociology Development Studies Industry Studies	Sociology of Science	Political Science International Political Economy	Economic Geography International Political Economy
Object of enquiry	Inter-firm networks in global industries	Heterogeneous networks of association between human and non-human actors	Variations in national institutions and systems of capitalism	Global network configurations and regional development
Orienting concepts	Value-adding chains Governance models Organizational learning Industrial upgrading and rents	Relational networks Human and non-human actants Immutable mobiles Topological surfaces	Organization of production regimes Market-related institutions Modes of coordination	Value creation, enhancement, and capture Corporate, collective and institutional power Societal, network and territorial embeddedness Strategic coupling
Intellectual influences	World systems theory International business Trade economics	Sociology of science Poststructuralism	Classical political economy Institutionalism	Relational economic geography GCC/GVC, ANT, VoC

Source: adapted from Coe (2009: iv. 556–62, table 1), with permission from Elsevier.

business systems', or 'national systems of innovation'.[26] The argument here is that different societies exhibit significant social and institutional variation—owing to differences in culture, polity, education systems, financial regulations, and so on—and therefore embody different production and welfare regimes, labour market practices, and capacities for state economic management. These variations will leave a distinctive imprint on firms that originate from, and/or are located in, particular national territories. The downsides of such an approach include an inclination towards developing rather crude and static typologies of national formations, on the one hand, and a tendency to neglect intra-national variation in political, institutional, and economic formations, on the other. What is added from a GPN perspective, however, is the recognition that institutional-cum-territorial logics matter for global production network actors. They are not just background context, as seems to be inferred in many GCC/GVC-styled analyses, but important shapers of why such actors do things in particular ways in particular places. And, of course, different capitalist territorial formations are also the *outcome* of global production networks dynamics. In other words, the on-the-ground developmental consequences of these dynamics are kept in view. We need an approach more capable of holding in balance the transformative effects of global production networks in the various economies where they are situated, and the ways in which national conditions shape their operations in particular countries and regions. The analytical necessity, therefore, is to unpack the *mutual transformation* of both the firms/networks and the places in which they are embedded.

An Outline of GPN 1.0

If we build upon elements of the cognate approaches introduced above, the initial GPN conceptual framework, here known as GPN 1.0, emphasizes the complex intra-, inter-, and extra-firm networks involved in any economic activity, and how these are structured both organizationally and geographically.[27] It is intended to delimit the globally organized nexus of interconnected functions and operations of firms and extra-firm institutions through which goods and services are produced, distributed, and consumed. The central concern of any GPN analysis should not simply be about considering the networks in their own terms, but should reveal the dynamic *developmental impacts* on territories interconnected through these networks (see Figure 1.1 for a graphical representation).

From the time of its first appearance, the GPN approach has deliberately distinguished itself from the antecedents discussed in four key respects (these are all consolidated and developed more fully in Chapter 2). First, through the explicit consideration of *extra-firm networks*, it necessarily brings into view

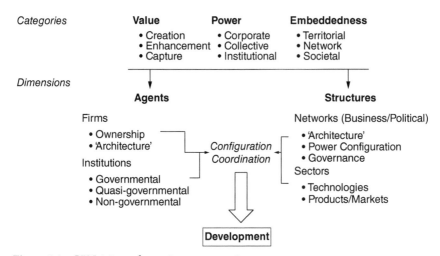

Figure 1.1. GPN 1.0: a schematic representation
Source: adapted with permission from Henderson et al. (2002: figure 1) (<http://www.tandfonline.com>).

the broad range of extra-firm institutions—for example, supranational organizations, government agencies, trade unions, employer associations, NGOs, and consumer groups—that have the potential to shape firm activities in the particular locations that are enrolled into global production networks. In this way, it seeks to move beyond the prioritization of inter-firm networks in GCC/GVC accounts, and brings extra-firm actors into global production networks, rather than seeing them as part of the wider context. Second, GPN analysis is innately *multi-scalar*, and considers the interactions and mutual constitution of all spatial scales from the local to the global. As already noted, while GVC research has become more attuned to sub-national scales of analysis in particular, there is still a tendency to foreground the national and the global in such work. Third, it is an avowedly *network* approach that seeks to move beyond the analytical limitations of the chain notion. Production systems are seen as networked and recursive meshes of intersecting vertical and horizontal connections in order to avoid deterministic linear interpretations of how production systems operate and how value is generated and distributed. The choice of the term 'network' in GPN analysis is not mere semantics, therefore, but reflects a particular ontological understanding of how socio-economic systems are organized and function. Fourth, the *governance* characteristics of global production networks are taken to be much more complex, contingent, and variable over time than is suggested in many GCC/GVC analyses. While recent work under the GVC banner has offered more nuanced typologies of governance modes within global value chains, there is still little consideration of how governance is shaped by the wider regulatory and institutional context in which all firms are situated.

The mobilization of the GPN framework depends on the operationalization of three interrelated variables. First, processes of *value creation, enhancement, and capture* are scrutinized. Second, the distribution and operation of *power* of different forms within global production networks is considered. Third, the *embeddedness* of global production networks—or how they constitute and are reconstituted by the ongoing economic, social, and political arrangements of the places they inhabit—is investigated. The consideration of embeddedness is a distinctive characteristic of the GPN perspective—the notions of value and power being central to all commodity/value chains approaches—and is reflective of a desire to highlight the important sociocultural and institutional contexts of all economic activities. We now briefly introduce each of these three pillars in turn.

In GPN 1.0 the term *value* is used in two ways. To begin, it evokes the traditional political economy notion of the surplus value that is created through a production process converting labour power into products and services to be exchanged for more than the labour value embedded in those commodities. Moreover, value also refers to the various forms of economic rent that can be realized through market as well as non-market transactions within global production networks. Rent is created in a situation where a firm has access to scarce resources that can insulate it from competition by creating barriers to entry for competing firms. Firms in global production networks may be able to generate rents in a number of ways (Kaplinsky 1998, 2005): from asymmetric access to key product and process technologies (techno-logical rents), from the particular talents of their labour force (human resource rents), from particular organizational skills such as just-in-time production techniques (organizational rents), from various inter-firm relationships involving the management of production linkages with other firms (relational rents), or from establishing brand-name prominence in major markets (brand rents). In certain sectors and circumstances additional exogenous rents may accrue to some firms as a consequence of preferential access to natural resources (resource rents), the impacts of favourable government policies (policy rents), the uneven availability of infrastructure (infrastructure rents), and the nature of the financial system (financial rents).

Several implications flow from this broad interpretation of value and its realization. While rents provide a source of sustainable income, they require considerable investment over time, meaning that they are both cumulative and dynamic. Furthermore, particular firms will not be able to create all these different forms of rent, but rather will specialize to a degree in certain kinds of inter- and extra-firm network relations. Last but not least, value may take on different forms as it is transferred through global production networks. Once the value characteristics of a given global production network have been delimited, it is then possible to think dynamically about the potential for *value enhancement* through firm-to-firm processes of knowledge and technology transfer, and industrial upgrading. Ultimately, it is important to consider which firms, and which locations, in the global production network succeed in *capturing value*, and this consideration leads directly to the second key GPN variable, power.

Power in a production network context can be thought of as the ability of one actor to affect the behaviour of another actor in a manner contrary to the second actor's interests. It can also reflect the ability of one actor to resist an unwanted imposition by another actor. This interpretation of power is based upon three assumptions. First, power is seen as relational, meaning that it is not a commodity that can be accrued and stored up like money or land, but rather it varies according to the actors involved in the network, the resources they have at their disposal, and the manner with which they are mobilized. Second, and relatedly, power structures at a given point in a network will influence and be influenced by power structures at other stages of the network. Power relations are therefore transaction specific. A global production network can be seen as a series of exchange relationships, and variations in the power balance along the network will affect the ability of its members to capture value. Third, any given inter-firm relation cannot be purely about power, as there is always a measure of mutual interest and dependency involved. While the relationships among participants are rarely symmetrical, firms in a production network to some degree depend on each other and work together for mutual benefit. These understandings of corporate power need to be augmented, however, by the recognition of other sources of power relations—most notably the institutional power held by the state and various supra-state organizations, and the collective power of labour unions, trade associations, NGOs, and the like—that may also shape the structure and nature of global production networks.

Finally, there are three specific yet interrelated forms of *embeddedness* employed within the GPN framework—societal, network, and territorial.[28] Societal embeddedness connotes the importance for economic action of the cultural, institutional, and historical origins of the economic actor in question. As such, it closely relates to the varieties of capitalism literature introduced earlier. For example, when a company invests overseas it takes with it some of the social and cultural attributes that it has acquired during its evolution within the context of its home base. These can include attitudes towards labour-management relations, working conditions and welfare benefits, how supplier networks should be organized, and the appropriate role for host country governments in the business environment. Network embeddedness refers to the network structure—that is, the degree of functional and social connectivity within a global production network, the stability of its agents' relations, and the importance of the network for its participants. In addition to inter-firm relations, network embeddedness also takes account of the broader institutional structures including extra-firm agents (for example, government and non-government organizations such as trade unions) that are often involved. It highlights the connections between the heterogeneous actors that constitute a global production network, regardless of their location, and is therefore not restricted to one geographic scale.

Territorial embeddedness captures how firms and related organizations are anchored in different places. Global production networks do not merely locate in particular places; they may become embedded there in the sense that they absorb, and in some cases become constrained by, the economic activities and social dynamics that already exist in those places. This anchoring will reflect a firm's dependence on the particular resources, labour markets, state policies, and so on, found in particular places. A key element of territorial embeddedness is the extent and nature of the relationships formed between firms performing different roles within global production networks (for example, lead firms and generic suppliers). These forms of embeddedness, both on their own and together, will clearly affect the prospects for economic and social development in given locations.

In sum, notions of value, power, and embeddedness are used to explore the sector-specific configuration and coordination of global production networks by firm and extra-firm actors. Importantly, GPN analysis seeks to operate at the intersections of structure and agency—that is, it is *structurationist* in inclination and orientation.[29] While the primary focus is to understand the global economy through the strategies of economic actors, it is always attuned to the wider structural and capitalist constraints upon those actions, and the ways in which strategies and actions can in turn rework and reshape these wider structural constraints.

GPN and (Regional) Economic Development

With the outline of GPN 1.0 in place, we can now move on to consider how these ideas might help us understand patterns of uneven economic development in a globalizing world.[30] GPN analysis posits that the key locus for understanding economic development is the *sub-national region*: firms are situated in particular places, not national economies, and all regions have distinctive institutional conditions that shape development practices and processes. It is thus the basic geographical building block through which patterns of economic growth and decline should be interpreted. The GPN perspective pays analytical attention both to endogenous growth factors within specific regions and also to the strategic needs of extra-local actors coordinating global production networks—that is, lead firms. Regional development can thus be conceptualized as a dynamic outcome of the complex interaction between region-specific networks and global production networks within the context of changing regional governance structures. It is these interactive

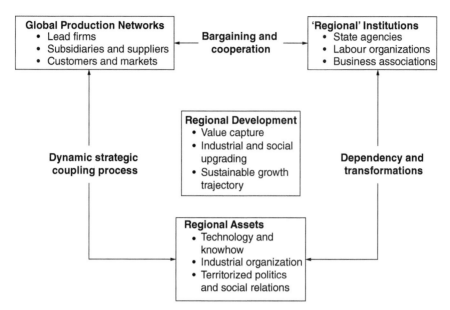

Figure 1.2. GPN 1.0: strategic coupling and regional development
Source: adapted from Coe et al. (2004: 470, figure 1). Copyright © 2004, John Wiley and Sons.

effects that contribute to regional development, not inherent regional advantages or rigid configurations of globalization processes. Despite certain path-dependent trajectories, regional development remains a highly contingent process that cannot be predicted a priori.

In this view, endogenous factors are necessary, but insufficient, to generate regional growth in an era in which competition is increasingly global. There is no doubt that, for development to take place, a region must benefit from economies of scale and scope derived from the local human, technological, and institutional resource base. In Figure 1.2, the term 'regional assets' is used to describe this necessary precondition for regional development. In general, these assets can produce two types of economies. On the one hand, economies of scale can be achieved in certain regions through highly localized concentrations of specific knowledge, skills, and expertise. On the other hand, economies of scope can exist if these regions are able to reap the intangible benefits of learning and the cooperative atmosphere embedded in these agglomerations. GPN analysis suggests that economies of scale and scope embedded within specific regions are advantageous to those regions—and bring about regional development—only insofar as such region-specific economies can complement the strategic needs of lead firms in global production networks. As shown in Figure 1.2, when such a complementary effect exists between regions and global production networks, a developmental process of *strategic coupling* will take place through which the advantages of regions interact positively with the strategic needs of actors in these global production networks. Regional development therefore depends on the coupling process that evolves over time in relation to the rapidly changing strategic needs of global production networks and the rather slower transformations in regional economies of scale and scope.

The notion of strategic coupling has three important characteristics.[31] First, it is strategic in that it needs intentional and active intervention on the part of both regional institutions and powerful global production network actors to occur. Second, it is time–space contingent, as it is subject to change and is a temporary coalition between local and non-local actors. Third, it transcends territorial boundaries as actors from different spatial scales interact. In other words, many of the key strategic decisions that determine the nature of coupling within a particular region are taken outside its bounds by actors associated with other spatial scales (for example, national, global). Importantly, the strategic coupling of local actors (firms and extra-firm organizations) with lead firms in global production networks should not be construed as a functionalist argument, because this coupling process is not automatic and always successful. The process needs to be unpacked and analyzed, because it changes over time and in different geographical contexts. Moreover, access to the enabling mechanisms and technologies for this coupling may be highly uneven geographically. Regional development can be fruitfully thought of in evolutionary terms as being shaped by periods of strategic coupling in sequence with phases of decoupling and subsequent recoupling.[32]

In Figure 1.2, the coupling process is seen to work through the processes of value creation, enhancement, and capture identified earlier. The fact that a region is 'plugged into' a global production network does not automatically guarantee a positive developmental outcome, because local actors may be creating value that does not maximize the region's economic potential. Hence, regional assets can become an advantage for regional development *only if* they fit the strategic needs of global production networks. This process requires the presence of appropriate institutional structures that simultaneously promote regional advantages and enhance the region's articulation into global production networks. It is crucial here that the notion of regional institutions includes not only regionally specific institutions, but also local arms of national/supranational bodies (for example, a trade union's local chapters), and extra-local institutions that affect activities within the region without necessarily having a presence (for example, a national tax authority). These multi-scalar 'regional' institutions are important because they can provide the glue that ties down global production networks in particular localities. Generally, the more a region is articulated into global production networks, the more likely it is able to reap the benefits of economies of scale and scope in these networks, but the less likely it is able to control its own fate.

However, in certain circumstances, regional institutions may mobilize their region-specific assets to bargain with lead firms in ways that mean power relations are not necessarily one-way in favour of the latter. The bargaining position of these regional institutions is particularly high when their region-specific assets are highly complementary to the strategic needs of lead firms in global production networks.[33]

GPN 2.0: A DYNAMIC THEORY OF GLOBAL PRODUCTION NETWORKS

Building upon elements of the GCC approach and other cognate approaches (for example, actor–network theory and the varieties of capitalism approach), the initial GPN 1.0 framework in economic geography and international political economy emphasizes the complex firm networks and territorial institutions involved in all economic activity, and how these are structured both organizationally and geographically.[34] It has been successful in offering a flexible, geographical framework for mapping the shifting configurations of global production networks. However, despite its aim 'to provide a more generally applicable conceptualisation of the GPN' (Henderson et al. 2002: 444) and its influential role as a heuristic framework in economic–geographical research and the wider social sciences, GPN 1.0 in many ways remains an inadequately developed *conceptualization* of global production networks. Though the initial framing identifies three interrelated 'conceptual categories' of value, embeddedness, and power, it has not explicitly developed and specified the *causal mechanisms* linking these elements to the dynamic configurations of global production networks. The still nascent stage of GPN 1.0 conceptualization has led commentators to argue that existing approaches are not sufficiently 'explanatory' and 'causal' to provide a coherent understanding of global production networks.[35]

Given the strong interest in global production networks in the academic literature and the international policy arena, we believe the epistemological context is now ripe to embark upon a more ambitious round of theoretical innovation that seeks to break significant new ground and inform subsequent rounds of empirical research.[36] In denoting GPN 2.0, we try in this book to initiate a step-change towards greater analytical precision and explanatory power in a theory of global production networks. In some instances this involves paring back the ambition of the original approach in order to provide more clarity and analytical traction; in some it involves giving more space to relatively underplayed actors and influences in GPN 1.0; and in others it involves deeper conceptualization of the dynamic forces underpinning the

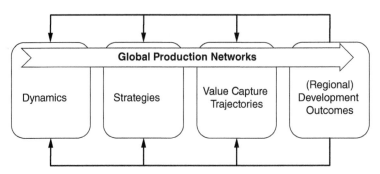

Figure 1.3. GPN 2.0: a theoretical schema

formation and operation of global production networks. In the final section of this introductory chapter we therefore briefly distil the contributions and advances that we seek to make in the chapters that follow. The central impulse is to enhance the ability of GPN thinking to contribute to *explanations* of patterns of uneven territorial development in the global economy.

Our core approach to this challenge is to seek to uncover the causal links depicted in Figure 1.3's main directional arrow. We aim to connect through, conceptually, from the structural capitalist dynamics that underpin global production network formation and operation to the on-the-ground development outcomes for regional economies. The underlying capitalist dynamics encompass key dimensions such as costs-cum-capabilities, markets, finance, and risk, and together distil the inherent imperatives of contemporary global capitalism. These dynamics are key variables that drive the strategies adopted by economic actors in (re)configuring their global production networks and, ultimately, the developmental outcomes in different industries, regions, and countries. Oddly, these competitive dynamics are little theorized in the existing GVC/GPN literatures, which are more concerned with certain aspects of the operation of such chains and networks *once* they are formed. With these causal drivers in place, we can then consider how they shape the strategies of different kinds of firms in global production networks. These firms can organize their activities through different configurations of intra-, inter-, and extra-firm network relationships, and we conceptualize how these configurations are shaped by different intersections of the underlying dynamics. In turn, we move on to consider the consequences of these causal mechanisms— comprising varying dynamics and strategies—for firms in global production networks. We use the concept of 'value capture trajectories' to frame in dynamic terms how firms are able, or not, to capture the gains from enrolment in global production networks. Finally, we seek to understand the impacts on territorial development by exploring how firm value capture trajectories can coalesce in particular places into dominant modes and types of strategic coupling, with different potential for value capture at the regional and the national levels.

The global production network becomes the overarching concept for making the connections between the conceptual elements of Figure 1.3, and our analytical focus is first and foremost on the various actors that constitute these networks. As the reverse arrows in the figure suggest, however, there are, of course, feedback mechanisms and recursive loops between these constituent elements. We do not wish to set things up as overly deterministic; indeed, one of the benefits of GPN 1.0 analysis has arguably been its eschewing of simple and linear lines of causation and its openness to multiple influences. At the same time, our quest for enhanced explanation in GPN 2.0 requires us to identify dominant lines of causality between global production networks and territorial economic development. The extent to which those lines are deflected or challenged in different geographical and industrial settings in part becomes an empirical question.

Previous research has tended to concentrate only on certain elements of Figure 1.3. GVC research has largely focused on the strategies of certain kinds of actors (often lead firms) and how they are able to extract value from other actors (usually key suppliers). GPN 1.0 has introduced sensitivity to geographical and institutional context, proffered a more nuanced reading of governance, and, through the notion of strategic coupling, started to probe the territorial development implications of enrolment in global production networks. The development of GPN 2.0, however, requires three different kinds of conceptual 'move' in order to make significant progress towards revealing the connections depicted in Figure 1.3 as a whole. First, we step back and offer greater precision with respect to the constituent elements and actors of a global production network. This is necessary because of the widespread adoption of the existing GPN framework and the sometime misinterpretation of some of its key terms and categories. Second, as mentioned above, we back up from the conventional focus on inter-firm relationships to reveal the underlying forces or dynamics driving the strategies and actions of the different types of firms embedded in global production networks. By developing this dynamic analysis of the emergence and evolution of network formation, we will eventually be able to explain more effectively the diverse industrial and territorial outcomes of these capitalist processes. Third, we move forward from considering the firm level outcomes of global production network enrolment to conceptualize further their intersections with territorial regional economies and the development impacts therein. This requires more explicit conceptualization of the inherent territoriality of global production networks.

In sum, GPN 2.0 should not be thought of as a fundamental break from GPN 1.0 thinking. It shares the same ontological and epistemological foundations (that is, the basic codes), and remains an actor-centric approach that understands the global economy as a mesh of networks of value activity performed by these actors in organizationally complex ways and territorially specific contexts. We continue to emphasize sectoral and geographical complexity, are still avowedly multi-scalar in orientation, and retain the same central question of seeking to understand uneven geographical development at both the national and sub-national scales within the global economy. The core categories of value, power, and embeddedness remain foundational (albeit with the latter somewhat reinterpreted through the notion of horizontal territorial interfaces, as we will explain in Chapter 2). At the same time, in GPN 2.0 we seek to offer a step-change in conceptual development by moving beyond the heuristic framing offered in Figure 1.1 to reveal the causal connections inherent to Figure 1.3. Put another way, we endeavour to offer greater analytical purchase on the processes of network formation, coordination, and configuration that are at the centre of Figure 1.1, and to unpack their connections to development that are simply captured as one large arrow in that diagram. As noted above, effecting that transition from GPN 1.0 to 2.0 requires a range of different conceptual moves.

A final caveat is in order here. It is important to reiterate that this book is primarily a work of conceptual development. It aims to be a theoretical exposition of GPN analysis that provides a way forward for future research. It does not seek to provide a geographically and sectorally exhaustive catalogue of real-world global production network structures and dynamics. Nor can it hope to review the vast array of empirical studies of particular industries and places that have respectively mobilized the GCC, GVC, and GPN frameworks (and combinations thereof) since the mid-1990s. Rather our use of empirical evidence in this book is, by design, highly selective and merely illustrative in order to put our abstract ideas into a more digestible form. In turn and when appropriate, we use endnotes extensively to offer a window onto the wider literature and to highlight those studies that we have found particularly fruitful in analytical terms (these tend to be studies that have engaged in conceptual development, rather than simple applications of the various frameworks).

That said, the existing empirical literature, with notable exceptions that we draw upon in the book, still exhibits something of a 'productionist' bias with the majority of case studies drawn from manufacturing industries. This bias is also possibly accentuated by the term 'production' in conceptions of global production networks. As we will explain in the next chapter, however, production is clearly *not* simply manufacturing but instead encompasses a wide range of value activity, such as commodity inputs, research and development, producer services, distribution, and so on. In drawing upon the existing literature in our book, we may be prone to creating a similar impression, but, as we try to make clear, we see GPN analysis as something that can and should be applied to *all* industries within the global economy. Most importantly, a plethora of business services, including finance, logistics, information technology services, and human resource management, can be considered as both strategically important inputs to a wide range of global production networks, but also as organized through global production networks in their own right. Equally, there are relatively few studies on the role of consumer dynamics upon which to draw. As will become clear in Chapters 2 and 3, however, both consumers and market demand more generally play an integral role in the theoretical framework we develop in the book.

The remainder of the book unfolds over five chapters. Chapter 2 consolidates our existing theoretical understanding of the *organization* of global production networks and reconceptualizes the key actors, network forms, and territorial dimensions of these networks. The chapter strengthens the toolkit provided by GPN 1.0 in three ways. First, we profile the growing range of intermediaries that broker and mediate inter-firm and extra-firm relations within such systems. Second, we conceptualize the aggregation of multiple global production networks into industries, as well as other forms of intra-industry and inter-industry intersections of global production networks. Third, we develop the hitherto under-theorized territoriality dimension by distilling the vertical and horizontal scalar dimensions of global production networks. Altogether, the chapter offers a more precise set of vocabularies for capturing the complex geographical configurations of global production networks in both network and territorial terms.

Chapter 3 represents the first of the three critical steps in our development of GPN theory by conceptualizing the *dynamic drivers* of value activity in global production networks.[37] In theorizing these capitalist imperatives within the competitive context of time–space compression, we identify three dynamic forces. First, we develop the concept of the cost–capability ratio to explore how firm actors seek to manage actively their various assets (for example, labour, technology, knowhow, and capital) within the context of dynamic global production networks. Second, with respect to market development we look at how issues of market reach and access, market dominance, time-to-market, and shifting customer behaviour and preferences are integral to all global production networks. Third, the growing importance of financial discipline—in terms of pressures from investors and shareholders and access to finance—is profiled. Finally, we intersect these three dynamics with notions of risk management relating to unpredictable economic, product, regulatory, labour, and environmental factors.

Chapter 4 takes a second critical step towards theory development by connecting the dynamic drivers considered in the preceding chapter to the *strategies* of the key corporate actors within global production networks. Extending existing work by drilling down beneath the industry level, we seek to reveal sectoral and firm complexity and variability. Four sets of strategies are explained in this chapter in relation to the dynamic drivers in Chapter 3. At the intra-firm level, we conceptualize internalization as a firm-specific strategy for organizing global production networks driven by particular sets of competitive dynamics. At the inter-firm level, two strategies are particularly prominent in the contemporary organization of global production networks—coordination/control and partnership. Lastly, extra-firm bargaining is explored as the strategic interface through which capitalist firms interact with extra-firm actors. Taken together, these two chapters develop the causal mechanisms of global production networks.

Chapter 5 uses the preceding analysis of the organization, dynamics, and strategies of global production networks to explain the diverse patterns of uneven economic *development* within the global economy. As such, it completes the book's three-step approach to theorizing economic development in an interconnected world with global production networks as the central driver. We develop the concept of 'value capture trajectories' as a new way of thinking about the highly varied and dynamic outcomes for firms both articulated into, and disarticulated from, global production networks. In turn, the developmental implications of those value trajectories are analyzed through the lens of the different modes and types of *strategic coupling* that may become apparent at the sub-national regional level. We also discuss how these dynamic modes of coupling are themselves highly contested by a range of actors both within and beyond the constituent global production networks.

Looking forward, our theory development in this book is intended to stimulate and inform a longer-term theoretical-cum-empirical research programme in the social sciences. Accordingly, in Chapter 6 we move from theory to *praxis*. We demonstrate how GPN 2.0 offers several distinct advantages over the understandings of global economic change embodied within the GVC research agenda, studies of varieties of capitalism and comparative institutionalism, and economic models premised on international trade theory. The aim is to distil the value added that may accrue from mobilizing the kind of theoretical approach developed in this book. Finally, we delve into the politics and practice of adopting the GPN perspective as an analytical tool for use by development policy-makers at different spatial scales.

NOTES

1. See, e.g., OECD (2011, 2013), WTO and IDE-JETRO (2011), Elms and Low (2013), IMF (2013), OECD-WTO-UNCTAD (2013), UNCTAD (2013a, b), Gereffi (2014), and Neilson (2014).
2. In this book and Yeung and Coe (2015), we use the acronym 'GPN' to denote theory or literature, and 'global production networks' to refer to the empirical phenomenon. The same distinction applies to 'GCC' and 'global commodity chains', and 'GVC' and 'global value chains'.
3. Readers looking for such information are advised to consult Peter Dicken's *Global Shift* (2011, 2015), which remains the definitive work on how globalization has

fundamentally reshaped the contours of the global economy. For an early but excellent assessment of the effects of the 'great recession' on the contours of the global economy, see Cattaneo et al. (2010b).

4. The business historian Alfred Chandler has produced two useful and complementary accounts of Fordism and American capitalism in *The Visible Hand* (1977) and *Scale and Scope* (1990).

5. For other important studies of this new competition in an era of flexible specialization, see Scott (1988), Storper and Walker (1989), Best (1990), Hirst and Zeitlin (1996), Storper (1997), and Storper and Salais (1997).

6. Propulsive industries are generally seen to be dynamic industries characterized by a high level of technological use and an extensive market. They are instrumental in driving growth in other industries to which they are linked.

7. Space constraints at this point preclude the possibility of dealing fully with other important issues about market structures, inter-firm/network rivalries, regulation, and so on that characterize different forms of global production system (see Hess and Yeung 2006a; Coe et al. 2008b). Chapter 3, however, will focus specifically on three contemporary dynamic forces in the form of cost–capability ratios (e.g. labour, technology, knowhow, and capital), market development (e.g. reach and access, dominance, time-to-market, customer behaviour and preferences), and financial discipline (e.g. investor and shareholder pressure, and access to finance).

8. See Fröbel et al. (1980) for one of the earliest analyses of this emergence of the new international division of labour, particularly in the textiles and garments industry.

9. For some empirical studies of this international relocation, see Henderson (1989), Gourevitch et al. (2000), Ernst (2005), Feenstra and Hamilton (2006), Scott (2006a), Lüthje et al. (2013), and Ferrarini and Hummels (2014).

10. These two processes of innovation flexibility and timely responsiveness constitute what Teece and Pisano (1994) call 'dynamic capabilities'. For selected work by perceptive scholars of business competition, see Schoenberger (1997), Kenney and Florida (2004), Mathews (2005, 2006), and Teece (2009).

11. By the late 1990s and the early 2000s, the world electronics industry had experienced another 'revolution' with the emergence of contract manufacturing as the key platform for achieving maximum production efficiency through enormous economies of scale and highly sophisticated supply chain management (Hobday 2001; Sturgeon 2002, 2003; Berger and Lester 2005). Chang (2008) makes a strong case for the role of modularization in enabling Samsung to compete against others consumer electronics giants such as Sony.

12. For more theoretical elaboration on time-to-market, see Stalk (1988), Best (1990), Stalk and Hout (1990), and Schoenberger (1994, 1997).

13. One of the best-known approaches to studying how technology disrupts lead firms and their market dominant positions is Christensen's 'disruptive innovation model' (see Christensen 1997; Christensen and Raynor 2003; Christensen et al. 2004).

14. See more details on these technological and logistical platforms in Macher et al. (2002) and Coe (2014).

15. For powerful studies of these transnational knowledge communities, see Saxenian (2006) and Saxenian and Sabel (2008).

16. Most importantly, these include Porter's work (1985, 1990) on value chains, Kogut's writing (1985) on value added chains, and Hopkins and Wallerstein's notion (1986) of commodity chains.

17. This GCC literature is enormous and reviewing it thoroughly could constitute a book in its own right! Key references include Gereffi and Korzeniewicz (1990, 1994), Gereffi (1994, 1995, 1999), and Bair (2009). For more recent attempts to revitalize the world-systems origins of the GCC framework, see Brown et al. (2010), Mahutga (2012, 2014), and Bair (2014).

18. This fourth dimension was added after the initial formulation; see Gereffi (1995).

19. For a cross section of GCC work, see Clancy (1998) on tourism, Gereffi (1999) and Bair and Gereffi (2001) on apparel, Gwynne (1999) on fruit, Fold (2002) on cocoa, Gellert (2003) on timber, Power and Hallencreutz (2007) on music, Birch (2008) on biotechnology, and Topik (2009) on coffee.

20. One clear evidence of this 'theoretical deficit' in the GCC literature is that, despite two well-known edited volumes explicating global commodity chains (Gereffi and Korzeniewicz 1994; Bair 2009), none of its key proponents has advanced further GCC theorization in a single book-length publication. Indeed in the GCC–GVC literature more broadly, the leading conceptual frameworks have been developed through several book chapters (e.g. Gereffi 1994, 2005) and journal articles (e.g. Humphrey and Schmitz 2002a; Gereffi et al. 2005).

21. For more on different approaches to global value chain governance, see Ponte and Gibbon (2005), Gibbon and Ponte (2008), and Gibbon et al. (2008). For a later attempt at 'modular' theory-building with respect to global value chain governance, see Ponte and Sturgeon (2014).

22. Important contributions here are offered by Humphrey and Schmitz (2002a, b), Schmitz (2004), Kaplinsky (2005), and Pietrobelli and Rabellotti (2011). Following Kaplinsky and Morris (2001), discussion of upgrading often identifies four types: *process* upgrading, whereby the production system is made more efficient, perhaps through superior technology; *product* upgrading, in which firms move into more sophisticated product lines; *functional* upgrading, in which they acquire new functions to increase their value added; and *chain or inter-sectoral* upgrading, whereby firms move into new categories of production altogether.

23. For more, see Neilson (2014). As Neilson argues, the uptake of the GVC lexicon in development circles is something of a double-edged sword, with critical elements of the original framework being 'lost in translation'. For an even more critical reading, see Fernández (2014), who argues that GVC research has been fully incorporated into the global neoliberal policy toolkit. We will revisit some of these issues of politics and practice in the final chapter of this book.

24. For more, see Murdoch (1998), Hetherington and Law (2000), Law (2004), and Latour (2005). For an early application to global coffee networks, see Whatmore and Thorne (1997). A contemporary illustration can be found in Ouma (2015).

25. Dicken et al. (2001) was the first such paper in GPN 1.0 to develop a network conception of the global economy, drawing upon both GCC and ANT work.

26. In what is broadly known as the varieties of capitalism (VoC) literature, scholars have explained how variations in national political–economic institutions shape the nature and behaviour of firms and enterprises from these national economies.

It is beyond the scope of this book to explain different varieties of capitalism and their business systems (for more, see Whitley 1992, 1999; Berger and Dore 1996; Whitley and Kristensen 1996, 1997; Crouch and Streeck 1997; Hollingsworth and Boyer 1999; Hall and Soskice 2001; Hancké et al. 2007; Hancké 2009; Morgan and Whitley 2012). The inherent constraints of this literature have led economic geographers to pursue the more nuanced and nimble notion of 'variegated capitalism' (Peck and Theodore 2007). We will revisit this literature from the perspective of GPN 2.0 in Chapter 6.

27. The key theoretical statements concerning the GPN approach can be found in the following: Dicken et al. (2001), Henderson et al. (2002), Coe et al. (2004, 2008a), Hess and Yeung (2006b); Yeung (2009b, 2014), Coe and Hess (2011) and Coe (2012). Interestingly, at the same time as the GPN approach was first emerging from economic geography, the same term was being developed by Dieter Ernst and colleagues (e.g. Ernst and Kim 2002). This latter approach had a strong focus on technological innovation, and by the later 2000s had developed into the notion of global innovation networks (GINs) (see Ernst 2009; also Parrilli et al. 2013).

28. Since the mid-1980s, networks and embeddedness have come to dominate the conceptual lexicon in economic sociology, organization studies, and strategic management (Guillén et al. 2003; Smelser and Swedberg 2005; Krippner and Alvarez 2007). Sociologists have been particularly interested in social network analysis since the 1920s and the 1930s (Kilduff and Tsai 2003). This genre of work focuses on social interaction as the micro-foundation of society. It was not until the mid-1980s, however, that the idea of economic action being embedded in networks of ongoing social relations was resurrected by the influential work of Granovetter (1985). Following Karl Polanyi's (1944) *The Great Transformation*, Granovetter argued against the atomistic reading of economic relations in transaction cost economics associated with Williamson (1975, 1985). Since then, this idea of embeddedness and networks has strongly reverberated through management and organization studies. An enormous range of theoretical and empirical studies has focused on how network embeddedness can enhance business formation and firm performance (Dacin et al. 1999; Meyer et al. 2011) and value chain activity (Bair 2008). For geographical takes on networks and embeddedness, see reviews in Yeung (1994, 2008), Hess (2004, 2008), and Grabher (2006).

29. Structuration is heavily associated with the sociologist Anthony Giddens (e.g. 1979, 1984). Giddens's structuration theory sought to overcome the 'phoney war' in the social sciences between macro- and micro-perspectives and to transcend the limits of both voluntarism and determinism by seeing structure and agency as being brought into action simultaneously. Giddens explained social life as being continually produced and reproduced through a process of structuration. From this perspective, both structure and agency were implicated in every moment of social interaction. In turn, semantic rules, resources (e.g. authority and property), and moral rules were seen as the modalities connecting structure and action, through both repetitive conduct and long-term institutional change.

30. These ideas of GPN 1.0 and regional development are initially developed in Coe et al. (2004) and further refined in Yeung (2009b).

31. MacKinnon (2012) distils no less than ten dimensions of strategic coupling processes—namely: mode of entry, status of affiliates, type of region (source or host), nature of regional assets (distinctive–generic), type of coupling (organic, strategic, structural), degree of coupling (full–none), depth of coupling (deep–shallow), power relations (symmetric–asymmetric, the latter leading to institutional capture), development outcomes (development–dependency), and exposure to decoupling (low–high). This is an important intervention, and provides a useful framework and lexicon for describing strategic coupling dynamics. A shortcoming, however, is that the framework is driven by its close links with the literature on TNC subsidiaries and their roles and capacities, but is less effective at capturing the subcontracted nature of production in many global production networks. We will develop further this concept of different modes of strategic coupling in Chapter 5.

32. It is important, therefore, that research should focus as much on periods when links between global production networks and regional economies are broken and remade, and the actors and events shaping such transitions, as on periods when the links are productive. This resonates with related calls to look at the ruptures (Coe and Hess 2011) and disarticulations (Bair and Werner 2011a) that may occur between global production networks and regional economies. We will develop this argument much more fully in Chapter 5.

33. A range of empirical work in East Asia has both demonstrated the utility of the strategic coupling concept and made considerable headway in demonstrating the different forms that strategic coupling may take. For instance, three key modes of strategic coupling that have driven economic growth in Asia have been identified in Yeung (2009b)—namely: international partnerships between lead firms and local firms in which development takes place through direct connections of regions into global production networks (e.g. Taiwan, Singapore); indigenous innovation through 'national champions' backed by state industrial policy over a period of decades (e.g. South Korean *chaebol*); and production platforms wherein regions are incorporated into global divisions of labour coordinated by lead firms and their Asian strategic partners (e.g. coastal China). Yang (2009) contrasted two modes of coupling with the same sectoral and national context, comparing the explicit coupling (i.e. actively driven by local government) between Taiwanese OEMs/ODMs and global lead firms in Suzhou's notebook personal computer cluster with the implicit bottom-up coupling dynamics associated with Taiwanese firms in Dongguan's desktop cluster. In a similar vein, Yang et al. (2009) identified geographically varied strategic coupling across three science parks in Taiwan, while in another study of the computer manufacturing industry in China, Yang and Coe (2009) argued that the nature of strategic coupling between global production networks and regional production clusters varied owing to both the different functionalities of those clusters within the broader global production network and the ways in which they were shaped by local institutional and economic contexts.

34. In the preceding section, we largely characterized GPN 1.0 as a coherent approach, but the reality is a dynamic body of work that has developed over some fifteen

years through an ongoing dialogue between the initial progenitors (including the current authors), collaborators, and critics (both supportive and sceptical).

35. See, notably, Hudson (2008), Sunley (2008), and Starosta (2010a).
36. It may also, we hope, represent a theoretical contribution and potential 'export' from the field of economic geography to the wider social sciences (cf. Yeung and Lin 2003; Dicken 2004).
37. Interestingly, while earlier GVC and GPN research has provided many insights into the nature of the operation of such production systems once they have become established, it has focused far less on the underlying structural imperatives that drive their formation and the strategies of key corporate actors. This is in some ways a surprising diagnosis, given the origins of the initial 1994 formulation of the global commodity chain approach in world-systems theory. In a thought-provoking paper, Starosta (2010a; see also 2010b) critiques GPN (and also GCC/GVC) approaches as being inherently empiricist and overly concerned with meso- and micro-levels of enquiry. He points to a tendency to identify the strongest lead firms in the system, and then explain the nature of the system in relation to that dominance, without adequately explaining how that dominance is produced and contested.

2

Organization

Global production networks are synonymous with economic globalization—the former as the key organizational platform for industrial and service production on a worldwide basis and the latter as a highly contested set of political–economic processes. This and the following two chapters collectively aim to explain how the organizational dynamics of economic globalization can serve as a powerful impetus for structural change in different national economies. This dynamic is particularly relevant in globalizing industries such as agro-food, apparel, automobiles, information and communications technologies (ICT), advanced producer services, finance, logistics, and retail. From a development perspective, under the right conditions the emergence of global production networks can provide an unprecedented opportunity for domestic firms and producers to acquire market access, capital, technology, knowledge, and capabilities from beyond their home economies. Their learning may now no longer be limited to domestic economic and institutional endowments, but rather is increasingly grounded in *trans-local* networks of economic activity that go well beyond the bureaucratic control and organizational confines of their home states and associated economic actors. In this process, domestic firms are progressively dis-embedded from their home economies and become gradually re-embedded in global production networks of various kinds.[1] This process of re-embedding represents a form of actor-specific stabilizing tactic, as described in Fligstein's *The Architecture of Markets* (2001), enabling firms to re-create a new conception of control that simultaneously allows them to move away from a structural dependence on the home economy towards new possibilities for growth in an interconnected global economy.

As we saw in Chapter 1, since the early 2000s considerable progress has been made in the social sciences towards the development of sophisticated conceptual frameworks for analyzing cross-border production networks, territorial formations, and economic development in this interconnected global economy. This genre of theoretical development has demonstrated the continuing unevenness in the territoriality of production and consumption, the differentiating role of structural and institutional conditions at various geographical scales, and the diverse responses and strategies of the firms, extra-firm organizations, and state institutions that shape the global economy across space and time. Global production network (GPN) theory postulates that the nature and trajectories of economic development in particular economies are highly dependent on the dynamic processes through which domestic firms are strategically coupled with, or emerge as lead firms in, global production networks. The explanatory power of GPN 2.0 hinges on its analytical capability of accounting for the complex organization of global production networks and the different strategies of economic and non-economic actors in these networks in the face of competitive dynamics in global industries. Industrial transformation and economic development therefore cannot be fully understood if an analysis is limited only to a particular economic agent (for example, the firm or the industry), geographical scale (for example, the state or a region within a national economy), or economic dimension (for example, trading tasks or trade in intermediate goods and services). Instead, a GPN analysis requires attention to multiple actors and their differentiated value activities across multiple geographical scales.

As the overarching conceptual departure point for the remaining chapters of this book, this chapter delimits the main building blocks of GPN theory for the analysis of economic development. In so doing, it consciously breaks with both methodological individualism and state-centric forms of social science. It takes stock of our existing understanding of the organization of global production networks and reconceptualizes value activity, key actors, networks, and their territoriality. We believe such an organizational delimitation of global production networks is necessary because of the wide adoption of the existing GPN framework and the varied and sometimes inconsistent ways in which its key terms and categories have been mobilized. The first three sections of this chapter focus on redefining value activity, actors, and networks—three indispensable analytical devices in any GPN analysis. We define the concept of *production* as the collective participation in value-adding activity by a variety of actors in different sectors, industries, and locations to create finished goods or services. These actors can be business firms and extra-firm institutions that are brought together by intermediaries connecting multiple actors in global production systems. These intermediaries play an important functional role in enabling the effective realization of value activity. This organizational constellation of value activity is best conceived as a form of network. We argue, therefore, for a network conception of the global economy in which economic activity becomes increasingly organized through network relationships within, between, and beyond individual firms and extra-firm institutions. The emergence of global production networks is underpinned by this organizational shift from intra-firm hierarchical control, as typified by Fordism (see Chapter 1), to inter-firm and extra-firm networks. In the penultimate section, we offer further conceptualization of a significant lacuna in GPN 1.0—territoriality. Despite the role of territoriality being a widely recognized advancement within the GPN framework, the territoriality of global production networks remains quite elusive and underdeveloped. We attempt to advance this geographical political economy thinking by reconceptualizing the global–local verticality of scales and intra-national horizontal interfaces in the spatial organization of global production networks.[2] Overall, this chapter conceptually clarifies and further develops the basic building blocks of GPN 2.0.

VALUE ACTIVITY

GPN analysis seeks to explain the nature and organization of global production networks, which involve both capitalist firms and diverse economies in organizationally complex and geographically extensive ways. To analyze the divergent trajectories of economic development, it explicitly recognizes the causal role of the strategic priorities and choices made by actors embedded in these economies and global production networks. These actors can be capitalist firms and state and non-state institutions. Their developmental action is primarily oriented towards the creation, enhancement, and capture of *value*. Of course, the constitution and significance of this value may vary from firms to extra-firm institutions. Even among capitalist firms, the production of value can be perceived differently, ranging from market dominance and industrial control to continual growth and sustained profitability. Among institutions, state agencies (for example, tax revenue) may view value differently from labour organizations (for example, wages), industry associations (for example, supplier linkages), consumer groups (for example, lower prices), and civil society organizations (for example, ethical and fair production). Nevertheless, it is useful to think of these firms and extra-firm institutions as primarily interested in value, with economic development (or decline, potentially) representing the contested outcome of their diverse conceptions and production of value.

In retrospect, the value chain concept associated with Porter's work (1980, 1985) provided an initial analytical category for the GPN framework—especially in relation to value and its contestation over space. This explicit concern with how value is created, enhanced, and captured in different geographical configurations of global production networks fundamentally underpinned GPN 1.0. As noted in Chapter 1, GPN analysis defines value in terms of both political economy notions of surplus value and more conventional understandings of economic rent or profit. Surplus value arises from the conversion of labour power into goods or services, and the subsequent difference between the labour value and exchange value of these goods or services. It is concerned with the employment, skills, working conditions, and social reproduction of labour in and through global production networks. By economic rent, we refer to profits accrued to firms and other economic actors that possess proprietary or unique branding, technologies, and expertise; management know-how and organizational relationships; and dominant or monopolistic market positions.[3] This combination of value generated from the labour process (surplus value) and industrial organization (economic rent) allows for the diverse ways in which value can be created, enhanced, and captured by *different actors* in the same global production network—some specializing in higher value-adding activities such as technological innovation and new market development in search of greater economic rent from consumption, with others relying on extraction of surplus value from low-cost labour in production. In short, value encompasses much more than the market value of goods or services, which represents value merely at the point of its exchange. Rather, value is a multifaceted concept incorporating the entire process of production, exchange, and consumption. In GPN 2.0, we continue with this line of conceptual delimitation by bringing together several strands of the analysis of value in an integrated form.

Another important contribution of the value chain concept to the development of GPN thinking is that it recognizes the conceptual inseparability of manufacturing and service activities in constituting economic production and value creation. In the original version of Porter's value chain, both kinds of economic activities were central to value chain processes. The conceptual significance of this integrated understanding of production in relation to the social divisions of labour becomes magnified through GPN analysis.[4] We simply cannot understand manufacturing activities, for instance, without a concomitant analysis of how these value activities are organized through a wide range of service tasks such as research and development (R&D), design, finance, logistics, distribution, and servicing. A recent joint report by the OECD–WTO–UNCTAD (2013: 16) estimates that, as intermediate inputs to global production, services contribute directly and indirectly to over 30 per cent of the total value added in all manufactured goods. In turn, several of these service activities are themselves organized and delivered through global production networks, as seen, for instance, in finance, advertising, logistics, and retailing.

In essence, economic production refers to an amalgamation of value activities that transform tangible materials and intangible inputs into manufactured products and/or services for industrial customers or final consumers. 'Production' in GPN analysis, therefore, does not refer exclusively to manufacturing activity. Rather, it encompasses all forms of economic activity, from resource extraction to manufacturing and services, involved in the creation, enhancement, and retention of value. Some of these activities may be concerned with *value creation*—a process through which a residual economic surplus is generated by the transformation of materials and inputs into a new product or the provision of new services by a group of interrelated actors, irrespective of whether these actors are organized in the form of craft production, vertically integrated production, or inter-firm production networks. Firms are the primary nexus through which such value creation is produced, but extra-firm actors such as the state and labour organizations can also contribute to value creation through direct subsidies (for example, grants and loans), indirect investment (for example, infrastructure and education), and skill development (for example, training enterprises). This value creation through new products or services usually begins with the original innovator or developer, and it eventually leads to the market success of these products or services. Depending on their differential capacity to define and control the final market for these products or services, different actors receive disproportionate returns from their participation in this process of value creation. The social and geographical distribution of this value becomes the most critical question for any theory of economic development.

Economic surplus, however, need not come only from value creation. It can also be generated through *value enhancement*, whereby actors add tangible or intangible inputs to an existing good or service in order to make it more valuable. This value enhancement process does not necessarily entail the production of new goods or services. It can be accomplished through the Schumpeterian-style entrepreneurship of bringing together 'new combinations' (Schumpeter 1934: 66) of existing materials and/or ideas. Technological innovation and knowledge are central to such value enhancement processes. Upgrading the technologies and skills of existing firms and suppliers can also increase their propensity to offer such value enhancement.[5]

As value activities created or enhanced by actors generate economic surpluses in geographically diverse ensembles, the most crucial determinant of development outcomes becomes the ability and capacity of these actors and related institutions to retain and/or capture these surpluses. It is one thing for an economic actor to create and/or enhance value in a global production network. It is quite another for this value to be retained and captured partially or fully by that actor *in situ*. *Value capture* thus becomes the most important strategic imperative for actors and institutions in any global production network. This value capture is both actor-specific and territorially specific in that the same actor (for example, a transnational corporation) may capture the value created/enhanced in one location, but shift it to another place through intra-firm transactions (for example, transfer pricing). Equally, local actors may capture more value and retain it in the same place through territorially specific social relations of production (for example, 'buy local' movements). We will return to this territorialization of value capture in greater detail in Chapter 5. Overall, our conception of value is concerned with both the dynamics of value production and their territorial specificities.

ACTORS

Value creation, enhancement, and retention are intimately linked to the ways in which value activities are organized. This primary concern with the organization of value activities—be they resource, manufacturing, or service-related—in global production networks necessarily brings us to the delimitation of the actors in these networks: that is, *who* are involved in value activities, and how do they coordinate, control, and govern these activities? Three groups of economic and non-economic actors are particularly integral to the constitution of a global production network—firms, extra-firm actors, and intermediaries. Such a network cannot operate without the simultaneous presence of these groups. We should point out, however, that these three groups of actors are not meant to be functionally equivalent and commensurable. Our actor-specific conception of global production differs from the stage-based view of value and production chains in the existing literature.[6] In this view, illustrated schematically in Figure 2.1, value activity is typically broken down into several stages of production—including the sourcing of material inputs, manufacturing or processing, logistics, distribution, and/or retailing—within the broader context of financial, technological, and regulatory regimes. This focus on production functions within the value chain approach, however, does not shed sufficient light on the complex motivations and strategies of the different interest groups and competing institutional fragments involved in the organization and governance of global production.

By focusing on firm and extra-firm actors, GPN 2.0 analyzes this diversity of interests and strategies in the different functional segments associated with globally organized value activity. Instead of thinking merely about how R&D, branding, and design activity can offer more value than labour-intensive assembly or retail sales in the production function of a product or service, our approach identifies specific actors that control and produce such value activity within the same or different functional segments. Are these higher-value activities located within a specific group of firms in a global production network, or are they more widely co-produced and shared in two or more groups of firms in various territorial ensembles? Even within the same firm, does the corporate headquarters view value activity in the same way as its subsidiaries at home and/or abroad? Do finance, marketing, engineering, and manufacturing divisions within the firm hold similar strategic views of the

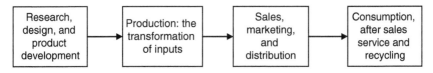

Figure 2.1. A stage-based approach to (global) value or production chains

firm's integration into a global production network? How are other extra-firm actors involved in the production of value activity? Moreover, as global production has become more sophisticated and complex over time, new economic actors that intermediate these inter-firm and extra-firm relations have also emerged as powerful brokers and standards-setters in the organization of these value activities. Despite their ability to arbitrage access to unique repertoires of information (for example, about markets and finance) and knowledge (for example, concerning production and technologies) in diverse networks, these intermediaries have not been well conceptualized in the existing literature. Our analytical task in this section is thus to elaborate on these three important groups of actors that together co-constitute a global production network and make it work.

Firms

Business firms are the basic building blocks of a global production network. While we view firms and their interrelationships as constituting and driving production networks, at the same time we are aware of the different types of ownership and varying national origins of firms. Ownership types can range from privately held corporations (for example, family firms) and publicly traded firms (for example, listed on stock exchanges) to enterprises with substantial or majority equity control by group-based shareholders (for example, cooperatives) and institutions (for example, state-owned enterprises). Their national origins (for example, Anglo-American, Scandinavian, continental European, Japanese, Chinese, and so on) can be equally significant in shaping the organizational cultures and strategic predispositions of these firms in global production networks.[7] At this point, however, it is useful for us to hold these two firm-specific variables constant, bearing in mind that considerations of ownership type and national origin will apply to firms in all roles and functions of a global production network, such as lead firms, strategic partners, suppliers, and customers. We will, therefore, leave these firm-specific variations to our conceptualization of global production network dynamics and actor-specific strategies in the next two chapters.

Taking this initial step of differentiating firms on the basis of their roles and functions in a global production network, we can identify in Table 2.1 a variety of firms, namely lead firms, strategic partners, specialized suppliers (industry-specific or multi/cross-industrial), generic suppliers, and customers. In GPN 2.0, a global production network necessarily entails the central role of one globally significant *lead firm*, and its organizational coordination and control and territorial configuration of a sufficient number of intra-firm affiliates, strategic partners, suppliers, customers, and extra-firm institutions. Three clarifications are useful in relation to this definition. First, the necessary presence of a global lead firm differentiates a global production network from a (global) commodity chain because the latter may not be organized around a single lead firm. This lead firm should be clearly identifiable within a particular industry, which may of course be characterized by the existence of multiple lead firms. A lead firm's industrial position can be measured in terms of market power (for example, revenue or share) or product definition (for example, branding, technology, or knowhow). A firm involved in multiple industries may play different functional roles—for example, being a lead firm in one industry and a supplier in another. By defining each global production network on the basis of a single lead firm, we should be able to avoid much of the definitional and conceptual confusion in the existing literature around what constitutes a global value chain or a global production network.[8] Our definition allows for methodological clarity that in turn makes it easier to identify a global production network as constituted by a lead firm and other firm and extra-firm actors.

Second, by 'significant', we mean a global lead firm that is defined by its firm-specific power and organizational capacity in exercising market control through product and market definition, rather than merely by its leadership in manufacturing processes and technologies or service provision. For example, a lead firm that is strong in branding and/or marketing may take control of market and product definition over another manufacturer or service provider in the same industry (for example, agro-food, electronics, and apparel). Its asymmetric capacity to exercise corporate power allows a lead firm to influence the investment and decisions of other firms and extra-firm institutions and to integrate them into its global production network in order to complete different value processes. In short, a lead firm is significant because it has the capacity to coordinate and control directly its production network—be it in the role of a buyer, producer, coordinator, controller, or market-maker, or a composite of one or more of these roles. As we will explain in the next section on networks, this coordination and control can be realized in varying degrees in relation to other actors in the same network and broader structural dynamics.[9]

Third, a lead firm internalizing all the value activities involved in producing a product or service (see Figure 2.1) may constitute a vertically integrated network of intra-firm affiliates. But it is not a global production network until it externalizes some of this value activity to a sufficient number of other firms. We define this sufficiency not in terms of the absolute number of firms external to a lead firm, but rather in terms of their organizational roles and functions. A global production network must have three or more roles, as described in Table 2.1, performed by different and independent firms such as a lead firm and its strategic partners or external suppliers and customers. In the existing literature, a chain or a network is often vaguely defined in sectoral terms by counting the number of lead firms (buyers or producers) and their suppliers. This dyadic conception of firm roles and functions in a global

Table 2.1. Firms as actors in a global production network

Global production network actors	Role	Value activity	Examples in manufacturing	Examples in service industries
Lead firms	Coordination and control	Product and market definition	Apple and Samsung (ICT); Toyota (automobiles)	HSBC (banking); Singapore Airlines (transport)
Strategic partners	Partial or complete solutions to lead firms	Co-design and development in manufacturing or advanced services	Hon Hai or Flextronics (ICT); ZF (automobiles)	IBM Banking (banking); Boeing or Airbus (transport)
Specialized suppliers (industry-specific)	Dedicated supplies to support lead firms and/or their partners	High-value modules, components, or products	Intel (ICT); Delphi and Denso (automobiles)	Microsoft (ICT); Fidelity or Schroders (banking); Amadeus (transport)
Specialized suppliers (multi-industrial)	Critical supplies to lead firms or partners	Cross-industrial intermediate goods or services	DHL (ICT); Panasonic Automotive (automobiles)	DHL (banking); Panasonic Avionics (transport)
Generic suppliers	Arm's length providers of supplies	Standardized and low-value products or services	Plastics in ICT and automobile manufacturing	Cleaning in banking and transport services
Key customers	Transfer of value to lead firms	Intermediate or final consumption	Other lead firms or consumers	Other lead firms or consumers

Source: Yeung and Coe (2015: table 3); © 2014 Clark University.

production network can be problematic because it does not account fully for the critically important range of diverse roles undertaken by the same firm or different firms in the same network. In our conception, a global production network is really meaningful if there are at least three such roles and functions involved in the global organization of production. More crucially, the existing literature does not allow for the same firm performing simultaneously different roles in two or more global production networks. Its conception of firms tends to be static, and locks firms into a particular lead firm or a supplier role in an existing organizational arrangement. In contrast, our conception allows a firm to serve as a lead firm in one network and a specialized supplier in another.

With these caveats, we can now proceed to characterize in more detail the role of lead firms in global production networks. We postulate that global lead firms exist in most manufacturing, service, and resource industries. Good examples are Apple, Hewlett-Packard, and Google in the ICT industry, Sony, Philips, and Samsung in consumer electronics, Toyota and General Motors in automobile, The Gap, Nike, and Adidas in apparel and footwear, AT&T and Vodafone in telecommunications, Citicorp and HSBC in banking, Hilton and Marriott in hospitality, British Airways and Singapore Airlines in passenger air travel, Wal-Mart and Tesco in retail, UPS and DHL in logistics, Exxon-Mobil and Shell in oil and gas, BHP and Rio Tinto in mining, Kraft and Nestlé in agro-food, and so on. Tables 2.2 and 2.3 list some of the most influential brand name lead firms in apparel and electronics. In the manufacturing sector, and through their *intra-firm affiliates* in different locations, global lead firms often specialize in the upstream activities of R&D and downstream activities of branding, marketing, and post-sale services. These lead firms are commonly engaged in original equipment manufacturing (OEM) and original brand manufacturing (OBM). While they continue to engage in high-value manufacturing activities and services (for example, branding and marketing), these global lead firms are increasingly compelled to outsource a large portion of their product categories to suppliers that are external manufacturers providing partial or complete manufacturing solutions. Since the 1970s, as noted in Chapter 1, this breakdown in vertical or intra-firm integration has led to the proliferation of horizontal or *inter-firm* production networks. In most global industries—for instance, ICT, apparel, toys, and footwear—large contract manufacturers have emerged to offer both technological solutions and massive economies of scale and scope to their lead firm customers. In many cases, these independent manufacturers have graduated from their earlier role as low-cost OEM suppliers to become increasingly involved in original design manufacturing (ODM), offering partial or complete design and manufacturing services to OEM lead firms.

When OEM and OBM lead firms eventually undertake no manufacturing and rely exclusively upon such ODMs for manufacturing their products, we

Table 2.2. Brand name lead firms in apparel

Lead firm type	Type of brand	Description	Examples
Retailers: mass merchants	Private label: the retailer owns or licenses the final product brand, but in almost all cases, the retailer does not own manufacturing.	Department/discount stores that carry private label, exclusive, or licensed brands that are available only in the retailers' stores in addition to other brands.	JCPenney, Macy's, Marks & Spencer, Sears, Target, Tesco, Walmart
Retailers: speciality and apparel		Retailer develops proprietary label brands that commonly include the store's name.	Abercrombie & Fitch, American Eagle, Gap, H&M, Limited Brands, Mango, NEXT
Brand marketer	National brand: the manufacturer is also the brand owner, and goods are distributed through multiple retail outlets.	Firm owns the brand name, but not manufacturing—that is, 'manufacturers without factories'. Products are sold at a variety of retail outlets.	Ben Sherman, Diesel, Gucci, Hugo Boss, Levi's, Liz Claiborne, Nike, Polo
Brand manufacturer		Firm owns brand name and manufacturing; it typically coordinates supply of intermediate inputs to its production networks, often in countries with reciprocal trade agreements.	VF, Fruit of the Loom, Gildan, Hanesbrands, Inditex (Zara)

Source: adapted from Gereffi and Frederick (2010: table 5.8). © World Bank, <http://hdl.handle.net/10986/2509>, Creative Commons Attribution license, CC BY 3.0 IGO.

conceive these latter firms as *strategic partners* to global lead firms because of their mutually dependent relationships. Through various organizational arrangements, global lead firms now rely more on the design, manufacturing, and logistic services of their strategic partners (see Table 2.1). As noted by Sturgeon and Lester (2004: 43):

> Today, suppliers must provide a capability for independent process development and an ability to perform a wide range of value adding functions associated with the manufacturing process, including help with product and component design, component sourcing, inventory management, testing, packaging, and outbound logistics. Lead firms are also demanding that suppliers have the ability to support the lead firm's operations and market-serving activities around the world.

Table 2.3. Brand name lead firms in electronics

Main market segments	Examples	
	Products	Lead firms
Computers	Enterprise computing systems, PCs (desktop, notebook, netbook), embedded computers	IBM, Fujitsu, Siemens, Hewlett-Packard, Dell, Apple, Acer, Lenovo
Computer peripherals and other office equipment	Printers, fax machines, copiers, scanners	Hewlett-Packard, Xerox, Epson, Kodak, Canon, Lexmark, Acer, Fujitsu, Sharp
Consumer electronics	Game consoles, television, home audio and video, portable audio and video, mobile phone handsets, musical equipment, toys	Toshiba, NEC, Vizio, Sony, Sharp, Apple, Nintendo, Microsoft, Samsung, LG, NEC, Matsushita, Hitachi, Microsoft, HTC, Philips
Server and storage devices	Portable, internal, external, backup systems, storage services	Toshiba, Western Digital, EMC, NetApp, Hewlett-Packard, Hitachi, Seagate, Maxtor, LeCie, Quantum
Networking	Public telecommunications, private telecommunications, networks, Internet, mobile phone infrastructure	Alcatel, Nortel, Cisco, Motorola, Juniper, Huawei, Ericsson, Nokia, Tellabs
Automotive electronics	Entertainment, communication, vehicle control (braking, acceleration, traction, suspension), vehicle navigation	TomTom, Garmin, Clarion, Toyota, General Motors, Renault, Bosch, Siemens
Medical electronics	Consumer medical, diagnostics and testing, imaging, telemedicine, meters and monitoring, implants, fitness	General Electric, Philips, Medtronic, Varian
Industrial electronics	Security and surveillance, factory automation, building automation, military systems, aircraft, aerospace, banking and ATM, transportation	Diebold, Siemens, Rockwell, Philips, Omron, Dover
Military and aerospace electronics	Ground combat systems, aircraft, sea-based systems, eavesdropping and surveillance, satellites, missile guidance and intercept	L-3 Communications, Lockheed Martin, Boeing, BAE Systems, Northrop Grumman, General Dynamics, EADS, Finmeccanica, United Technologies

Source: Sturgeon and Kawagami (2010: table 7.4). © World Bank, <http://hdl.handle.net/10986/2509>, Creative Commons Attribution license, CC BY 3.0 IGO.

Because of their firm-specific capability in offering value added services extending well beyond manufacturing production (for example, joint product and technological development), these partners are strategically important to their global lead firm customers within the same global production networks. In many ways, their relationships with global lead firms resemble a partnership more than a customer–supplier transactional relationship. In short, global lead firms and strategic partners enter into inter-organizational relations of strong mutual interdependence in order to compete as a network of interdependent firms. We will address these inter-firm partnerships in greater detail in Chapter 4.

In industries producing intermediate goods, there are highly specialized producers of high-value components, modules, machinery, and equipment for global lead firms in both manufacturing and service industries. These producers can also be thought of as strategic partners to their key customers (Table 2.1). Typical examples are microprocessor chip manufacturers to computer makers, machine tools and equipment suppliers to leading automobile and semiconductor manufacturers, shipbuilders to marine transport service providers, and aircraft manufacturers to passenger airlines. In many of these industries, the organizational relationships between producers and customers are highly complex and strategic because substantial proprietary information and knowledge (for example, relating to strategic plans or market development) are shared between them. The transaction values are also very high because of the high costs of producing machines or equipment customized to the production and service requirements of key customers that are global lead firms in their respective industries.

In the service sector, lead firms are often market leaders in terms of brand names, the unique value proposition of the service offering, and marketing capabilities. They develop outsourcing relationships with independent suppliers of manufactured goods and services. In telecommunications services, for example, global lead firms enter into strategic partnerships with equipment suppliers such as producers of telecommunications equipment and mobile handsets. These producers can be lead firms in their own global production networks. There are therefore overlapping and even cross-industry global production networks with organizational interstices occupied by the same firm. A lead firm in one production network can be a strategic partner to a lead firm in another network. As will be explained and illustrated in the next section on networks, the key to distinguishing such organizational positionality of one firm (for example, as a lead firm or a strategic partner) rests with its capacity to exercise power and control, sometimes through collaborative efforts, in coordinating a particular global production network.[10]

Apart from lead firms and strategic partners, a global production network invariably involves a variety of *independent suppliers* in manufacturing and service industries. These suppliers can be further divided into specialized suppliers and generic suppliers (see Table 2.1). As specialized suppliers, firms can provide manufactured goods (for example, parts and components) and services (for example, OEM assembly) or producer services (for example, legal services or logistics) that are well integrated into the value activity coordinated by a particular global lead firm. The role performed by these specialized suppliers can be industry-specific or crossing different industries. In manufacturing, a specialized supplier may provide components (for example, ball bearings) to one or more global production networks in the same industry (for example, automobiles). Other specialized suppliers can provide parts or modules (for example, Panasonic's audio-visual systems or ABB's motors) for manufacturing products in various industries (for example, electronics, automobiles, power systems, and aviation). Specialized suppliers in the service sector are often providers of advanced producer services such as finance, legal services, logistics, management consultancy, wholesale and distribution, and so on. Some of them serve as specialized suppliers to other firms in the same industry (for example, financial products and management consultancy for banking institutions). Other providers offer specialized services to lead firms from a variety of industries (for example, logistics firms servicing banking institutions and semiconductor manufacturers).

Over time, some of these specialized suppliers may emerge to become strategic partners to global lead firms when their inter-firm relationships are underpinned by much greater asset specificity and mutual dependency. On the other hand, generic suppliers are those that offer fairly standardized and relatively low-value products or services to other firms in the same global production network, such as the lead firm, its strategic partners, and/or specialized suppliers. These client firms usually face low switching costs when they choose from diverse generic suppliers of goods (for example, regular plastic parts) or services (for example, office cleaning).

Finally, no global production network can be complete without *key customers* who pay for the goods or services produced by a variety of other firms in spatially dispersed territories. The consumption of the goods or services produced through global production networks represents the ultimate realization of value transferred from these customers to global lead firms for further distribution to other firms in the same network. For manufacturers of intermediate or capital goods and suppliers of producer services, these key customers can entail other lead firms in manufacturing and service industries. Inter-firm relationships thus prevail in the organizational configuration of these global production networks. In the ICT industry, the key customers for mobile devices made by lead firms such as Apple and Samsung are telecommunications services firms (for example, AT&T and Vodafone) that package these devices as part of their wireless communications services in various regional and national markets. In services, commercial banks count on key corporate customers who raise funds through debt financing and require other financial services. These customers can be lead firms in their respective global production networks. In air transport, cargo services are extremely important to the effective functioning of many global production networks through which lightweight products are manufactured worldwide.

Extra-Firm Actors

Apart from managing their intra-firm affiliates and inter-firm organizational relationships with other firms in the same global production network, lead firms must also engage with extra-firm actors such as the state, international organizations, labour groups, consumers, and civil society organizations in the diverse localities that are articulated into these networks. These state and non-state institutions can be highly significant *extra-firm* actors shaping value activity in different global production networks. While not meant to be exhaustive, Table 2.4 summarizes the main role and value activity of these extra-firm actors. The role of the *state* in economic governance is well recognized in the literature on development.[11] The state can participate directly in firm activity through direct equity investment and favourable industrial policies. By taking up equity positions in firms within global production networks, the state can influence the configuration and governance of these networks through its ownership of lead firms. Some of today's global lead firms are indeed such state-owned enterprises (for example, Huawei and Petrobras) or government-linked companies (for example, Singapore Airlines and Renault).[12]

Table 2.4. Extra-firm actors in a global production network

Global production network actors	Role	Value activity	Areas of influence	Impact on firm activity
The state	Promotion and regulation	Ownership, industrial policies, innovations, and market rules	Capital, land, and labour markets; taxation; social and environmental concerns	Country of origin effect Different levels of state institutions Bargaining dynamics and value capture
International organizations	Global rules, agreements, and regulation	International sanctions and codes of conducts	Finance, labour, business ethics, and environment	Global
Labour groups	Firm-specific governance and extra-firm pressures	Collective bargaining	Wages and working conditions	Local, national, and international
Consumers	Buyers of final goods or services	Preferences and choices	Limited, unless through collective action	Mostly local or national
Civil society organizations	Ensuring corporate social responsibility	Lobbying and social sanctions	Ethical sourcing, gender equality, and environmental sustainability	Mix of local, national, and international

Apart from the equity option, the state can promote specific firms through industrial policies that offer preferential grants, loans, and tax benefits. These policies may help stimulate particular kinds of value activity, such as R&D, design, and branding, which matter most to the development trajectory of a particular regional or national economy. In East Asia, for example, the prominence of the ICT industry in South Korea, Taiwan, and Singapore is clearly a direct outcome of extra-firm initiatives in the form of state-led industrial policy.[13] However, the successful articulation of these economies and their domestic firms into ICT global production networks owes as much to firm-specific strategies as to direct state sponsorship through policy interventions. National firms have, over time, developed their own technological innovations and organizational capabilities that enable them to enter into cooperative inter-firm relations with global lead firms. In some states, particularly those in developing economies, there are substantial differences in the state's role across different regions within their national economies. Some regional states (for example, Karnataka in India and the coastal provinces of China) have instigated highly effective industrial policies that in turn provide crucial impetus for connecting their regional centres (for example, Bangalore and Shanghai) with lead firms in global production networks.

Moreover, the state at various geographical scales (for example, national, regional, and local) can set and enforce formal and informal rules and regulations that favour particular configurations of global production networks. This regulatory role of the state has often been discussed in the existing literature.[14] Suffice to say that the state's role as a regulator depends very much on its bureaucratic capacity and institutional legitimacy and therefore varies significantly across and within national formations. In principle, state regulation can extend from labour and land issues to financial markets, and from health and safety issues to environmental concerns. While most firms in global production networks are subject to some or all of these regulatory influences, their responses are again highly variable. Firms from diverse countries of origin are often embedded in different regulatory relationships with their home states. In national economies with a more liberal market stance (for example, the United States and the United Kingdom), state regulation tends to be more formalized and less beholden to particular actors in global production networks. For example, labour market policies are generally applicable to all firms, irrespective of whether they participate in a global production network. In more coordinated market states such as Germany and Japan, however, the regulatory role can be more targeted, including sector-specific regulations and closer policy coordination of distinct interest groups in global production networks.

In recent decades, many national states have 'up-scaled' their regulatory functions to *international organizations* such as the World Trade Organization (WTO) and the International Monetary Fund (IMF) that are vested with increasing regulatory authority over key policy instruments and enforcement mechanisms, such as anti-dumping actions and protection of intellectual property rights, financial sector liberalization, and fiscal prudence in public finance. As production becomes more globally dispersed, international organizations have also developed important codes of conduct for labour conditions (for example, International Labour Organization) and business and investment ethics (for example, the United Nations Conference on Trade and Development (UNCTAD)). Taken together, these international actors, sanctioned and supported by national states, play a significant and often complementary role to state regulation of global production networks.

In addition to the state and international organizations, we witness a variety of other non-state actors in global production networks (Table 2.4). Through their collective action, these non-state actors—such as labour groups, consumers and civil society organizations, and transnational advocacy networks—are important extra-firm actors because they can facilitate or disrupt the efficient functioning of global production networks.[15] *Labour organizations* are obviously important here because all firms are organizational devices bringing together the collective value production by labour—whether they are workers, managers, professionals, and so on. Similar to the state, the role of labour organizations as an extra-firm actor varies substantially across national economies. In national systems with historically substantial labour involvement in industrial governance (for example, Germany), the governance of different production networks entails more than just lead firms in inter-firm relations, incorporating both firms and labour in the (re)configuration of value activities in industrial production.[16] In national economies with weak labour organizations (for example, parts of the Global South), value extraction by firms in global production networks tends to be given almost a free rein. In other words, we expect a continuum, from very strong to very weak, in the role of labour organizations in co-governing value activity by firms in global production networks.

For manufacturers of finished goods and providers of consumer services, the notion of final customers refers to individual *consumers* in various national economies. As extra-firm actors, these consumers can engage global lead firms through their individual and/or collective action in the form of consumption preferences and choices, boycotting, litigation, and so on.

While these consumers often have little direct control over the value activity in the global production of these goods and services, their active role in a global production network can be enhanced through extra-firm collective action such as consumer groups and advocacy organizations. These *civil society organizations* can translate consumer preferences and views into collective pressure on particular firms and extra-firm actors (for example, the state) in global production networks. While recognizing their importance in addressing consumer and other social concerns (for example, gender issues and the environment) in the value activity of global production networks, these organizations can be highly diverse in their objectives and interests. Their legitimacy and effectiveness again vary enormously across localities, making it analytically very difficult for us to prescribe a priori a particular role for their involvement in disparate global production networks. In reality, this role can be better illustrated through empirical studies because of its sectoral and geographical specificities. For example, ethical and fair trade initiatives in developed countries, strongly advocated by the state and civil society organizations, are generally more effective in influencing sourcing strategies of certain kinds of lead firms, such as major retailers and their domestic and foreign suppliers in the agro-food and apparel industries.[17]

In other industries such as electronics and automobiles, these initiatives have much less purchase in shaping how lead firms coordinate their global production networks. Instead, we are witnessing the growing importance of what Büthe and Mattli (2011) term the 'new global rulers' through the privatization of regulation. These non-state global setters of standards and norms in global industries play an increasingly vital role in the governance of inter-firm relations. For example, the influence of the credit-rating agencies extends far beyond that of financial institutions such as banks, affecting global lead firms and their strategic partners seeking funding in different capital markets. This pressure in turn shapes their production and sourcing strategies (see more about this in Chapter 3). Private associations and consortiums in high-tech industries are also highly crucial in setting new industrial standards and technological parameters that profoundly influence the value activities of lead firms, their strategic partners, and customers. We describe these new global players as *intermediaries* because they often intermediate diverse interests and objectives of firms and extra-firm actors in global production networks spanning most industries.

Intermediaries

In our conception, intermediaries bridge and connect multiple actors in a global production network, allowing them to engage in value activity of mutual benefit. These intermediaries can be firms or extra-firm actors; they are therefore not a third category of actors. Instead, intermediaries are conceptualized in relation to their *functional role* in global production networks. Indeed, some intermediaries (for example, financial institutions or logistics firms) are lead firms in their own industry-specific global production networks. In this case, intermediation leads to the intersection of multiple networks across different industries. Extra-firm intermediaries can be business and industry associations that represent and engage the collective interest of firms in a particular national and/or industrial context. The participation

Table 2.5. Intermediaries as enablers in a global production network

Global production network actors	Role	Value activity	Areas of influence
Financial intermediaries	Credits, information and knowledge services	Managing financial risks and promoting new innovation and investments	Credit lines, financial advice, investment evaluations, value projections, tax strategies, etc.
Logistics providers	Connecting lead firms with their strategic partners, global suppliers, and final consumers	Efficiency, speed, and flexibility of the entire production network	Production operation, information and inventory management, and just-in-time delivery
Intermediaries in standards	Establishment, enforcement, and harmonization of protocols and codified knowledge Consultancy and information providers	Compliance, certification, and private regulation	Production (e.g. labour and environment) Consumption (e.g. quality and safety) Innovation (e.g. standardization, protocols, and interfaces)

of these intermediaries ensures the provision of unique inputs, mostly intangible in nature, to make these networks work. While illuminating the complex power relations governing lead firms and their suppliers in cross-border production networks, past research has not paid much attention to these power brokers, who enable the effective functioning of global production networks. In this section and Table 2.5, we attempt to incorporate and conceptualize three such critical intermediaries: finance, logistics, and standards.[18]

A few caveats are necessary here. First, our choice reflects the enormous market power of these service providers in the 2000s and beyond. We do not deny the continued significance of other more traditional intermediaries, such as sourcing agents in apparel, toys, and footwear, import–export traders in electronics, and wholesale distributors in automobiles and food.[19] The under-theorization of these new intermediaries in global production networks, nevertheless, represents a missing link in our existing knowledge base. We believe the initial work done in this area needs to be significantly extended. Second, each of these service providers clearly serves as an important actor in contemporary economic systems. But their role in most global production networks is neither the same as lead firms, nor equivalent to that of strategic partners or suppliers. These intermediaries should be conceived of as enablers that global production networks need to function effectively. Third, intermediaries are necessarily the 'go-betweens' among key actors in global production networks. In this sense, they intermediate diverse interests between, say, lead firms, their partners, suppliers, customers, and other extra-firm institutions. In some cases, global lead firms task these intermediaries (for example, consultancies and advisory agencies) to govern their relationships with other actors in global production networks. In other instances, state institutions may flex their muscles with respect to these intermediaries (for example, financial lending practices) in order to put regulatory pressure on global lead firms. Fourth, intermediaries (for example, logistics providers) often engage in deep integration with lead firms and other actors in global production networks and control a significant amount of proprietary information critical to the successful operation of a particular global production network.

Let us now consider the role of *financial intermediaries*. The financialization of the global economy since the breakdown of the Bretton Woods system in the 1970s has undoubtedly put finance at the forefront of global capitalism.[20] But how does finance play an intermediating role in global production networks? During the Fordist era of vertical integration and mass production, hierarchically organized multidivisional firms tended to use retained earnings and debts (for example, bank borrowing) to fund their productive activity. While the largest and most dominant Fordist firms issued public offerings in stock exchanges, the extent of the capital market's penetration into everyday corporate life was relatively modest even in the United States and United Kingdom—the archetypes of Anglo-American capitalism. In the contemporary era, however, the massive securitization of corporate assets and financial re-engineering of firms, revolutionized by such intermediaries as investment banks in corporate finance, has brought finance into the core of the globalization of production networks. Global lead firms are now no longer masters of their own destiny. Their CEOs are increasingly driven by shareholder interests and credit ratings in capital markets. In short, a GPN analysis engaging directly with these financial intermediaries can illuminate better the functioning and operation of global production networks.[21]

More specifically, we consider four particular ways in which finance intermediates global production networks. First, global finance impinges directly on value creation, enhancement, and retention in global production networks. This is perhaps the most important role of finance in intermediation. The enormous complexity in managing financial risks such as interest and exchange rates in global production challenges even the most powerful global lead firms. The kind of financial knowledge and expertise required to handle these risks has gone far beyond the capability of their in-house finance teams and treasury departments. These lead firms often look to financial intermediaries to provide critical services so that these firms can *actually* capture substantial value from their productive activity. These services include credit lines, financial advice, investment evaluations, value projections, tax strategies, and so on. Moreover, these financial intermediaries may provide additional services such as arranging credit for key partners and suppliers of global lead firms and handling financial transactions between them. In so doing, these financial intermediaries play a substantial role in greasing the wheels of global production networks.

Second, finance intermediates the innovative trajectories of global production networks. As the innovation of new products and services requires massive investment in new technologies, expertise, and knowhow, financial intermediaries play an indispensable role in loan syndication, risk calculations, market projections, and earnings estimations associated with these new products and services. Behind the introduction of successive generations of iPhones and iPads, for example, Apple needs to engage a number of financial intermediaries to ensure the market success of its products. In order for a telecommunications service provider to bid for a new broadband service project, it needs to bring in financial intermediaries to ensure the availability of syndicated credits at the best rates and the mitigation of market uncertainties associated with these medium-term projects. As such, finance penetrates deeply into the core functions of any global production network—the configuration of value activities and new innovations.

Third, financial reporting is of considerable importance for value calculation among lead firms in global production networks because the tendency towards short-term reporting in most capital markets compels these firms to reduce their time horizon in production planning and supplier relationships. Financial intermediaries can help lead firms to plan and restructure their existing production networks in order to respond more effectively to this pressure. Fourth, greater access to capital markets can fundamentally reshape the relationship between ownership and management, particularly in publicly listed lead firms, which in turn requires adjustments to the time horizons of corporate performance, value capture expectations, and firm-specific governance models. Through their advisory services and credit provision, financial intermediaries can enable global lead firms to make these adjustments successfully.[22]

The increasingly indispensable role of finance as an intermediary in global production networks sits alongside the rise of *logistics* in making these networks truly global in their spatial reach. In general, logistics refers to the entire process of planning, implementing, and managing the movement and storage of raw materials, components, finished goods, and associated knowledge from the point of origin to the point of consumption.[23] It is about more than just supply chain management because logistics providers increasingly engage in backward integration by helping lead firms establish and/or relocate their production operations and manufacturing facilities. This pre-production role of logistics intermediaries distinguishes them from specialized suppliers, such as supply chain managers, which do not have the same depth and breadth of logistical capabilities. Meanwhile, some logistics providers integrate forward to reach out to final consumers on behalf of global lead firms and their strategic partners. These providers intermediate lead firms' demand for high quality and efficient distribution services and their strategic partners' high-speed and high-volume production arrangements. Logistics providers are thereby becoming more embedded in entire production networks spearheaded by global lead firms and are developing longer-term cooperative relationships that connect together these lead firms and their strategic partners and global suppliers.

In the logistics literature, firms are categorized into first, second, third, and fourth party providers. First party logistics refers to the in-house provision of transport, warehousing, and other supply chain and distribution functions within global lead firms. Second party logistics is characterized by the outsourcing of these functions to an external service provider, known as a specialized supplier in Table 2.1. But this intermediation is specific to a particular customer and does not yet constitute a production network comprising of two or more actors engaging in inter-firm relations. For logistics to play a truly intermediating role in global production networks, third and fourth party logistics should also be considered. In the former, two or more firms within a particular production network agree to contract the same service provider to take care of their entire logistics requirements. This intermediary is involved in value activity that stretches between R&D, production, marketing, and distribution of a particular good or service. Between R&D in a lead firm and production in overseas partners, for example, a third party logistics (3PL) provider such as DHL or UPS may be responsible for information sharing, transfer of documents, blueprints, prototypes, and delivery from suppliers of materials and components. The same service requirement also exists between production and marketing/distribution. A global lead firm is likely to demand speedy time-to-market from a 3PL, in collaboration with strategic partners such as contract manufacturers. This 3PL must also work with strategic partners that are particularly concerned with continuous manufacturing operation, efficient inventory management, and just-in-time production to save costs and to capture more value. Overall, it is clear that the intermediating role of a 3PL in a global production network can be highly complex; it can be a make or break factor in the creation, enhancement, and retention of value among actors in a network. In recent years, a new form of logistics intermediary has emerged to integrate actors in global production networks with logistics service providers. These fourth party logistics (4PLs) providers are effectively market integrators that specialize in more than just logistics (such as 3PLs). They have to provide non-asset and skills-based services, such as financial and management consulting, software development and integration, brokerage of transport and import/export requirements, and so on.

If finance and logistics are obvious intermediaries shaping the configuration, operationalization, and governance of global production networks, *standards intermediaries* are far less tangible and visible in their imprints on these networks. By standards, we mean intermediaries that are involved in the establishment, enforcement, and harmonization of protocols and codified knowledge and specifications in the global production of goods and services. Table 2.6 summarizes the major attributes and actors involved in these standards. To Nadvi (2008), compliance with these standards has become a *sine qua non* for any actor to participate in global production networks. At the international level, these standards can refer to production (for example, labour and environmental) and consumption domains (for example, quality and safety).[24] International standards can pose a significant barrier of entry into global production networks because of the high economic, social, and institutional costs associated with their compliance. A change in international standards can also impinge on existing network configuration and governance, producing distinct losers and winners. At the industry level, standards are highly important in fostering technological innovations and new services in areas such as telecommunications and biotechnology.[25] Industrial

Table 2.6. Standards as intermediaries in global production networks

Attribute of standard	Variability
Field of application	• Quality assurance • Environmental • Health and safety • Labour • Social/economic • Ethical
Form	• Codes of conduct • Label • Standard
Coverage	• Firm/commodity chain-specific • Sector specific • Generic
Key actors	• International business • International NGOs • International trade unions • International organizations
Certification process	• First, second, or third party • Private-sector auditors • NGOs • Government
Regulatory implications	• Legally mandatory • Market competition requirement • Voluntary
Geographical scale	• Regional (e.g. a US state) • National • Macro-regional (e.g. the EU) • Global (e.g. the UN Global Compact)

Source: adapted from Nadvi and Waltring (2004: table 3.2). With permission.

standards are critical to vertical specialization among key actors in global production networks. Without common technical interfaces and modularity standards in constituent components and subsystems, it is doubtful that the worlds of production in electronics and automobiles could be as highly globalizing as they are.

Now that the intermediating power of international and industrial standards is rendered more visible, it is useful to introduce the key intermediaries that establish and enforce these standards. In general, we can conceive a wide range of institutions as being involved. International organizations such as the International Organization for Standardization (ISO) and the United Nations' Food and Agriculture Organization (FAO) tend to be more prominent in setting standards that should be complied with on a global basis. But the actual implementation of these standards on the ground falls to an assortment of intermediaries such as quasi-state institutions, civil society organizations, transnational advocacy networks, and inspection agencies. Because of this diversity in intermediaries at the level of implementation and compliance, global standards are really 'global' only in name. Their concrete realization in governing production networks varies significantly across different jurisdictions and institutional contexts.[26] For example, while global standards on labour conditions are well recognized and established, many suppliers to brand name global lead firms (e.g. retailers) continue to flout these standards.

In comparison, industrial standards are often better enforced and produce tangible outcomes in shaping the configuration of global production networks. By setting new technological and product or service standards, important intermediaries such as industry associations and certification agencies play a dominant role in intermediating diverse interfaces within global production networks—for example, between lead firms and their strategic partners, between customers and their suppliers, between producers and consumers, and so on. In terms of technological standards, lead firms, and industry associations are often actively involved in setting standards, albeit with radically different vested interests. A lead firm and its key partners and suppliers can reap exceptional profits and capture high levels of value if their technology becomes the industry standard. Well-known examples are automobiles (for example, energy efficiency and safety standards), computer operating systems (for example, MS-DOS versus UNIX), electronics (for example, Blue-ray versus HD in DVD technology), and mobile telecommunications (for example, GSM versus CDMA and iOS versus Android). In industries where compliance to common standards is required (for example, agriculture and services), certification agencies become crucial intermediaries between customers and suppliers in disparate global production networks. For example, organic food certification and ethical trade initiatives have relegated much of the certification power in governing agro-food production networks to independent, and often private, agencies. Compliance with labour standards is also increasingly monitored and verified by specialized social audit firms such as Cal-Safety, Global Social Compliance, and Veritas. The rise of these new private regulators has complicated existing governance relations among firms in production networks.[27]

As global standards are becoming a more standard operating procedure for governing global production networks, both existing actors in these networks and new actors trying to enter into these networks require new knowledge about these standards and their implications. With global standards come a whole array of specialized providers of such knowhow about the nature of, and compliance with, these standards, whether at the international or the industry level. The massive demand for this knowhow has created a whole new industry of standards consultancy and service providers that intermediate the ways in which actors in networks conform to and/or evade these standards. For example, ethical and labour standards are increasingly tied to corporate social responsibility (CSR). Global lead firms are particularly susceptible to CSR liabilities because of the risk of substantial reputational damage. These firms often actively involve CSR consultants and specialists to re-examine and re-evaluate their entire production networks and to monitor ethical and labour code implementation in order to minimize CSR liabilities and potential damage. These consultants in turn wield tremendous leverage over other actors in the networks (for example, local suppliers). Similar to the intermediation role of logistics service providers, these standards consultancies capitalize on their intangible and tacit knowhow of international and industrial standards to mediate the competing interests among lead firms, strategic partners, local suppliers, and consumers in global production networks.

NETWORKS

The above section has presented three functional groups of actors—firms, extra-firm actors, and intermediaries—that play the most significant roles in shaping the configuration and governance of value activity in the global economy. The interrelationships between these actors are necessarily complex. As a collective and complementary process, the creation, enhancement, and retention of value do not begin and end with a global lead firm in a linear chain-like manner. Rather, we need a network conception of this organizationally complex and geographically extensive process of configuring value activities because of the mutually interactive and recursive nature of the relationships involved. As outlined in Chapter 1, we argue in this book that the organization of diverse manufacturing and service activities by a wide range of actors and institutions in multiple locations is best understood conceptually as a global production *network*. For the purpose of methodo-logical clarity, we begin the identification and analysis of each network by identifying a global lead firm and then building in a wide range of other related firms and extra-firm actors in order to constitute fully this network.

Our network conception also points to the diversity of organizational modes through which any particular global production network can be con-figured and coordinated. The governance of global production networks cannot simply be assigned solely to lead firms in a static and hierarchical manner, because of the often contested and evolutionary relationships between lead firms and other actors in inter- and extra-firm settings.[28] The politics of governance goes beyond the partial equilibrium view expressed in the existing value chain governance approach. Reflecting on this issue, Levy (2008: 944) argues that the GPN approach should pay 'attention to the agency of actors in mobilizing and deploying resources, forging alliances, shaping regulatory structures, and framing issues. From this perspective, GPNs resem-ble contested organizational fields in which actors struggle over the construc-tion of economic relationships, governance structures, institutional rules and norms, and discursive frames'. In short, global production networks are constituted by and through actors that in turn are shaped by the various dynamic logics of global competition.

In particular, we conceive economic actors such as the firm not as individ-ual agents *per se*, but as a constitutive part of the wider network through which emergent power and strategic effects are realized over time and in different territorial ensembles. Firms are not standalone 'black boxes', but rather actively contested organizational devices for the accumulation, mobilization, and deployment of resources and competencies in the production and extrac-tion of value. This dynamic conception of actors and their power relations improves on earlier work on value chain governance that focuses primarily on transactional linkages between firms (for example, buyer and supplier rela-tionships). Focusing analytically on the articulation of firms into global flows of capital, labour, and knowledge, GPN analysis also ventures beyond a state-centric interpretation of economic development. We argue that this articula-tion in search of new and complementary assets for value production and extraction is a firm-specific organizational choice based, crucially, on the emergent dynamic capabilities of firms and their evolving relations with other firm and extra-firm actors. Our conception therefore places significant analytical emphasis on firms and their strategic action *in* and *through* global production networks.[29] As argued in Henderson et al.'s earlier influential work (2002: 438) on global production networks,

> if the object of our endeavours is the possibilities for economic development and
> prosperity, then we should recognize that in order to speak authoritatively on
> these issues, we need to study what firms do, where they do it, why they do it, why

they are allowed to do it, and how they organize the doing of it across different geographic scales.

In the following two subsections, we describe the distinct organizational configurations and power relations of actors in global production networks.

Configurations

This subsection attempts to illustrate some possible configurations of a stylized global production network and explains how such multiple networks can intersect both to form an industry and to bridge different industries. This attempt brings us closer to understanding how actors and industries intersect in various global production networks and how these intersections can be aggregated up to form different industries and sectors. Figure 2.2 describes two common organizational configurations of global production networks, each with a distinctive lead firm and encompassing a wide range of other firm and extra-firm actors. In the first configuration, known as a *strategic partnership model*, a global lead firm engages another firm as a strategic partner to provide partial or complete solutions for its product or service delivery to key customers. This inter-firm partnership criss-crosses with tangible and intangible inputs from specialized suppliers and intersects with broader structural initiatives intermediated by industrial associations such as standardization and modularization.

In the manufacturing sector, the strategic partner is likely to be a total solution provider such as supply chain managers in apparel (for example, Li & Fung) or contract manufacturers in ICT (for example, Hon Hai Precision). In services such as transport, a strategic partner can be a manufacturer of major transport equipment such as aircraft-makers (for example, Boeing and Airbus) and shipbuilders (for example, Hyundai Heavy Industries). To deliver the finished products to the customers of the lead firm, a strategic partner has to engage with logistics service providers. Responsible for most, if not all, of the manufacturing activity, it is also subject to lobbying pressures from extra-firm actors such as labour organizations that push for better working conditions and higher labour standards in its factories. Specialized suppliers such as platform leaders are also involved in the branding and marketing activity of the lead firm, as it reaches out to its customers (for example, 'Intel Inside' in personal computers). Consumer groups may exert pressures to ensure the corporate social responsibility of a lead firm. Overall, this configuration of a global production network places a significant degree of analytical attention on the complex inter-firm relationship between the lead firm and its strategic partner in the context of other inter- and extra-firm intersections. Coordination and governance in this model tends to be shared between the lead firm

(a) Strategic partnership model: e.g. apparels, ICT, transport

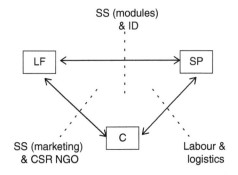

(b) Lead firm-centric model: e.g. automobiles, ICT, banking

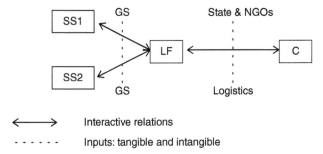

Figure 2.2. Two organizational configurations of a global production network

Note: LF = lead firm; SP = strategic partner; C = customer; SS = specialized supplier; GS = generic supplier; ID = industry association; NGO = non-government organization.

and its strategic partner. The model can be commonly observed in both manufacturing (for example, apparel and ICT) and service industries (for example, transport).

By contrast, the second configuration of a global production network in Figure 2.2 does not provide for the role of a strategic partner. Instead, this is a *lead firm-centric model* of organizing a global production network in which the lead firm dominates and drives the entire network. This model is often observed in such industries as automobiles, ICT, and banking. In each of these industries, we can identify lead firms that take charge of a significant proportion of the production of goods or services. In the automobile and ICT industries, a lead firm may bring together material inputs from specialized suppliers (for example, key modules and core components) and generic suppliers (for example, plastic parts) to produce finished or intermediate goods (for example, semiconductors). Because of their firm-specific choices (for example, technological and strategic concerns), these lead firms prefer to internalize much of the production process in order to exercise greater control over the quality and delivery of their products to customers. This delivery and distribution may involve other firms such as logistics and retail service providers. As the manufacturers of these products, lead firms are subject to lobbying and other interventions from state and non-state actors. In the service industries, major banks, for example, are lead firms that draw upon material and intangible inputs from their specialized suppliers (for example, computer hardware and information systems) to offer financial products and services to their corporate customers and individual consumers. In this lead firm-centric model, our analytical focus tends primarily to fall on the lead firm and its forward and backward linkages with specialized suppliers and key customers. Other inter- and extra-firm actors may mediate these linkages such that the governance power of the lead firm in this network is partially constrained.

Taken together, these two illustrative configurations of global production networks are premised on the organizational roles of diverse actors such as lead firms, strategic partners, suppliers, and extra-firm actors. While each configuration tends to resonate more strongly in particular sectors and industries, we do expect *both* configurations to be possibly found in the same sector or industry. These configurations may also evolve in a dynamic fashion over time. In the automobile industry, for example, which is generally characterized by the lead firm-centric model, a specialized supplier of core components (for example, gear boxes) or services (for example, automobile design and distribution) may, over time, take up the role of a strategic partner through firm-specific initiatives or industry-wide transformations. This dynamic evolution can lead to a reconfiguration of the global production network from a lead firm-centric model to a strategic partnership model. In a similar vein, the intense inter-firm relationship between a lead firm and its strategic partner can disintegrate over time when the latter ventures into product or market definition—the core competence and function of the lead firm—by developing its own branding and products. Under threat from its strategic partner, this lead firm may internalize some or all of its manufacturing activity. It may also engage with another solution provider, even though this new inter-firm relation may be less strategic and mutually dependent. Equally, the strategic partner may evolve to become a lead firm and thus exit its partnership with the lead firm. In these dynamic scenarios, a strategic partnership configuration may be transformed into a lead firm-centric model of global production networks.

Moving beyond the dynamic configuration of a single global production network, we can now consider how multiple networks can aggregate and intersect. This aggregation is conceptually significant because it allows us to overcome the 'unit of analysis dilemma' identified by Bair (2005: 166)—how firm-level investigations of value chains can be aggregated and mapped onto larger units of analysis such as the regional or the national economy.[30] Our conception also provides a clear and consistent approach to analyzing domestic and international linkages in global production networks across different industries. In Figure 2.3, we map out three such organizational possibilities: (a) aggregation of multiple global production networks to form an industry; (b) intra-industry intersection of global production networks through common strategic partners or specialized suppliers; and (c) inter-industry intersection of global production networks through firms undertaking different roles in different global production networks.[31] In the first possibility (Figure 2.3(a)), we can aggregate multiple production networks, some global and some local, to form an entire industry. The personal computer industry, for example, is comprised of multiple global production networks, each having one lead firm and resembling either model in Figure 2.2. The top ten global lead firms and other firms involved in their global production networks can be readily aggregated to form almost the entire global computer industry. But to account fully for the computer industry in a particular regional or national economy, other local firms in the same industry may matter, even though their production and marketing activity may be oriented towards the domestic economy. A more complete GPN analysis may therefore bring in these local firms that are not yet integrated into any global production network. In this way, an industry can be thought of as an aggregation of multiple global production networks and localized firms.

As we move from one global production network to another *within* the same industry, we often observe that several major partners or suppliers tend to provide manufacturing or other value activity to multiple lead firms. We call this *intra-industry intersection* of multiple global production networks (see Figure 2.3(b)). In the ICT industry (B1), for example, single or multiple ODMs or EMS providers can serve the manufacturing needs of several brand name lead firms. These manufacturers become the nodes through which the global production networks of these lead firms intersect. In the retail sector (B2), major food and confectionery producers (for example, Cadbury and Kraft) may supply multiple lead firm customers (for example, Wal-Mart and Tesco). While lead firms in these industries do not intersect with each other, they tend to share common strategic partners and/or specialized suppliers, leading to criss-crossing of their global production networks.

More importantly for the analysis of firm strategies and developmental outcomes (Chapters 4 and 5, respectively), our conception of global production networks allows for *inter-industry intersections* that enable cross-sectoral and inter-industrial analysis of economic development. In these intersections of multiple global production networks across industries, we can begin by identifying a nodal firm that performs multiple roles in these industries—it may be a lead firm in one industry and a specialized supplier or a customer in

(a) Aggregation: formation of an industry

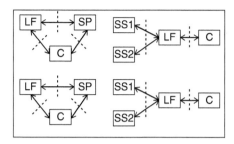

(b) Intra-industry intersection

B1. A common strategic partner

B2. A common specialized supplier

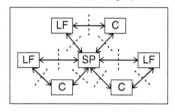
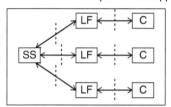

(c) Inter-industry intersections

C1. Customer as a lead firm

C2. Lead firm as a specialized supplier

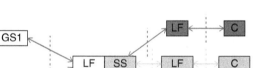
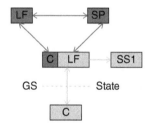

C3. Common ownership

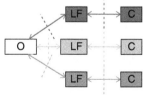

Figure 2.3. Multiple global production networks: industry and intersections

Notes: Each container box in (a) and (b) or each level of shading in (c) represents an industry or sector. LF = lead firm; SP = strategic partner; C = customer; SS = specialized supplier; GS = generic supplier; O = owner.

another industry. Three such inter-industry intersections can be identified in Figure 2.3(c). First, a lead firm in one global production network serves as a *customer* in another network and influences the strategic partnership relations in the latter network (C1). For example, Singapore Airlines is a global lead firm in the passenger air transport industry, coordinating its global production network of transport services. But it is also a key customer of Boeing, a global lead firm in the aerospace industry. In this manufacturing industry, Boeing partners with leading specialized engine suppliers such as Rolls-Royce, GE Aviation, and Pratt & Whitney to produce cutting-edge transport equipment for passenger service providers. By working with a specific engine supplier, Rolls-Royce, Singapore Airlines can effectively shape the strategic partnership between Boeing and its engine-makers. In both industries, we identify the global lead firms (that is, Singapore Airlines and Boeing) and examine their interrelationships (with strategic partners) that in turn influence the dynamic configuration of their respective global production networks across different industries.

Second, an inter-industry intersection can occur when a lead firm in one global production network serves as a *specialized supplier* to multiple lead firms in several industries. In C2, this intersection is particularly prevalent in the context of service lead firms serving as a specialized supplier to multiple partners and/or customers in different industries. Good examples are logistics, finance, and retailing. In each of these service industries, a global lead firm can coordinate and control its own global production network and, yet, each network can connect to multiple customers that are lead firms in diverse industries (shown in different shadings). A logistics global lead firm such as DHL can serve the organizational needs of a great variety of manufacturing and service industries. As a specialized service supplier, it can connect the flow of goods and services among various global production networks in these industries. In retail, giants such as Wal-Mart and Tesco are clearly lead firms in their own right, exerting huge control over their myriad supply networks. But in functional terms, their primary role is to distribute the products and services of other lead firms, ranging from food to non-food products such as health and electronics.[32]

Third, common ownership of multiple lead firms or strategic partners can lead to inter-industry intersections (as in C3). This is particularly evident in the case of business groups or conglomerates in which the ultimate holding company may control several firms that serve as lead firms, strategic partners, or specialized suppliers in multiple industries.[33] Some of the world's largest business groups tend to control several lead firms that straddle diverse industries and sectors. Japan's Sony, for example, controls major lead firms in two industries—electronics, and media and entertainment. Until its split in 2013, the former News Corp controlled lead firms (Fox and News Corp) in media, entertainment, publishing, and so on. Hong Kong's Cheung Kong Holding, a leading property developer in Asia, controls Hutchison Whampoa, a global lead firm in operating ports and telecommunications. Through common ownership, the governance of many of these lead firms and therefore their global production networks in multiple industries can be better understood as a form of inter-industry intersection. Taken together, this actor-specific approach to defining global production networks offers a more explicit unpacking of these actors and their interrelationships, which constitute the evolutionary dynamics of global industries. It also helps illuminate the complex power relations of these inter-firm and extra-firm relations.

Power Relations

In our conception of value activities coordinated by multiple actors, the complex interrelationships between the lead firm and other firms and extra-firm actors are both structural and relational in nature. As detailed in Chapter 1, a relational view of global production networks requires us to go beyond a structural analysis of the global economy that tends to adopt a zero-sum approach to asymmetric power distribution and network governance. In the organizational contexts of Figures 2.2 and 2.3, the structural approach tends to assume a unidirectional flow of power relation, usually from the lead firm to its partners and suppliers. This zero-sum approach often fails to account for the complex and recursive power relations among diverse actors in these networks. Instead, our relational analysis of global production networks focuses on the existence of differential power relations and authority systems within a network and their emergent effects on various actors.[34] A global production network reflects relational processes and uneven structures in which, and through which, corporate power is distributed, exercised, and governed. As noted by Coe et al. (2008b: 272; emphasis in original), production networks 'reflect the fundamental *structural* and *relational* nature of how production, distribution and consumption of goods and services are—indeed always have been—organized. Although they have undoubtedly become far more complex organizationally, as well as far more extensive geographically, production networks are a *generic* form of economic organization'.

Powerful lead firms are those that drive global production networks and make things happen. Their ability to do so depends on their asymmetric control and internalization of key resources (physical, political, economic, social, and technological). The network literature in economic sociology and strategic management has commonly suggested that power in a network is a structural function of a firm's positionality within the network (for example, centrality) or strength of association (for example, density).[35] This structural view of power and authority in a network, however, tells us little about the dynamic and qualitative nature of its constitutive relationships, such as supplier selection and control, degree of mutual trust, commitment and reciprocity in partnership, and durability and endurance under pressure, which is far more important than structural durability *per se*. It also suffers from an *ex ante* conception of clear role definitions among actors in a network by assuming a stable and identifiable set of power relations that are measurable and substitutable in quantitative terms.

Given the inherent dynamics and uncertainties associated with the constitution of global production networks, we view power and governance in both structural and relational terms. While we conceive these networks as having certain structural properties (for example, the differential roles of actors in Figure 2.2), we do not automatically assign and distribute certain power balances to each network of actors (for example, OEM lead firms have power 'over' their strategic partners). The fluidity of roles and functions among these actors in a network often destabilizes any a priori assumed form of power relations in network governance. As such, we define power as the capacity of an actor to exercise and achieve control over a particular strategic outcome in its own interests that can be realized only through the process of exercising. Power is as much a structural property as a contingent and contextually defined practice among interconnected actors in a network. This practice of power cannot take place in an organizational vacuum, but instead requires the concomitant presence of other actors in an evolving set of social relations. The control of resources, therefore, does not inadvertently imply that an actor is powerful until power is exercised in relation to other actors in the same network—such control is only a necessary, but not sufficient, condition for the allocation of power to any actor. In other words, power should be conceived as a relational practice embedded in the structural position within a network.

To understand further this constitution and practice of power relations in governing global production networks, it is useful to reconceptualize how *network embeddedness* serves as the main conduit through which firms and extra-firm actors become articulated into global production networks. Through their embedding in global production networks, economic actors from a particular economy are connected with other network members, irrespective of their origin or local anchoring in particular places. As argued in Henderson et al. (2002: 453), 'it is most notably the "architecture", durability and stability of these relations, both formal and informal, which determines the agents' individual network embeddedness (actor–network embeddedness) as well as the structure and evolution of the GPN as a whole'. Economic actors and their embedded relations with other actors in the same network are crucial in determining their collective power and the precise configuration and coordination of global production networks. In this dynamic configuration, actors draw upon divergent forms of power in order to take on an advantageous position in global production networks that favours their value creation, retention, and capture. Those economic actors occupying a leading role in their global production networks tend to benefit disproportionately from the value processes associated with the market success of their products and services. Other partners incorporated into the same network can also gain from enhanced opportunities to upgrade their operations and to improve on their collective surpluses. This relational positioning for greater value extraction becomes the *raison d'être* for actors to articulate into diverse global production networks.

By according a significant degree of relative autonomy to these economic actors, our approach acknowledges the contingent implications of actor-specific choices for the developmental outcomes of global production networks. While this theoretical framework offers useful analytical dimensions for understanding the causal mechanisms of economic development, it does not force a particular structural logic of network organization or power distribution onto geographically specific development outcomes. As the ultimate dependent variable, development cannot be 'read off' from a mono-causal chain of analytical logic, but should rather be understood as a contested and relational outcome of diverse configurations of global production networks in which actors and institutions in various territories and locations vie for a dominant position vis-à-vis each other in coordinating and controlling such networks and realizing their goal of value extraction. These contingent outcomes are reflected in the feedback mechanisms in Figure 1.3. In sum, actors in global production networks contest and play significant roles in shaping the configuration and governance of these networks. Their collective structural and relation interactions ensure the effective functioning of intricate production networks spanning national contexts, territorial ensembles, and regulatory authorities; they weave together these networks to make them truly global in nature and reach. But what does 'truly global' really mean in our understanding of these networks? We now turn to the final and, as yet, underdeveloped, question for this chapter—the territoriality of global production networks.

TERRITORIALITY

As with the earlier iteration, GPN 2.0 takes *territoriality* seriously because the 'where' question is extremely important in understanding how value creation, enhancement, and retention through global production networks matter for economic development in an interconnected world economy. It also constitutes an essential part of our language for describing the spatial dynamics of actors and value activity in these networks. We are interested in both the organizational configurations of global production networks and their geographical reach. Geography, however, is not just the physical surface on which these value activities are organized and performed.[36] Rather, geography can be an active space that shapes the territorial constitution and configuration of these network activities. While useful in analyzing *national* economic development in the global economy, the existing literature remains rather limited in its conception of territoriality, focusing primarily on the *global–national* scale.[37] Thus, while the global value chain concept has the potential to bring multiple geographical scales to the forefront of its analysis, the territoriality of these commodity/value chains remains weakly developed and under-theorized, reflecting, in part, the framework's origin in world-systems thinking.[38] Territoriality is highly aggregated in the existing GCC/GVC framework, which tends to identify the territorial units of analysis as either core/developed countries or periphery/developing countries. This is where GPN analysis can make a stronger claim, because it deals with how actors in various global production networks are anchored in different places and regions,[39] and yet operate at multiple scales—from the local and the regional to the national and the global.[40] While we concur with Lane and Probert's view (2009: 12) that 'GPNs do not exist in an anonymous global space but remain territorially embedded, albeit in multiple locations', we seek to venture further by explicitly reconceptualizing the territoriality of global production networks.

In GPN 2.0, territoriality refers to the spatial organization of global production network relations and development outcomes along two important dimensions: the vertical dimension of *global–local* scales and the *horizontal territorial* interface. In Figure 2.4, we illustrate this intersection of actor roles (the vertical dimension) with space (the horizontal dimension). On the vertical dimension in Figure 2.4(a), territoriality can be understood as multiple geographical scales along the global–local continuum—the global being the highest scale and the local the lowest. This spatial scope of actors, from the global to the local, is highly specific to the organizational configuration of each global production network. Some corporate functions are globally organized and implemented (for example, strategic planning and product mandates in headquarters), whereas other value activities can be reproduced in several supra-national regions (for example, manufacturing, sales, and servicing). Value activities in global production networks can also be highly local because crucial inputs and/or knowhow are grounded in particular localities. This localization of global production networks is particularly prevalent in the initial phase of producing goods and/or services. We can think of food production (for example, *terroir* and physical conditions) and high fashion (for example, designers and local buzz), for example. Despite the global presence of final consumers in these contrasting industries, their production networks can be highly localized in specific places (for example, Bordeaux wines and Mount Kenya coffee) and cities (for example, London, Milan, Paris, and New York).[41] In other industries, these value activities can be 'up-scaled' to specific regions within national economies when production takes place

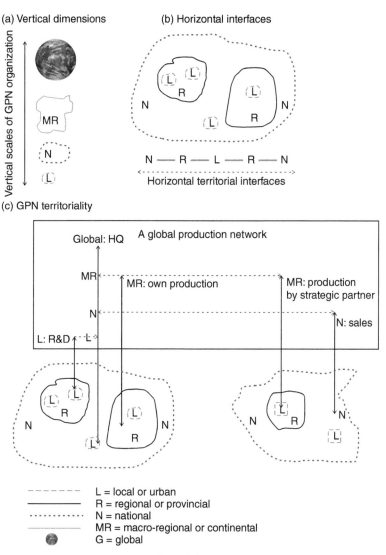

Figure 2.4. Territoriality of global production networks

in evolving industrial districts and regional complexes that offer significant agglomeration economies. In many globalizing industries (for example, apparel, automobiles, electronics, and machinery), the territorially specific advantages of cluster economies have been widely recognized as the key pillar for development in regional economies.[42] Both local and regional scales are also the critical terrains on which development outcomes of these value activities (for example, employment change, technological upgrading, and livelihoods) are played out. As will be developed fully in Chapter 5, the territoriality of global production networks and associated value capture trajectories and development outcomes hinge crucially on the different modes and types of strategic coupling between territorialized actors and their counterparts in these networks.

In the existing GCC/GVC analyses, at the national scale—the most common spatial unit used—the world economy is typically divided into developed and developing countries, both of which are respectively vying for sustained industrial dominance and industrial upgrading. In reality, however, the national scale in these studies represents merely a territorial 'container' of value chain activities. The analytical importance of this container conception of the national scale is concerned primarily with the institutional regulation of production, distribution, and retailing in global production networks because this regulatory function is often performed by the nation state.[43] Through its industrial and competition policy—often politically motivated—the state can directly shape the competitive dynamics of both producers and consumers in these networks. But, as argued in the earlier section on intermediaries, this primary role of national governments in regulating competition and in setting and implementing standards in global production networks varies significantly across national economies with diverse institutional capacities and political legitimacies. It can also be bypassed through regulatory activity championed by international organizations and cross-national industry associations 'from above' (international scale), or even private providers 'from below' (local and regional scale). Hence, while the national scale is perhaps the most visible and easily identifiable one in any GCC/GVC analysis, we believe it has less efficacy in explaining developmental outcomes than has hitherto been argued in the literature. Instead, the lower scales (local and regional) and higher scales (macro-regional and international) are as, and in some cases more, significant in understanding both the organizational dynamics and development outcomes of global production networks.

If we take this multi-scalar view of territoriality seriously, the 'global' in global production networks is really a metaphorical device to bring together all of the above scales—local, regional, national, macro-regional, and international—in our conceptualization of the spatial organization and geographical reach of these networks. Very few production networks are truly global in their organizational integration of constituent value activities, with the exception perhaps of final distribution (for example, retailing) and consumption. Even in automobiles, presumably one of the most sophisticated consumer goods with a global appeal and market, most lead firms (assemblers) continue to rely on main parts and components produced by their suppliers *within* the same home country (national scale) or home continent (macro-regional scale). Owing to such strategic considerations as just-in-time production and firm-specific tacit knowledge, these assemblers have developed intricate production networks that are highly integrated in both organizational and territorial terms. Most assemblers in Germany, Japan, and South Korea, for example, rely on first-tiered suppliers located in close proximity to their plants. Even when these assemblers internationalize their full production to new locations (for example, China, Thailand, Mexico, and Canada), they continue to source from their main suppliers, who follow their clients to these new locations. Macro-regional institutional arrangements such as the North American Free Trade Agreement (NAFTA) and the common market of the European Union have also encouraged this macro-regional clustering of automobile producers and their supplier networks. Virtually none of today's lead firms in the automobile industry can claim to be a truly global producer deploying modules and components from all over the world and engaging in sequential production of an automobile using facilities located in all major continents. They are at best 'world producers' with a geographically extensive production presence in different continents and production networks concentrating in each of these macro-regions.[44]

In electronics, an equally globalizing industry in terms of markets and final consumption, production networks are hardly global either. While the production of modern electronics products is quite globalized, it tends to be highly concentrated in macro-regions such as East and South-East Asia, Western Europe, and North America. Extensive knowledge and supplier networks are present in these regions to facilitate R&D and market control by lead firms, high-speed and volume manufacturing by their strategic partners, and cost-competitive component supply from different firms worldwide. Still, the global production networks of most electronics products remain tightly organized around only a limited number of major firms and regions within nation states.[45] The production of an iPhone 4, for example, is heavily dependent on major inputs from Apple (USA), Samsung (South Korea), and Infineon (Germany).[46] The total value added of US$120.76 by these three firms alone accounts for 62 per cent of the US$194.04 factory gate price of the finished iPhone 4. In most electronics products sold in global markets, very few components are sourced from some of the largest and most populated regions of the world—Africa, South Asia, Latin America, and the Middle East.

The idea of a global production network, then, should be understood territorially as a spatial ensemble of different local and regionally centred value activities. While the final goods and services are global in their consumption, their production is far less integrated globally than the literature has suggested. Instead, the globality of these networks should be reconceptualized along the global–local continuum as a dynamic scalar configuration of value activities across diverse localities, urban and regional economies, nation states, and macro-regional formations. In Figure 2.4(a), the functional activities within a lead firm and across other actors in the same production network can be organized in various territorial configurations; some are highly localized (for example, R&D) while others are regional and global in nature (for example, headquarters functions and production activity). This multi-scalar vertical conception of the territoriality of global production networks allows for a more nuanced understanding of their configuration and development implications.

As illustrated in Figure 2.4(b), this vertical dimension of organizing global production networks intersects with horizontal territorial interfaces, which are defined as the lateral incorporation of space—from localities (L) within regions (R) to regions within a national space-economy (N). This intersection refers to the spatial form of grounding value activity known as *territorial embeddedness*. In other words, value activity must always be located somewhere. Here, we can think of the territorial configurations of value activity by actors within the nation state—the most obvious territorial container of different regions and localities. But our conception does not end with the national scale. Instead, we conceive the vertical organization and flow of value activity in multiple scales from the local to the global, and yet, each of these organizational scales can be horizontally embedded within any national territorial formation, aggregating from localities to regional ensembles and from these regions to the national economy. In short, our conception incorporates both organizational scales (vertical dimension) of network actors and their territorial embedding (horizontal interfaces). The two are necessarily interconnected because, irrespective of their vertical scales of organization, actors in global production networks must eventually 'touch down' in specific territorial ensembles—be they local, regional, or national. Once this touching-down occurs, value activity tends to spread across different localities and regions along horizontal interfaces. Such processes can include geographical spillover in technological innovation, the spatial diffusion of management and marketing practices, and the spatial integration of production activity.

Let us explain with further examples. Within a specific *locality*, Figure 2.4(c) shows a lead firm and the location of its global headquarters function (for example, Hewlett-Packard). In fact, many of today's global lead firms operate their headquarters functions out of only a few localities, such as global cities or their founders' places of origin. Meanwhile, another locality within the same country hosts the local R&D activity of this particular global production network (for example, component design services for its manufacturing plant nearby). Thinking territorially, we can also envisage the diffusion and spillover of value activity to adjacent localities and clusters. This lateral expansion of value activity within the same scale can serve as an important possibility for local upgrading. This is where territoriality matters most, because, even though their developmental outcomes may be disproportional and contested, different localities can be gradually articulated into global production networks, and possibilities for value capture can be enhanced.

At the regional scale, we often witness inter-regional competition in value activity associated with the horizontal integration and expansion of global production networks. This inter-regional intersection is illustrated in Figure 2.4(c) when production activity within a particular global production network is located in high-growth regions of national economies in two contrasting continents—one performed by the lead firm's own manufacturing facility (for example, in California, USA) and another by its strategic partner (for example, in China's Shenzhen). As described vividly in Lüthje et al.'s *From Silicon Valley to Shenzhen* (2013), both regional economies are drawn into an intricate set of competitive and cooperative relations—competitive between these manufacturing plants and cooperative between the lead firm and its strategic partner (for example, Singapore's Venture Corp). These inter-regional dynamics can also be found in two regions of the same national economy. The relocation of labour-intensive assembly work from coastal localities to inland regions of China, for example, represents a significant challenge for relatively more developed regional economies in Shenzhen, Guangdong, Fujian, and Zhejiang.[47]

This inter-regional rivalry, nevertheless, is not unique to developing countries. Intense inter-regional competition drives technological innovation and employment shifts within advanced economies. In the United States, for example, different regions and states compete against each other for high value added jobs and activities (for example, Silicon Valley, Research Triangle, and Route 128).[48] At the same time, lead firms in these regions of California, North Carolina, and Massachusetts are facing severe competitive pressures in the vertical dimension from other leading national firms and their production networks in Western Europe (for example, the UK and Germany) and East Asia (for example, Japan and South Korea). This juxtaposition of inter-regional competition within the USA and international competition among American, European, and Asian firms represents the most intriguing territoriality of global production networks.

Though rather complex, this intersection of organizational and territorial configurations is precisely the reality of today's global production networks. Understanding this vertical–horizontal interface in the territoriality of value activity is critical to how we can resolve the analytical dilemma of production networks operating on a global scale and, yet, producing very local and regional impacts. As argued by Breznitz (2007: 23):

> There has been no study that systematically examines how product fragmentation shapes the development of emerging industrial countries. Such an account would need to explain why some activities occur in specific locations, as well as clarify whether particular development strategies resonate better with specific stages in the global product networks. What the literature offers are only suggestions for research frameworks on the governance and power relations in different types of product chains, or case studies about particular industries in specific locations.

In GPN thinking, we argue that the territoriality of production networks should not be construed exclusively at one spatial scale. A value chain analysis fetishizing the global scale for assessing value capture and industrial upgrading tells us little about how the reconfiguration and changing governance of value activity can impact differentially on localities and regions with diverse resource endowments, institutional settings, and growth trajectories. Equally, a value chain analysis specific to the local scale may be too myopic because it tends to take for grant powerful extra-local processes and forces that operate at wider scales. By explicitly incorporating the interfaces of these vertical–horizontal dimensions into our conception of territoriality in GPN 2.0, we can develop a better understanding of how and why development can occur in particular localities and regions at the same time as national development strategies may fail to 'resonate better', in Breznitz's terms (2007), with the competitive dynamics of global production networks.

CONCLUSION

The historical antecedents of our conception of global production networks are complex and variegated. This chapter has offered a *geographical political economy* take that starts to integrate these different, and yet disparate, strands of conceptualization into the basic building blocks of a coherent theory in order to analyze the evolutionary dynamics in the global space-economy and their consequences for economic development. By carefully delimiting and drawing diverse actors (for example, firms), extra-firm institutions (for example, states, civil society organizations, and intermediaries), and territories (for example, local and regional economies) into a common conceptual framework, this chapter has provided the initial elements of a comprehensive conceptual apparatus sensitive to processes that operate at multiple geographical scales and are driven by differentiated power relations among actors and institutions in global production networks. By directing its analytical attention onto dynamic intra-firm capabilities, complex inter-firm networks, and institutionalized extra-firm relations, this conceptual effort towards GPN 2.0 differentiates it from the earlier iteration (GPN 1.0) by reframing our conception of value activity, providing a clearer methodological approach to defining global production networks and their intra- and inter-industry intersections, and developing further the territoriality of these networks. It offers a more comprehensive and flexible analytical structure, and allows for a wider range of development pathways and outcomes in an era of accelerated global competition. Global production networks serve as the primary organizational device for firms and extra-firm actors to engage more effectively with the possibilities and perils of an interconnected world. Developing the differentiated agency of actors and networks across geographical scales, this approach enables us to understand multiple development possibilities in diverse territorial formations. Importantly, it goes beyond the persistent tendency in existing studies of economic development to focus exclusively on self-contained national political economies.

As will be developed more fully in the next three chapters, GPN theory focuses on the key organizational mechanisms connecting both the economic actors and political forces internal to regional and national economies and trans-national flows spearheaded by lead firms in global production networks. As such, economic development is viewed as a trans-local dynamic process of growth and change whereby multiple actors operate at a variety of geographical scales. The dynamic articulation of these actors into different global production networks constitutes the central nexus of economic development, as these networks bring together geographically dispersed assets and capabilities in a recursive and cumulative process of inducing and stimulating growth and development. The coordination and configuration of global production networks by these actors have important consequences for value creation, retention, and capture in multiple localities and economies. Industrial transformation and developmental outcomes are not just dreamt up in official state plans or corporate boardrooms, but rather are the contingent effects of diverse actors creating and responding strategically to different competitive dynamics in global production networks. In the next two chapters, we will elaborate in depth these competitive dynamics and the strategies pursued by actors in global production networks.

NOTES

1. See a fuller argument in Yeung (2013, 2014).
2. This territoriality of global production networks will be fully illustrated in Chapter 5, where we address the core issue of strategic coupling in sub-national regional development.
3. In earlier work (Henderson et al. 2002; Coe et al. 2004), and as discussed in Chapter 1, we followed Kaplinsky's delimitation (1998) of various types of economic rents. We now find this distinction a little too categorical and prefer to provide an integrated conception of economic rent and its constituent elements.
4. In their *The New Social Economy*, Sayer and Walker (1992) make a convincing case about this indivisibility of manufacturing and service activity in the contemporary understanding of the capitalist social division of labour. For an early analysis of the service sector nexus of commodity chains, see Jones and Kierzkowski (1990) and Rabach and Kim (1994). For more contemporary studies of services in GVCs, see Gereffi and Fernandez-Stark (2010), Fernandez-Stark et al. (2011), and Low (2013).

5. See Crescenzi et al. (2014), for instance, who provide a European study of the role of technological innovation in global production networks.
6. See the example of UNCTAD's *World Investment Report 2013: Global Value Chains: Investment and Trade for Development* (UNCTAD 2013b), in which GVCs are typically measured and analyzed in terms of stages and functions in global production and the national economies performing these roles (also Elms and Low 2013; IMF 2013; OECD 2013; OECD-WTO-UNCTAD 2013).
7. This argument has been well rehearsed in the varieties of capitalism (VoC) literature introduced in Chapter 1, which argues that variations in institutional structures and business systems significantly explain the sources and variations of resource and capability endowments enjoyed by capitalist firms from different home economies. Contrary to the convergence accounts about the emergence of global firms, this work highlights how firms are heavily shaped by the national culture, political ideology, political institutions, and economic institutions of their home country (Doremus et al. 1998). See Lane and Probert (2009) for a comparative analysis of how German, American, and British firms differ in the organization and control of their apparel global production networks. We will return to the VoC literature in Chapter 6 to demonstrate how GPN theory adds new analytical value.
8. Indeed, the existing literature cited in Chapter 1 tends to define such a chain or network as an entire global industry such as apparel, automobiles, or agro-food. Inter-firm relations in such analyses are often between or among firms in a particular segment or subset of a global production network—e.g. buyers and their suppliers, assemblers and module producers, producers and distributors, and so on. See further elaborations in De Marchi et al. (2014) and Ponte and Sturgeon (2014).
9. Our conception of a global lead firm is necessarily broader than the one commonly used in the literature, in which a lead firm is defined by its capacity to set and enforce 'critical parameters' for value chain governance (Humphrey and Schmitz 2002b: 7–8). These parameters range from product definitions and process standards to the schedule, quantity, and price of products to be supplied. In this conception, a lead firm is often viewed as either a buyer or a producer in different value chains. GPN 2.0 explicitly recognizes the multiple roles of a lead firm that can be a buyer to its suppliers, a producer for its customers, a coordinator of standards and technologies, and a controller of material and intangible flows— all in the *same* global production network. As noted in Chapter 1, because of its analytical interest in value chain organization and governance, this genre of research generally does not consider how inter-firm relations in value chains are connected with the broader dynamics of industrial transformation in specific local, regional, and national economies. In addition, our conception of a global lead firm extends beyond Petrovic and Hamilton's idea (2011) of market-makers, which tends to focus on large retailers, commonly known as global buyers, and neglects market leaders in resource extraction, manufacturing, and advanced producer service sectors.
10. In the case of the global electronics industry, Sturgeon and Kawakami (2010, 2011a) observe that highly specialized component suppliers or service providers

such as Intel (CPU chipsets) and Microsoft (software operating systems) are by themselves major platform leaders wielding significant power over brand name computer lead firms and their contract manufacturers (see also Gawer and Cusumano 2002; Gawer 2010).

11. Some of the best-known works are Amsden (1989), Wade (1990), Evans (1995), and Chang (2002). Two of the World Bank's publications have also hailed the market-enhancing role of the state in development (World Bank 1993; Lin 2012a). For a more recent reprise of these ideas, see Whittaker et al. (2010), Ros (2013), and Yeung (2014).

12. The distinction here is between public enterprises that are directly owned and managed by the state, and firms in which the state has a direct or indirect stake and yet leaves the management to professional managers.

13. For the role of the state in steering the ICT industry in these three economies, see Evans (1995), Mathews and Cho (2000), Amsden and Chu (2003), and Breznitz (2007). Wong (2011), however, argues that the state becomes less effective in nurturing high-tech industries that are imbued with inherent uncertainties, such as biotechnology.

14. See Dicken (2011) for an excellent introduction to the key themes and issues in this literature, while Smith (2014) theorizes the links between states and global production networks in more depth. For more on the state as a multi-scalar formation—a widely accepted interpretation in economic geography at least—see Brenner et al. (2003), Swyngedouw (2004), and Keil and Mahon (2009).

15. See more details on the politics of these advocacy networks in Keck and Sikkink's *Activists beyond Borders* (1988).

16. For more details on the German industrial system, see Herrigel (1996, 2010).

17. For studies of such initiatives and their inherent tensions and challenges, see Blowfield (2000), Freidberg (2004), Barrientos and Dolan (2006), Pickles (2006), Hughes et al. (2008), Barnett et al. (2011), Pickles and Smith (2011, 2015), Dunaway (2014), and Rossi et al. (2014).

18. Our list is not meant to be exhaustive. Other critical intermediaries providing advanced business services are management consultants, legal services, recruitment agencies, and so on. But space constraints mean we focus here on these three. See Hassler (2004) for a case of labour recruitment agencies as intermediaries.

19. Good examples of these intermediaries are supply chain managers (e.g. Hong Kong's Li and Fung) and trading companies (e.g. Japan's *sogo shosha*). See Sturgeon et al. (2011: 241–3) on Li & Fung, and Hamilton and Kao (2011: 191–4) on *sogo shosha*. Gibbon and Ponte (2008) offer a historical analysis of the emergence of purchasing agents and supply management in the context of American manufacturing firms.

20. Two very useful accounts of these dynamics are provided by Langley (2008) and Krippner (2011).

21. On the rise of shareholder value in corporate governance, see Lazonick and O'Sullivan (2000). We will explain more fully the role of financial discipline in driving the dynamics of global production networks in the next chapter.

22. We thank John Pickles for these two important points.

23. See Bonacich and Wilson (2008), Bonacich and Hamilton (2011), and Coe (2014) for contemporary analyses of logistics in global production networks. A central

argument of the last of these pieces is that leading logistics providers can themselves be thought of as lead firms within their own global production networks, engaging and coordinating a wide variety of suppliers and subcontractors in delivering specialized logistics services.

24. Despite the intangibility of standards, the existing literature has paid some attention to the role of international standards in value chain governance in general (e.g. Kaplinsky 2010; Ponte et al. 2011a) and in agro-food industries in particular (Mutersbaugh 2005; Ponte and Gibbon 2005; Morgan et al. 2006; Neilson and Pritchard 2009; Ouma 2010; Lee et al. 2012). Quark's work (2013) on the international cotton trade shows how different actors, institutions, and states rival each other in order to influence standard-setting processes and to set the rules defining quality and enabling dispute adjudication.

25. See Hess and Coe (2006) for an in-depth study of standards in mobile telecommunications.

26. See Ouma (2010, 2015) for a fascinating study of how private actors in standards governance play a highly significant role in the restructuring and market access of Kenya's horticulture industry.

27. For studies of the role of international standards in governing labour in global production networks, see Pun (2005), Nadvi (2008), Lane and Probert (2009), Barrientos et al. (2011), Posthuma and Nathan (2011), Dunaway (2014), Rossi et al. (2014), and Pickles and Smith (2015).

28. Our dynamic view of global production networks differs from the dyadic approach in the theoretical work on the governance of global value chains. In this latter approach, the analytical emphasis is placed on characterizing the governance of the *entire* value chain on the basis of these discrete and dyadic (network) coordination relations between lead firms and their immediate (first-tier) suppliers. As pointed out critically by Bair (2008: 354), what characterizes this dyadic coordination relation in one part of the value chain (e.g. between a lead firm and its first-tier supplier) may not necessarily be applicable to other inter-firm relations further down the same chain (e.g. between the first-tier supplier and other tiers of suppliers). The privileging of this dyadic relation is rather limiting because it does not allow for multiple logics, as is the case in our network approach, in understanding the organization and configuration of global industries. It also underscores the analytical problem of the chain (sequential) approach to theorizing these global industries. The same problem is also evident in the supply chain management literature (see Gattorna 2010). While the term 'supply chain' was first used by Keith Oliver, a logistics consultant, in 1982, Gattorna (2013: 226) argues that 'the more accurate term these days would be value networks'. To him, 'networks they are, spreading from local to domestic national trading environments, becoming regional as more countries are involved in strategic sourcing and/or distribution strategy, and ultimately, global. The complexity of these "networks-of-networks" increases exponentially as the geographic scope widens, and the number of links (both transport and electronic transactions) and nodes (facilities of all types and activities within) increases'.

29. For a complementary view of such dynamic articulations, see Pickles and Smith (2015). GPN 2.0's approach of articulating different actors into global production

networks contrasts with the 'disarticulation perspective' of Bair and Werner (2011a) and Bair et al. (2013), who examine the processes and consequences of these actors being excluded from global value chains and production networks. See also Neilson and Pritchard (2009) for a study of everyday social relations and practices in relation to such value chain struggles.

30. Critiquing the literature on GVC governance, Gibbon (2008: 38) similarly argues that 'there is a danger that this formulation loses sight of the overall configuration of chains, as opposed to the content of specific links within them. Depending on the complexity of a given commodity, there will be any number of "make or buy"-type decisions needing to be made by a wide variety of agents at different links along a chain. The model suggested by Gereffi et al. is ideal for examining each of these individually. But it provides us with little indication of how to move from this level of analysis to a characterization of the overall pattern of decisions along a chain'.

31. Here we are simply identifying the 'building blocks' of a GPN analysis; we will draw out more specific characteristics of these intersections and dynamic trajectories in Chapter 5.

32. See Hamilton et al. (2011) for an analysis of the importance of these very large retailers in reshaping the global economy.

33. For general work on business groups in the global economy, see Khanna and Palepu (1997), Khanna and Yafeh (2007, 2010), and Colpan et al. (2010).

34. For a relational view on networks, see Dicken et al. (2001), Yeung (1998, 2005a, b, 2009c), and Hess (2008). This multiplicity of power relations is also found in Ponte and Sturgeon's reinterpretation (2014) of GVC governance into unipolar, bipolar, and multipolar forms.

35. For some classic studies of the structural properties of social networks, see Burt (1982, 1992, 2005, 2010), White (1992, 2002), Nohria and Eccles (1992), and Gulati (2007).

36. This notion of geography is particularly common in the international business literature: e.g. Dunning (1998, 2009), Porter (2000), Buckley and Ghauri (2004), Mudambi (2008), and Beugelsdijk and Mudambi (2013). See a critique in Yeung (2009c).

37. While, as we saw in Chapter 1, Gereffi et al's initial formulation (1994: 2) of GCCs did offer a sense of multi-scalarity, their subsequent analyses and those of their followers tend to focus on the global–national scale at the expense of local and sub-national scales (e.g. urban and regional). In their refinement of the governance structures in GVCs, Gereffi et al. (2005) and Sturgeon (2009) continue to operate through specific industries at the global scale and give little analytical attention to how governance in these global industries is linked to industrial transformation in specific local, regional, and national economies. Some exceptions to this general observation about the existing literature are Bair and Gereffi (2001), Humphrey and Schmitz (2002a), Cammet (2006), Pietrobelli and Rabellotti (2007), and Neilson and Pritchard (2009). For a general review of related studies of local clusters in GVCs and GPNs, see Parrilli et al. (2013). Meanwhile, most analyses in international economics rely on input–output tables and international trade data to examine GVC activity such as production

fragmentation (Arndt and Kierzkowski 2001) and 'task-trading' (Grossman and Rossi-Hansberg, 2008). These studies are often couched at the *national* scale, as if countries are inserted into GVCs and become economic actors in their own right. See examples in Elms and Low (2013), IMF (2013), Milberg and Winkler (2013), OECD (2013), OECD-WTO-UNCTAD (2013), and UNCTAD (2013b).

38. See Bair (2005: 154–5; 2008: 347–8) for useful reviews of such a world-systems conception of commodity chains originating from the work of Terence Hopkins and Immanuel Wallerstein.

39. A quick note on our definition of the term 'region' is important here. From this point onwards, we use the term 'region' to denote a sub-national territorial unit. However, we will use the term 'macro-region' or 'supra-national region' to describe a continental unit of territorial organization, such as Europe or Asia, or a smaller grouping of contiguous countries therein—for instance, the Association of South-East Asian Nations (ASEAN) states.

40. See examples of such multi-scalar analysis of global production networks in Coe et al. (2004), Yeung (2009b, d, 2010), and MacKinnon (2012). In Ponte and Sturgeon's (2014) recent modular theory-building approach to GVC governance, multi-scalarity refers *not* to geographical scales, but rather to micro-, meso-, and macro-scales of governance within GVC links, along GVCs, and of GVCs.

41. For studies of creative design in these cities, see Scott (2008), Sunley et al. (2011), and Tokatli (2011).

42. Some of the more influential studies are found in Saxenian (1994), Storper (1997, 2013), and Scott (1998, 2006b, 2012).

43. This institutional structuring by the nation state has been extensively developed in the VoC literature discussed in Chapter 1.

44. See also Lung et al. (2004) and Rugman (2005) for more on this regionalization perspective on global lead firms. On the regional production networks in the automobile industry, see Van Biesebroeck and Sturgeon (2010) and Sturgeon and Van Biesebroeck (2011). See J. D. Wilson (2013), Ferrarini and Hummels (2014), and Pickles and Smith (2015) for empirical studies of macro-regional production networks.

45. See Yeung (2007a), Ernst (2009), Sturgeon and Kawakami (2010, 2011a), and Lüthje et al. (2013) for studies of the global production networks in the electronics industry.

46. This example is based on OECD (2011) and Gereffi (2014).

47. See Zhu and Pickles (2014) for a study of this restructuring process as 'go up' (upgrading), 'go West' (cheaper regions), and 'go out' (outsourcing to South-East Asia) in China's apparel industry.

48. For the interventionist role of the US federal state in driving this technological competition in different regions, see Block and Keller (2011) and Weiss (2014).

3

Dynamics

In an increasingly interconnected world, heightened competition in the global economy takes place in tandem with the emergence of global production networks in most industries and sectors. As we noted in Chapter 1, global competition among firms, their embedded global production networks, and diverse economies has become more intensified since the late 1980s because of the capitalist imperatives of cost reduction, increasing production flexibility, and compression in time-to-market. To overcome these competitive challenges and to sustain their value extraction goals, lead firms and their strategic partners in global production networks have developed a variety of spatial, organizational, and technological fixes. The impact of these fixes on economic development depends critically on the ways in which firm and extra-firm actors in regional and national economies are articulated into global production networks. Global production network (GPN) theory internalizes the globalizing nature of inter-firm competition and cooperation into its dynamic analysis of developmental trajectories in specific economies. More importantly, we argue that this articulation is shaped by the complex interaction between firm-specific fixes to the competitive dynamics of global production networks and territorially specific coupling mechanisms in different industries and economies. Situated in the context of extra-firm institutions seeking better value capture for their stakeholders, the developmental outcomes of this interaction are therefore likely to be diverse and variable.

Predicated on Chapter 2's conceptual specification of basic building blocks in GPN theory, this chapter begins our elucidation of causal mechanisms. It represents the first critical step in our effort towards GPN 2.0 by explaining the dynamic drivers of value activity in global production networks.[1] Revisiting Figure 1.3, we argue that these capitalist dynamics become the *raison d'être* of global production networks that in turn prompt and explain the strategies of economic actors and their consequences for uneven economic development in different regional and national economies. In unpacking these capitalist imperatives within the competitive context of time–space compression, we identify three dynamic forces in the form of *optimizing cost-capability ratios*, *sustaining market development*, and *working with financial discipline*. While the existing literature on global commodity chains (GCC) and global value chains (GVC) introduced in Chapter 1 has paid much attention to cost reduction rationalities in governing buyer-driven commodity chains and the importance of technological leadership in producer-driven commodity chains, few such studies have brought together these two considerations and integrated them into a dynamic concept such as the cost-capability ratio. Even fewer studies in this literature have placed sufficient explanatory emphasis on market development and financial discipline in their analyses of global production in different industries and sectors.[2] While Bair (2005: 154) recognizes that 'adherents of both the GCC and GVC approaches share an interest in understanding how the concept of a value-added chain can inform firm-level strategies of industrial upgrading', few existing studies have theorized in depth the broader dynamic forces to which these firm-level strategies are responding and whose causal effects these strategies are mitigating.[3]

Our purpose in this chapter is not to reinvent the wheel by rehearsing existing theoretical explanations in these earlier studies.[4] We also do not pretend to be exhaustive in our reframing of the dynamic forces shaping capitalist production. Nor do we attempt to develop a parsimonious model purporting to explain all the general dynamics of what in reality is a highly complex and differentiated world of global production networks.[5] Here we seek to theorize and integrate what we consider to be the most powerful dynamics driving and shaping actors in their organization and configuration of global production networks. We intentionally choose to focus on the capitalist dynamics that matter for *economic actors* in global production networks, eschewing the industry-level approach in earlier theorizations of industrial governance or the international focus in economic models of outsourcing. We believe that different economic actors even in the same industry and national economy will negotiate and respond to these dynamics in drastically different ways such that industry- or national-level generalizations, such as buyer- or producer-driven chain governance or international outsourcing as production fragmentation and trading tasks, are often hard to sustain. Our conceptual focus on economic actors—lead firms and their partners/suppliers, extra-firm institutions, and intermediaries—is also critical because the dynamic drivers of global production network formation and evolution are first and foremost economic in nature. This focus does not sideline or render passive the critical role of extra-firm actors such as the state and labour organizations. As described further in this chapter (and more fully in Chapter 5), they play an integral role in shaping the broader competitive dynamics confronting firm-specific economic actors. To us, the three dynamic forces we analyze in this chapter are the necessary causal conditions for explaining actor-specific strategies in these networks, and which in turn produce diverse empirical developmental outcomes; they are the independent variables for us to explain *why* global production networks are organized and governed in certain ways and their multifarious consequences for economic development.

In the next three sections, each of these three forces and its causal effects on actors in global production networks is specified. The sequence of presenting these dynamic forces corresponds to their relative historical importance, with cost considerations as the primary dynamic force in the early origin of most value activity in global production networks. Over time, market development and financial discipline have become equally, if not more, critical in shaping the organizational and spatial configurations of global production networks. To exemplify how these dynamic forces actually work in driving various global production networks, we primarily draw upon empirical examples from three of the most globalizing manufacturing industries—electronics, automobiles, and apparels, but we also use other sectoral cases where appropriate. As noted in Chapter 1 and in order to focus on theory development, our approach to empirical evidence will necessarily be brief and illustrative rather than detailed and exhaustive. More empirical cases and territorial outcomes will be addressed in the following two chapters. The final section brings together these three dynamics of global production networks under the conceptual umbrella of 'managing uncertainty and risk'. Here, we integrate these competitive dynamics with risk considerations that are almost completely missing in the existing GVC and GPN frameworks.[6] Overall, this chapter provides the theoretical foundations for specifying causal explanations in a GPN analysis of economic development.

OPTIMIZING COST–CAPABILITY RATIOS

Since Gereffi and Korzeniewicz's seminal work (1994), two decades of empirical research into the emergence and governance of global commodity/value chains have clearly confirmed the importance of cost-based competition in driving the globalization of production organized around spatially dispersed networks of lead firms and their global suppliers. The incessant competitive pressure in advanced capitalist economies to lower prices of goods and services in end markets compelled lead firms, mostly vertically integrated through to the late 1970s, to reconsider their cost structures. These structures were reflected in both direct and indirect costs—direct costs comprising material inputs, labour wages, fixed assets, and other production-related payments; indirect costs relating to transaction costs with customers and suppliers, payments for goodwill and trademarks, investment in proprietary knowhow, and costs associated with raising finance.[7] Direct costs associated with production, particularly wages, became the most obvious arena for optimization. Internationalization to lower wage cost locations, through establishing direct subsidiaries or subcontracting to third-party suppliers, opened an entirely new window of opportunity for these vertically integrated lead firms.[8]

With hindsight, this capitalist dynamic of cost reduction had clearly existed well before the rise to dominance of Fordism in the early twentieth century. But its causal effect on market competition and industrial organization has been much more pronounced since the emergence of global production networks from the 1980s onwards. As lead firms were increasingly confronted with new competitors from within both advanced economies and newly industrialized economies (for example, Japan since the early 1970s and, later, the East Asian 'Tigers' since the early 1980s), cost considerations became paramount in corporate survival and business cycles. In short, the competitive pressure of cost reduction is not a benign force impinging on the development of global production networks spearheaded by lead firms. Rather, it is predominantly an integral and dynamic condition that must be continually pursued by all economic actors—firms and extra-firm institutions—in these networks.

This focus on cost as the fundamental driver of global production, however, overlooks the other side of the same coin—the capabilities of the firm. In lieu of an explicit theory of the firm in our conceptualization, it is useful to observe that a firm necessarily incurs costs in acquiring and mobilizing resources to complete its productive activity. A resource-based view of the firm allows us to appreciate better its inherent role as a capable and strategic organizer of productive assets and value activities.[9] In short, cost alone does not give us enough analytical purchase to define the firm as the key *actor* in a production network; cost must be theorized alongside capabilities to form a complete and actor-oriented view of the firm. A firm can therefore be thought of as a managerial device for optimizing the accumulation and deployment of its available resources underpinning its core capabilities, at the lowest possible cost. These firm-specific *capabilities* can be defined in terms of its productivity, technology, knowhow, and organizational capacities (for example, management routines and extra-firm repertoires).

As lead firms in advanced economies started to internationalize their production networks in earnest in response to fierce cost pressures in their home markets from the 1980s onwards, they began to engage local suppliers, initially to provide simple and basic materials and components for their local production. In the early phase of this development, most local suppliers— particularly those in developing and emerging economies—remained fairly weak in terms of firm-specific capabilities. Supplier capabilities, however, were relatively less critical than low production costs in determining the initial articulation of these local suppliers into evolving production networks orchestrated by lead firms. Just like costs, firm-specific capabilities are relative and can evolve in a recursive and dynamic manner in capitalist competition.

Through firm-specific learning and extra-firm initiatives (for example, industrial promotion and policy support by extra-firm institutions such as the developmental state), local suppliers can enhance their existing capabilities and/or develop new capabilities to achieve what GVC scholars call industrial upgrading.[10] In situations where increasingly capable local suppliers are able to take on more complex and higher value-added production activity, global lead firms can re-engineer their organizational strategy to focus on the highest value activities, such as new product and market development and more sophisticated technological innovation, and to capture more value from these new product life cycles. In other words, both local suppliers and their lead firm customers can engage in a recursive and co-evolutionary dynamic such that the former can benefit from growing firm-specific capabilities and the latter can capture even more value from their expanding global production networks.[11]

Cost–Capability Ratio: A Dynamic Concept of Co-Evolution

In this book, we use the dynamic concept of the cost–capability ratio to describe the optimization process that allows firms in global production networks to achieve greater firm-specific capabilities and value capture. We argue that, while cost reduction is clearly an important capitalist dynamic compelling lead firms to engage in outsourcing and subcontracting to independent suppliers at home and abroad, cost is a relative concept. It must be conceptualized in combination with the actor-specific capabilities of these lead firms and their suppliers in order to arrive at a complete picture of its causal influence on the formation and evolution of global production networks. Optimizing the cost–capability ratio presents a perennial challenge to lead firms if they are to weather global competition, and therefore significantly influences their strategic choices. The dynamics of optimizing the cost–capability ratio can help us understand why certain value activities are outsourced to independent suppliers by global lead firms, and why the mix of these activities changes over time in a particular global production network. This optimization process is therefore highly contingent on a firm's existing resource endowment and strategic direction in current and/or new markets under the influence, of course, of extra-firm institutions. The optimal cost–capability ratio varies from one firm to another. Some firms can achieve optimal ratios through cost reduction or building new capabilities, whereas others can accomplish improvements in both dimensions.

In Figure 3.1, we present four different scenarios of cost–capability ratios confronting both lead firms and their suppliers (domestic and abroad).[12] In general, a lead firm is most competitive if it enjoys a low cost–capability ratio that can be achieved through high capabilities with low costs (for example,

Lead firm

Capability	Cost	
	Low	High
Low	**C**: Market follower with weak long-term survival prospect	**D**: Market follower facing immediate exit
High	**A**: Highly competitive industrial leader	**B**: Industrial leader but subject to serious competitive pressures

Supplier

Capability	Cost	
	Low	High
Low	**A**: clear price-taker with no or little bargaining power	**D**: No prospect of securing value activity in global production networks
High	**B**: Highly competitive and may evolve into a strategic partner or even a lead firm (A or B)	**C**: No prospect of securing value activity in global production networks, except those supplying highly specialized modules and components (e.g. 'platform leaders') and essential services (e.g. customized or proprietary solutions)

Figure 3.1. A matrix of cost–capability ratios in global production networks
Source: Yeung and Coe (2015: table 1). © 2014 Clark University.

lead firm A). High firm-specific capabilities in productivity, technology and knowhow, and/or organizational routines require very substantial investment that tends to drive up overall costs, however.[13] Market leaders in most globalizing industries invest heavily in research and development (R&D), human resources, and marketing to sustain their cutting-edge products and/ or services. A low cost–capability ratio is therefore much harder to achieve when all value activity, including manufacturing production, takes place in the home economy because labour-related production costs in advanced economies tend to be high. A lead firm (B) with the next lowest cost–capability ratio tends to have high capabilities and high costs, a competitive scenario quite typical among lead firms in most advanced economies since the 1980s. To optimize its cost–capability ratio and to stay afloat in the context of global competition, a lead firm such as this tends to engage in international production through establishing in-house facilities abroad (that is, subsidiaries) or outsourcing to independent suppliers.[14] The successful establishment of a global production network will allow this lead firm (B) to reduce production costs and to move towards a more optimal ratio, characterized by lower overall costs and higher capabilities, that enables it to become a highly competitive industrial leader (lead firm A). Meanwhile, lead firm (C) suffers from declining firm-specific capabilities and, as a follower, an inability to control the definition of its market, even though its overall costs remain low. It needs to invest substantially in its capability building in order to move towards lead firm positions A or B. As a high-cost and low-capability lead firm, D has immediate options of market exit or stringent cost management in order to try and survive as lead firm C.

On the other hand, a supplier (A) with low production costs (particularly labour costs) and low firm-specific capabilities does not enjoy a good bargaining position when it first articulates into a global production network. It tends to be a price-taker and survives on the basis of its 'race to the bottom' cost structure (for example, low wages, substandard quality, or poor working and safety condition). Because of the low entry barriers associated with this mode of production, it can be easily substituted by other suppliers in the same or another low-cost location. As the scope for reducing its already low production costs is often limited, the competitive imperative for this supplier is therefore to move towards a lower cost–capability ratio by improving on its firm-specific capabilities in manufacturing (for example, quality, yield, design, and speed) and services (for example, product design, inventory management, logistics, and after sales support). With low production costs (for example, economies of scale and stringent cost control) and high capabilities (for example, innovation in production and management), a supplier (B) of intermediate or final products/service tends to be highly competitive and may be able to succeed in taking over significant outsourced value activity by lead firms in global production networks. A highly successful strategic partner (B) may take on the role of becoming a global lead firm (A or B) when it ventures into market definition through new brand development and product/service innovation. For a supplier with high costs (C), its articulation into global production networks is possible only if it has very high firm-specific capabilities that cannot be easily substituted. An example is suppliers of highly specialized products or services, known as platform leaders, which command a monopolistic position in intermediate markets (only Microsoft and Intel in the global ICT industry; see Chapter 2 n. 10). Otherwise, supplier C must seek to reduce costs and move towards the competitive position of supplier B. This scenario also applies to emerging lead firms from newly industrialized economies that have begun to experience higher cost–capability ratios owing to growing domestic costs and the inherent limits placed on their firm-specific capabilities (a function of the weaker national innovation systems developed by extra-firm institutions).

Overall, this dynamic concept of the cost–capability ratio can illuminate an important co-evolutionary process in successful global production networks in which both lead firms and their suppliers work to reduce their cost–capability ratios over time. By optimizing their ratios through international production and outsourcing, lead firms may be able to maintain or regain their industrial leadership in end markets. By articulating into the global production networks of these lead firms and enhancing their own firm-specific capabilities, independent suppliers can also optimize their ratios over time. Through inter-firm learning and deepening transactional relationships, these suppliers can evolve further to become strategic partners of global lead firms. Cost reduction alone, therefore, cannot be the *raison d'être* of evolving global production networks. Rather, costs and firm-specific capabilities directly relate to each other and are subject to change over time under global competition. Only by continuously optimizing cost–capability ratios can lead firms and their suppliers engage in this recursive process of sustaining or improving their competitive positions in the global economy.

Optimization in Global Industries

To put this abstract concept of optimizing cost–capability ratios into context, we now illustrate briefly how this capitalist dynamic has determined the evolutionary trajectories of some of the most globalizing industries—namely, electronics, automobiles, and apparel.[15] In these three industries, we observe the movement of global lead firms from vertically integrated original equipment manufacturers (OEMs) towards vertical specialization by brand name lead firms in electronics, global assemblers in automobiles, and global buyers in apparel. Meanwhile, suppliers in these three industries may evolve from low cost–low capability OEM suppliers to engage in (co-)design, logistics, and full package production. In the electronics industry, this co-evolutionary dynamic is most advanced when OEM suppliers emerge to become large-scale contract manufacturers taking over the entire manufacturing process and, sometimes, logistics and post-production services on behalf of their global brand name lead firms. This process of optimizing cost–capability ratios in both lead firms and their contract manufacturers is greatly facilitated by advancements in industrial standards (for example, product modularity) and production technologies (for example, computer-aided flexible manufacturing).[16] As observed by Sturgeon and Kawakami (2010: 263):

> Even though the specifications and information handed off between value chain functions in the electronics industry tend to be highly complex, the combination of information technology and well-known standards means that specifications can be codified and temporarily simplified, creating a pinch point in the flow of

tacit information that allows data to be transmitted across vast distances and to other firms.

In this environment of open standards and modular product architecture, suppliers to OEMs can improve their firm-specific capabilities, such as yield, productivity, and turnaround time, without making costly investments in dedicated production assets for a specific order or customer. Together with lead firm customers, these suppliers can achieve lower cost–capability ratios and higher economies of scope through finely distributed divisions of value activity in their global production networks.

When did this concern with optimizing the cost–capability ratio begin to assert its imperative on global lead firms? As early as the 1960s, American and European OEMs began to engage in international production in order to take advantage of lower labour costs in developing economies.[17] With the exception of the apparel and textile industry under import quota constraints, this emerging new international division of labour was underpinned more by lead firms establishing in-house affiliates abroad than by outsourcing to independent suppliers in low-cost locations. However, it was not until the early 1980s that optimizing the cost–capability ratio compelled lead firms to engage much more extensively in international outsourcing to independent suppliers. As we will detail later in this chapter, financial discipline in the home economy became the primary force steering OEM lead firms to move away from an emphasis on expanding domestic production through reinvestment of profits and retained earnings, to a more short-term focus on corporate downsizing and distributing dividends to increasingly demanding shareholders.[18] Milberg and Winkler (2013: 24) thus argue that 'we locate the logic of offshoring in the broader context of corporate strategies and their evolution since the 1980s. Faced with continued product market competition and a growing sense of the need for immediate gains in stock price, managers of large lead firms have increasingly looked to cost control as a means to maintain cost mark-ups'. Indeed, their data reproduced in Table 3.2 show that, on the basis of a compound annual growth rate (CAGR), declining import prices in the United States between 1986 and 2006 were highest in sectors with the most developed global production networks, such as computers, electrical and telecommunications products, agro-food, apparel, and footwear. By tapping into the lower cost–capability ratios of suppliers in their global production networks, American lead firms in these sectors were able to translate lower production costs abroad into lower import prices and greater corporate profits through the same or higher mark-ups.[19]

This primordial concern with cost control since the 1980s has profoundly shaped the co-evolutionary dynamics in global production networks. In the electronics industry, international outsourcing to lower-cost suppliers in newly industrializing economies began with lead firms' non-core functions,

Table 3.1. Relative import prices in the United States, 1986–2006

Sector	Description	CAGR (%)
75	Computer equipment and office machines	−7.81
76	Telecommunications and sound recording and reproducing apparatus and equipment	−4.81
07	Coffee, tea, cocoa, spices, and manufactures thereof	−3.27
77	Electrical machinery and equipment	−2.89
62	Rubber manufactures	−2.23
88	Photographic apparatus, equipment and supplies and optical goods	−2.13
81	Prefabricated buildings; plumbing, heat and lighting fixtures	−1.96
84	Articles of apparel and clothing accessories	−1.84
85	Footwear	−1.64
55	Essential oils; polishing and cleansing preparations	−1.63
82	Furniture and parts thereof	−1.60
89	Miscellaneous manufactured articles	−1.49
75	Textile yarn, fabrics, made-up articles, and related products	−1.43
87	Professional, scientific and controlling instruments and apparatus	−1.36
84	Travel goods, handbags, and similar containers	−1.16
78	Road vehicles	−1.11
59	Chemical materials and products	−1.05
69	Manufactures of metals	−1.03
64	Paper and paperboard, cut to size	−1.03
51	Organic chemicals	−1.02
03	Fish, crustaceans, aquatic invertebrates, and preparations thereof	−0.91
52	Inorganic chemicals	−0.86
01	Meat and meat preparations	−0.62
05	Vegetable, fruit and nuts, fresh or dried	−0.58
66	Non-metallic mineral manufactures	−0.55
74	General industrial machinery, equipment, and machine parts	−0.55
11	Beverages	−0.41
72	Machinery specialized for particular industries	−0.25
73	Metalworking machinery	−0.23
63	Cork and wood manufactures other than furniture	−0.21
54	Medicinal and pharmaceutical products	−0.01
67	Iron and steel	0.83
24	Cork and wood	1.07
25	Wood pulp and recovered paper	1.15
68	Nonferrous metals	3.14
28	Metalliferous ores and metal scrap	3.34
33	Petroleum, petroleum products and related materials	7.45

Note: CAGR = Compound Annual Growth Rate. Sectors numbers listed are two-digit SITC.
Source: adapted from Milberg and Winkler (2013: table 4.5).

particularly in the lower-end manufacturing of components, modules, and, later, entire product lines. In this early phase of international outsourcing, lead firms such as Dell and Hewlett-Packard retained some core manufacturing facilities in their home country to produce finished products to meet build-to-order demand and relied on their lower-cost suppliers for intermediate goods such as parts and components. Empirical studies by Sturgeon and Kawakami (2010) and Sturgeon and Memedovic (2011) show that world trade in these intermediate goods has tended to grow substantially after major recessions in the USA (for example, the burst of the 1985 personal computer bubble and the 2001 dot.com bubble) and regional crises (for example, the 1997 Asian financial crisis). This growth in intermediate goods trade indicates expanding global production networks, because American lead firms were reluctant to invest in new in-house production capacity and, instead, chose more aggressive implementation of international outsourcing to reduce production costs during crises or to meet rapidly growing post-crisis demand. As noted by Sturgeon and Memedovic (2011: 8), 'in good times and in bad, outsourcing and offshoring tended to become more common'.

In the apparel industry, cost differentials between lead firms and suppliers can be very substantial. For example, Dussel Peters (2008: 17) estimates that textiles (for example, fibres, yarns, and fabrics) generally account for as much as 50 per cent of the total cost of the final garment product. But China-made fabrics can be 50 per cent cheaper than equivalent US-made fabrics. Labour costs also remain low in those Asian economies endowed by an extremely large reserve army of labour. To Appelbaum (2008: 70), 'global competition between contractors competing for the orders of these "big buyers" has been a key factor in keeping labor costs down, since any factory that could not meet the price requirements of its clients risked losing business to another factory down the street or around the globe'. It is also important to note that cost-based competition is highly critical to service functions that require substantial labour inputs. Facilitated by technological innovation and international competition, a wider range of lead firms' business service functions, such as back office administration, sales, customer service, ICT support, and even applied R&D, can now be outsourced to international suppliers based in lower-cost locations (for example, India and the Philippines). Demand for these outsourced service functions comes not only from lead firms in manufacturing, but also from a wide range of service sector lead firms, such as those in finance, logistics and transport, tourism, healthcare, and so on.[20]

As international sourcing by lead firms has grown rapidly since the 1980s in response to cost pressures, the firm-specific capabilities of their suppliers must concomitantly increase in order to sustain the low cost–capability ratios underpinning successful global production networks. This capability development among an increasing range and diversity of suppliers corresponds with what Sturgeon and Lester (2004) and Sturgeon et al. (2011) term 'making the global supply base' in an era of global production networks. The co-evolution in supplier capabilities reduces the cost–capability ratios of key suppliers, further enhancing their competitiveness in securing more orders from their lead firm customers. Some of these more capable suppliers also engage in a greater range of value activity beyond manufacturing and cover a much wider geographical terrain to serve global lead firms. By the end of the 1990s, Sturgeon et al. (2011: 223) observe:

> retailers, branded merchandisers, and manufacturers, whether they were selling globally or simply seeking to cut operating costs to compete at home, could quite easily tap into supplier capabilities in multiple locations without the cost, risk, or time required to set up their own factories and nurture local supply chains from scratch. The new step was to simplify these supply relationships by using the same set of global suppliers in each of the regions where production was carried out.

More specifically, manufacturing suppliers in East Asia, predominantly those demand-responsive economies such as Taiwan, South Korea, and Singapore, managed to grow their firm-specific capabilities while keeping their overall costs in check.[21] From their initial role as suppliers to OEMs and large retailers in the 1960s through to the 1980s, these East Asian suppliers to global lead firms capitalized on favourable industrial policy and institutional support from their domestic developmental states, a clear case of the important role of extra-firm actors in shaping the context for the emergence of, and articulation into, global production networks.[22] These state-led efforts allowed for rapid human resource development, technological transfer through state-sponsored research institutes, and cost competitiveness through fiscal incentives and infrastructural support. Over time, these home-grown suppliers have continued to sustain their competitive positions in global production networks even though their domestic production costs are rising. This is primarily because the firm-specific capabilities of these suppliers increase at a much faster rate than their costs, resulting in sustained low cost–capability ratios. In electronics, Hobday (1995) found learning-by-doing to be the central mechanism through which East Asian suppliers developed their in-house production and, later, design and management capabilities. Their graduation from OEM suppliers to original design manufacturers (ODMs) and electronics manufacturing services (EMS) providers points to the emergence of a new class of very large global suppliers supporting brand name lead firms in the industry, as identified in Table 2.3. These East Asian suppliers can now provide a one-stop full service, ranging from product design to manufacturing within very short lead times to other more complicated aspects of cross-border integration such as logistics, inventory management, and post-sale services. This increasing integration of supplier capabilities and consolidation of sourcing options works well with lead firms' persistent desire to optimize cost–capability ratios throughout their entire global production networks.

In automobiles, the competitive pressure of lowering cost–capability ratios is even more intensely felt by large brand name assemblers, typically known as 'producers' (as opposed to 'buyers') in the literature. Since the mid-1980s when Japanese automakers began to dominate the world market, American and European assemblers have attempted to lower their cost–capability ratios by outsourcing more components, modules, and subsystems to third-party suppliers. This vertical specialization of large assemblers has led to the rapid rise and increasing role of large global suppliers from Germany (Bosch, ZF, Siemens VDO, Continental, and Luk), the USA (Lear, Delphi, Johnson Controls, Visteon, and TRW), Japan (Denso and Yazaki), France (Valeo), and so on. As observed by Van Biesebroeck and Sturgeon (2010: 212) and Sturgeon and Van Biesebroeck (2011: 184), these

> suppliers took on a much larger role in the automotive industry, often making radical leaps in competence and spatial coverage through the acquisition of firms with complementary assets and geographies. As automakers set up final assembly plants in new locations and tried to leverage common platforms over multiple products and multiple markets, they pressured their existing suppliers to move abroad with them. Increasingly, the ability to produce in all major production regions has become a precondition to being considered for a project.

Similarly to electronics and automobiles, the apparel industry has also experienced a supplier revolution in which giant transnational suppliers have replaced small-scale producers in single locations. As the brand name apparel firms listed in Table 2.2 have increasingly given up their in-house manufacturing facilities and sourced instead from these large suppliers, the demand for supplier capabilities has grown much larger and more complex. Table 3.2 demonstrates a wide variety of functional capabilities in apparel production, ranging from cut, make, trim (CMT) assembly and packaging to full-package service and global sourcing coordination and investment. These brand name lead firms, whether mass merchants or speciality retailers, have strong firm-specific capabilities in marketing, branding, and retail operations. But their capabilities in international sourcing and procurement are more limited in a world of rapidly growing breadth and specialization of apparel products and suppliers with strong production capabilities. This co-evolutionary dynamic explains why brand name lead firms increasingly seek strategic suppliers and intermediaries that can help them optimize their cost–capability ratios. In doing so, these suppliers and intermediaries experience a recursive process of further capability building through these new orders and supply contracts.

The above conceptualization has explained how the competitive dynamics of optimizing the cost–capability ratio has compelled lead firms to develop and/or expand their global production networks over time. Interestingly, this process is not a one-way street whereby a lead firm buys from captive suppliers just because the latter offer the lowest price for the components or products required. Instead, this causal dynamic operates in a recursive and co-evolutionary fashion through which lead firms and their suppliers interact and seek to achieve lower cost–capability ratios *for the network as a whole*— lead firms benefit from lower costs and suppliers develop greater firm-

Table 3.2. Supplier capabilities in apparel

Functional capabilities	Supplier tier	Country examples	Roles	Firm examples
Cut, make, trim (CMT) (assembly)	Marginal supplier	Cambodia, Mexico, Vietnam, Sub-Saharan Africa, the Caribbean	Manufacturing	Domestic firms and affiliates of foreign firms
Package contractor (OEM) sourcing	Preferred supplier Niche supplier	Bangladesh and Indonesia Sri Lanka	Manufacturing, sourcing, and inbound logistics	Domestic firms (e.g. Brandix Lanka) and affiliates of foreign firms
Full-package provider (ODM)	Strategic supplier	European Union, Turkey, India, China	Design and R&D, manufacturing, logistics, and distribution	Luen Thai (TW) and Esquel (HK)
Service providers	Coordinators and foreign investors	Hong Kong, Taiwan, Singapore, Malaysia, South Korea	Buying services, logistics and inventory management	Li & Fung (HK) and AMC (USA)

Note: TW = Taiwan; HK = Hong Kong.
Source: adapted from Gereffi and Frederick (2010: table 5.7). © World Bank, <http://hdl.handle.net/10986/ 2509>, Creative Commons Attribution license, CC BY 3.0 IGO.

specific capabilities. In all three global industries discussed here, the necessity of lowering cost–capability ratios has led to greater vertical specialization by brand name lead firms in advanced economies and more international outsourcing to suppliers in newly industrialized and developing economies.[23] As some of these suppliers gradually accumulate and develop further their firm-specific capabilities, global lead firms outsource even more value activity to them in order to achieve further lower cost–capability ratios and to stay competitive in their major markets. Capability development allows these suppliers to reduce their cost–capability ratios and to engage in functional, process, and even product upgrading. Ultimately, these co-evolutionary dynamics operate successfully only in *some* global production networks, leading to substantial industrial reorganization and consolidation over time. While this consideration of optimizing cost–capability ratio might be considered as 'productionist' in nature, we do not underestimate the equally critical role of non-production considerations, particularly market development and financial discipline, in driving the dynamic formation and transformation of any global production network, topics to which we now turn in the following two sections.

SUSTAINING MARKET DEVELOPMENT

The causal effects of market conditions on the geographical dynamics of global production were recognized in Gereffi's original formulation (1994, 1999) of buyer-driven global commodity chains in such labour-intensive industries as apparel, footwear, and toys.[24] In that formulation, market forces in advanced capitalist economies are embodied in the rise of large buyers, such as retailers, merchandisers, and their purchasing intermediaries, which in turn drive the internationalization of production and their overseas supplier networks. To satisfy growing demand and to maintain their competitive edge in rapidly expanding domestic markets, these large buyers place vast orders with their suppliers across a range of developing and newly industrialized economies and yet demand that the latter reduce the price of manufactured goods. As initially observed by Gereffi (1994: 104), 'we need to take a close look at the US retail sector, whose big buyers have fuelled much of the growth in consumer goods exports in the world economy. Changes in America's consumption patterns are one of the main factors that have given rise to flexible specialization in global manufacturing'. While adopting a somewhat US-centric viewpoint that underplayed the significance of buyers and retailers from Western Europe in particular, Gereffi was undoubtedly prescient in foregrounding the *market imperative* behind the formation and development of global production networks.[25] The nature of this market imperative embodied in consumption and market access, however, has not been adequately developed in the subsequent literature because much of its analytical focus tends to be placed on inter-firm governance and its implications for value capture and distribution along the value chain. It also has no place in the parsimonious models of international outsourcing that are primarily concerned with the declining costs of communications, transport, and transactions.

The Market Imperative

In this book, we argue that the dynamics of market development are not just about large buyers or producers bringing durable goods or services to mass consumers for their final consumption in pre-existing or externally defined end markets. This tends to be the standard analytical mandate of the marketing and international trade literature.[26] On the contrary, we conceptualize the market imperative as a complex and negotiated outcome of the producer–customer interface through which *both* producers and customers are actively involved in market creation. The emergence and changing configuration of global production networks represents an organizational outcome of this iterative process of market making. The market is therefore not an externally imposed structure in which producers and customers react and behave passively. Through their actor-specific practices, these economic agents create and shape such market structures.[27] Adopting this market-making perspective, Petrovic and Hamilton (2011: 32) argue that 'markets are not simple, spontaneously occurring, self-organizing structures. Rather, they are made, maintained, and reproduced by economic actors, typically large firms, that act as market-makers. The results of their actions are the markets of the modern economy—institutionally complex, consciously generated structures that enable and facilitate large numbers of transactions between large numbers of diverse trading partners'. Our GPN approach, nevertheless, differs somewhat from Hamilton et al.'s perspective (2011), which focuses predominantly on how retailers reshape global production, meaning that the role of other important market-makers such as consumers, suppliers, and intermediaries tends to be sidestepped in this buyer-driven view of market development.

Understanding the enduring dynamics of the market development process requires us to give as much analytical attention to customers and their behaviour as to producer strategies, ranging from merchandisers to manufacturers and distributors and the critical role of intermediaries such as traders, logistics, and standards enforcers. Market creation entails developing new demand conditions and supplier capabilities that are mutually reinforcing and geographically mutable. Intermediaries provide the necessary 'glue' to bind the complex relationships between these customers and suppliers. Focusing on both producers and customers in their dynamic shaping of global production networks, we examine the market imperative through four dimensions: reach and access, dominance and concentration, customer pressures, and time-to-market. Our general assumption is that the intermediaries described in Chapter 2 are deeply involved in all of these dimensions. The extra-firm actors described in Table 2.4 are also prominent in shaping the broader institutional and regulatory contexts in which these customer–producer relations are reproduced and engendered.

In general, a market for a product or service is measured in terms of the volume or size of demand, the rate of growth, and the nature of demand with respect to quality, standards, innovation, differentiation, and so on. Developing and sustaining *market reach and access* imposes strong competitive pressures on global lead firms, irrespective of their cost–capability ratios and producer roles in global production networks (for example, buyers or manufacturers of goods or providers of services). Lead firms with high cost–capability ratios are more compelled to reshape their production networks in order to maintain and/or redefine their market position. As market-makers, lead firms with low cost–capability ratios are better positioned to develop continually their access to new markets and benefit from their first-mover advantages in terms of market making. Extra-firm actors in the home markets tend to provide a supportive institutional context for this international market access. This support comes in the form of international trade negotiations, branding and other marketing support, inter-governmental agreements on standards, removal of other non-tariff barriers, and so on.

Meanwhile, international suppliers of intermediate or finished goods/services are subject to the same competitive pressures because access to markets in advanced economies through lead firms brings potentially larger orders, upgrading opportunities, and, ultimately, better value capture. Extra-firm institutions are often keen to support the development of this international market access by their home-based suppliers. Once a new market has been created through firm-specific entrepreneurial innovations (for example, new or recombinant technologies, products, or services), lead firms tend to seek *market domination* in order to capture as much value as possible from their proprietary products or services. This capitalist impulse towards market domination is evident even in the most globalizing industries, such as automobiles and electronics, in which industry-wide standards and other proprietary technologies serve as the frontiers of domination. Lead firms that succeed in optimizing their cost–capability ratios through reconfiguring their global production networks are likely to be dominant players with respect to market creation and domination in these industries. These markets are often characterized by oligopolistic competition among a few leading players. Increasing supplier capabilities also contribute to greater market concentration in the global supply base.[28] From the perspective of both lead firms and their major suppliers, the dynamics of market dominance clearly provide a strong incentive to develop and (re)configure global production networks.

The market imperative of global production networks, nevertheless, should not be defined entirely from the perspective of these producers of final goods or services (lead firms, suppliers, and so on). Customers can be just as critical in defining this market imperative. In general, customer refers to corporate users and individual consumers of goods and services in end markets. In corporate markets for goods or services, customers are typically business firms or extra-firm institutions oriented towards other intermediate markets or private individuals. We can think of producers in the global automobiles and electronics industries supplying to their corporate clients and institutional customers. In intermediate markets, corporate clients can be logistics firms purchasing automobiles to serve their business customers or semiconductor manufacturers buying high-tech equipment to make chips for other electronics producers. In end markets, corporate clients (for example, car rental firms or retail banks) or institutions (for example, state and non-state organizations) purchase finished goods and services to serve private consumers and individuals. These consumers and individuals also buy directly from producers of finished goods and services for their own consumption.

This simple distinction between intermediate and end markets points to substantially different *customer pressures* confronting producers. In intermediate markets, corporate and institutional customers tend to possess more specialized knowhow and firm-specific demand for finished goods or services. By virtue of their size and scale of purchasing, such customers enjoy substantially greater market power than individual consumers. But, since these corporate and institutional customers do not engage directly with consumers or private individuals, they intermediate the market imperative between producers and end users. On the other hand, end markets are fiercely competitive and fast moving precisely because of the extremely diverse nature of consumer demand and preferences. The market impulse of this diverse consumer behaviour is transmitted to producers through their corporate and non-corporate clients. Two dimensions of this market impulse are critical. First, consumers are very demanding in terms of pricing and quality such that producers (that is, lead firms and their key suppliers) can capture high levels of value only during the initial phase of the product life cycle. Once a product or service has become widely available and thus 'matured', competition from other producers will reduce the level of market dominance and value capture. It is in this context that *time-to-market* becomes part and parcel of the market imperative in driving the configuration of global production networks by producers. The more quickly a new product or service gets to the end market, the greater the initial value a lead firm can capture.[29] Second, consumer preferences evolve over time in response to broader institutional and societal changes, which are often spearheaded by extra-firm actors such as the state, international organizations, and consumer groups. In addition to economic factors such as price and quality, consumers are now better informed and take into account other non-economic considerations such as ethical and social responsibility and environmental impact in their consumption decisions. As we will discuss further below, these diverse consumer preferences have increasingly become a defining feature of the market imperative in shaping how producers develop and organize their global production networks.

Market Making in the Home Countries of Lead Firms

Having defined and explained the market imperative, we now examine how this dynamic operates in the global production of markets by buyers/producers, still predominantly found in advanced capitalist economies and their suppliers across a wide range of economies. The global production of markets is concerned not so much with value activity in the production of goods and services, but rather with the creation and sustaining of *demand* for these goods and services among final consumers and end users. In this process of market making, a distinctive organizational shift in core value activity and competence occurs among lead firm producers. This general shift towards market making is evident in the rise of merchandising as a core value activity and the concurrent decline of the manufacturing function in many lead firms. The retail revolution started in the post-war USA and quickly spread to other advanced economies, accelerating from the 1980s onwards. It was associated with the rise of large format retail stores, which not only led to massive growth in the retail industry itself, but more significantly, also transformed the global organization of value activity, as pointed out so effectively by Gereffi (1994: 104–8) in his analysis of buyer-driven global commodity chains. More recently, Hamilton and Petrovic (2011: 3) argue that 'the retail revolution should be understood as a more fundamental transformation in the organization of the overall global economy, the transformation that continues to change not only the world of retailing, or even the relative power between retailers and their suppliers, but also the shape of international trade, economic development, product worlds, and consumption practices'.[30]

The causal effect of this retail revolution on market development operates differently among the three major groups of economic actors in global production networks: lead firms, consumers, and suppliers. First, the impulses of market dominance and concentration drive the competitive dynamics of lead firms in their domestic markets. Beginning in the late 1980s, department stores in the USA, widely hailed as pioneers of the retail revolution in the 1960s, began to lose their market dominance to emerging retail formats such as supermarkets, hypermarkets, discount stores, and speciality stores. The process was quickly imitated in other advanced economies and, subsequently, has spread across much of the world in successive waves of what Thomas Reardon and colleagues call 'supermarketization' (Reardon et al. 2005).[31] This segmentation of the mass market led to immense competitive pressures on oligopolistic lead firms across these new retail formats to sustain their market position through optimizing their cost–capability ratios and developing or expanding global production networks.[32] As evidenced in Milberg and Winkler (2013: 110–11), offshoring to lower-cost suppliers has allowed these domestic lead firms to sustain their market dominance through strategic control of cheaper and/or more competitive imports into the home economy. These competitive imports tend to reduce the profits and market power of lead firms' domestic competitors. From this initial transformation in markets for general merchandise such as apparel, footwear, toys, and household goods, the retail revolution spread to newer and high-tech industries such as consumer electronics and Internet-enabled businesses (for example, Amazon, eBay, Alibaba) in the 1990s and thereafter. To sustain their market dominance, lead firms in global electronics industries such as personal computers, digital devices, and consumer electronics focus on market making through brand management, retailing, and post-sale services, and outsource the manufacturing of their products to lower-cost suppliers in newly industrialized and developing economies.[33]

Second, consumer behaviour and customer preferences have been transformed from a passive force to become a major influence on the strategic decisions of lead firms and their global suppliers. This shift is often supported and institutionalized by extra-firm actors such as state agencies, international organizations, and civil society organizations (see Table 2.4). In advanced economies, convergence in consumption practices towards certain types of retail markets, product worlds, and choice expectations has created a very large and powerful middle class who take seriously their consumer rights and sovereignty. In particular, consumers in these established markets are much more demanding towards lead firms on the quality, innovation, product differentiation, standards, and ethics inherent to their products and processes. Working through both non-firm institutions and personal consumption choices, their reception of global production orchestrated by lead firms in relation to outsourcing practices, working conditions, and environmental impacts also carries serious implications for lead firms' brand image and reputation. While market dominance creates a powerful incentive for lead firms to externalize or outsource their production in order to reduce accountability for the standards expected by their consumers in home markets, this market incentive is counterbalanced by growing levels of awareness among consumers who have much better access to information and resources to engage in collective action such as product boycotting and ethical campaigns.[34]

Third, the rise of this demand-driven retailing, a term coined by Hamilton and Petrovic (2011: 7), has been supported by rapidly growing and more capable supplier markets. As consumer demand increases contemporaneously with the retail revolution, a feedback loop is established in which retailers respond to greater demand with an ever greater supply of durable goods sourced from worldwide suppliers. This mutually reinforcing demand and supply of goods is necessarily underpinned by the development of a global supply market. In this market, suppliers in different locations compete for orders from large buyers on the basis of price, quality, and timely delivery. As conceptualized in the previous section, the most capable suppliers are able to optimize their cost–capability ratios to secure larger orders from global buyers.

The competitive dynamics of market creation in advanced economies operate through this interactive process of lead firms generating greater demand—in terms of both lower prices and higher standards/quality—from consumers and fulfilling that demand through engaging their suppliers in evolving global production networks. In this market dynamic, each of these three groups of actors attempts to maximize the value extracted from the production–consumption nexus: lead firms profiting from higher prices and lower costs, consumers demanding lower-cost products or services at higher standards/quality, and suppliers being squeezed in between these competing pressures and attempting to improve their cost–capability ratios and to yield to more stringent demand. And yet, all of them are subject to the ruthless imperatives of market reach and access, dominance and concentration, customer pressures, and time-to-market. What is missing in this consideration of sustaining market development, however, is the possibility of new markets and emerging consumers *beyond* the traditional home markets of global lead firms.

New Markets in the Global South

The rise of new markets in developing economies and the partial shift of end markets to the Global South in the 2000s have unleashed a significantly new market imperative that is different from the earlier retail revolution in advanced economies—the home markets for most global lead firms.[35] This new market imperative entails a massive increase in domestic consumption of finished goods and services, a demand structure skewed towards commodities, infrastructure, and light manufactured goods, and lower concern for product standards and quality levels. Since the 1990s, the rapid growth of the world's most populated economies—most notably China and India—has provided not only a low-cost global supply base for lead firms from advanced economies. More importantly, it has created new demand from literally billions of people for goods and services previously destined for consumption only in advanced economies. Table 3.3 shows that the global middle class is estimated to increase massively from 1.8 billion in 2009 to 4.9 billion people in 2030. Some 85 per cent of this growth is likely to be based in Asia's largest economies, led by China, India, and Indonesia. As noted recently by Victor Fung (2013: p. xx), Chairman of Li & Fung—one of the world's largest supply

Table 3.3. The changing global distribution of middle-class consumers, 2009 and 2030

Region	2009		2030	
	Number (millions)	Global share (%)	Number (millions)	Global share (%)
North America	338	18	322	7
Europe	664	36	680	14
Central and South America	181	10	313	6
Asia Pacific	525	28	3,228	66
Sub-Saharan Africa	32	2	107	2
Middle East and North Africa	105	6	234	5
World	1,845	100	4,884	100

Source: Based on data from Kharas (2010: table 2) <http://dx.doi.org/10.1787/5kmmp8lncrns-en>.

chain intermediaries, 'not so long ago it was common to assume that production took place in the East for consumption in the West. With the growth of the middle class in Asia and more policies to support domestic demand, however, the momentum for consumer growth is more likely to be in Asia than in the West'. In the post-2008 global financial crisis era, the continual growth of domestic demand in the Global South has provided much needed impetus for global lead firms to overcome market stagnation in advanced economies. As concluded by Kaplinsky and Farooki (2010: 139), 'just as growth is likely to be reduced or to stagnate in the northern economies in the future, so growth in Asia in general and in China and India in particular, is likely to be sustained. If nothing else, the relativities in growth paths between these two worlds in the past two decades are likely to be sustained, and even to increase'.

As the Global South takes on a more substantive role in the market development imperative of global lead firms, it is useful to examine the structure and nature of this growing domestic demand. After several decades of articulation into different global production networks, some of these emerging economies have developed extensive intermediate and end markets in their demand structures. In intermediate markets, emerging economies are characterized by their strong appetite for commodities such as agricultural crops and feeds, minerals, metals, forest products, and so on. These intermediate inputs are needed to support industries such as food, energy, construction, and manufacturing. In end markets, these emerging economies are no longer manufacturing products only for exports to advanced economies. They are increasingly becoming the final destination for such manufactured goods. This reconfiguration of global demand for intermediate inputs and final goods and services creates a powerful market imperative for existing lead firms from advanced economies and emerging domestic firms in these developing economies. The configuration and coordination of global production networks is, therefore, not just shaped by the competitive dynamic of decreasing cost–capability ratios driven by global lead firms through their suppliers in emerging economies. More crucially, these lead firms and their increasingly capable suppliers are actively reorganizing their inter-firm production networks in order to capture more value from this new market opportunity. Importantly, and as noted earlier, leading global buyers, most notably global retailers, have been expanding their operations internationally since the mid-1990s to take advantage of these global shifts in demand and patterns of middle-class growth. In doing so, the usual direction of flow of goods and services within global production networks can, in some instances, be reversed.

To capitalize on this new market imperative, global lead firms and their network partners and suppliers have recognized that the nature of this demand imperative is substantially different from that in advanced economies.

In his influential book *The Fortune at the Bottom of the Pyramid*, the late C. K. Prahalad (2005) argues that the vast market in the Global South, known as the bottom of the pyramid (BOP) market, represents a new challenge to the market development imperative of global lead firms. While some segments of this BOP market can be as brand conscious, globally connected, and ready for advanced technology as their counterparts in the developed world, the vast majority require a new market imperative from global lead firms and their suppliers; many of the latter can count on the BOP in their home markets. In particular, corporate customers and individual consumers in the BOP market tend to be less demanding on the product standards and quality controls described in Table 2.6. Institutional actors and state regulators in this market are also often more lax or weaker in enforcing quality standards and controls in production processes. This unique nature of demand in the BOP market in turn leads to lower entry barriers to new domestic and foreign firms, but puts more intense pressure on price competition and product functionality.

Competitive success via tapping into this vast BOP market, however, requires not just tweaking global products or services to fulfil this demand at lower costs, but rather a fundamentally new understanding of the nature of demand and a corresponding system of production networks. Global lead firms are therefore compelled to develop new 'tuned-down' products or services for this BOP market through localized product innovation and R&D centres in these emerging economies. Successful product innovations can then be transferred to other BOP markets or even to mature markets in advanced economies. The delivery of these localized products or services also necessitates new and more decentralized distribution mechanisms and interfaces that are fundamentally different from the giant retail formats to which lead firms are so accustomed in their home markets. Meanwhile, suppliers to these lead firms can use home advantage, often supported by a favourable set of domestic extra-firm institutions, to enhance their existing firm-specific capabilities because of their proximity to customers and markets, and localized knowledge of consumption behaviour, the institutional context, and the business system. The more capable suppliers from the BOP markets are incentivized by this new market imperative to reorient their strategies to focus more on domestic or intra-macro regional markets, potentially enabling them to develop into lead firms in their own right. As predicted by Sturgeon and Kawakami (2010: 293) in the electronics industry:

> going forward, new industries and value chain combinations will inevitably include more firms—lead firms, contract manufacturers, component suppliers, and even platform leaders—based in newly developed and developing countries. We can anticipate, if nothing else, a spate of new lead firms born in developing countries without the expectation that they will need to move up the contract manufacturing ladder in their efforts to become branded companies. Today,

more GVC elements are available than ever before, either for sale or for hire, and it is only a matter of time before one, and then several new, world-beating electronics companies arise from the developing world to dominate some as-yet unknown product area in the ever-expanding electronics industry.

WORKING WITH FINANCIAL DISCIPLINE

The dynamics of optimizing cost–capability ratios and sustaining market development have profound causal effects on economic actors in global production networks. But these interrelated cost and market effects do not form a complete explanation of the evolution of firm-specific strategies and global production networks. From being a relatively obscure consideration in the early GCC literature during the 1990s, finance has come to the forefront of accounting for the evolutionary dynamics of these actors and networks in the 2010s. Just as production fragmentation and cross-border supplier networks since the 1980s have fascinated researchers interested in inter-firm governance and industrial development, a parallel and, in retrospect, perhaps much more significant phenomenon has dramatically transformed many of the world's dominant economies, with the USA and the United Kingdom being at the forefront of change. This is the transformative imperative of *financialization*, defined by Davis (2009: 93) in his *Managed by the Markets* as a powerful process through which 'financial considerations—market valuation—would drive choices about the boundaries and strategies of the firm. Firms would focus on doing one thing well, and that one thing was often determined by the stock market'.[36] A complete GPN theory must take into account the causal role of finance in disciplining the organization of capitalist production in the global economy.

In this book, we argue that the pressures and opportunities associated with financialization impinge on lead firms and compel their strategic shift towards global production by developing and expanding their global production networks. The causal dynamics of financial discipline work through actor-specific strategies and responses that in turn produce different spatial and organizational configurations of these networks (to be explained in the next chapter). Lead firms that succeed in meeting the demands of financial discipline through globalizing production tend to perform well in the financial market in terms of stock prices and executive rewards, prompting a further shift in their strategic emphasis towards a finance-driven approach to corporate growth and governance. In this iterative sense, financialization works hand-in-hand with global production networks to sustain capitalist accumulation. As argued by Milberg (2008: 445):

financialization has encouraged a restructuring of production, with firms narrowing their scope to core competence. And the rising ability of firms to disintegrate production vertically and internationally has allowed these firms to maintain cost mark-ups—and thus profits and shareholder value—even in a context of slower economic growth. The point is not that globalized production triggered financialization, but that global production strategies have helped to sustain financialization.

In what follows, we describe how this causal process plays out among lead firms and their global suppliers.

Financialization of Lead Firms

While the powerful disciplining effects of financialization on lead firm strategies have been better known since the 2000s, it is important to recognize that the process started as early as the 1970s, particularly in the USA. But the phenomenon did not originate from private-sector initiatives; it was rather an unintended outcome of the state-led transformation of financial markets—a clear reminder of the role of extra-firm institutions in shaping the competitive dynamics confronting economic actors in global production networks. Tracing the political origins of financialization in the USA in *Capitalizing on Crisis,* Krippner (2011) points to the strong urge of US state officials to tap into domestic and global capital markets in order to resolve pressing domestic political dilemmas arising from the crisis of Fordism and the collapse of the welfare state during the 1970s.[37] As a consequence of this political resolution, 'the basic elements that supported the financialization of the US economy—more critically, a rapid pace of credit expansion associated with domestic financial deregulation, large foreign capital inflows, and a monetary policy regime that "followed the market"—were put in place over the course of the 1980s and 1990s' (Krippner 2011: 143).[38]

Once unleashed, the financialization associated with this massive growth of domestic credit and foreign capital inflow has significantly transformed the nature and organization of many lead firms in the USA.[39] As more savings and credit are channelled into financial markets and investment products through mutual funds and financial asset management, lead firms do not need to depend exclusively on banks and other lending institutions to finance their investment and production.[40] They can now turn to capital markets to meet their investment requirements and to access finance on favourable terms, albeit with a catch—they have to fulfil the financial objectives of their investors, and these shareholders are singularly interested in higher and, often, short-term stock prices. This growing alignment of interests between non-financial lead firms and their disparate shareholders is increasingly underpinned by corporate re-engineering focusing on lead firms' core competences, the globalization of their production relations, and changing corporate governance norms (for example, very large executive compensation packages tied to share prices and the rise of CEOs with financial backgrounds) and forms (for example, greater separation between ownership and control and the direct role of institutional investors).[41]

Since the 1980s, this financialization of non-financial lead firms has produced profound incentives and pressures on corporate strategies and decisions. In terms of incentives, lead firms have begun to realize that more profits can be generated through short-term financial re-engineering of their existing operations than through longer-term industrial investment in new plants, equipment, technology, and products. Corporate financial officers find more profit sources in portfolio income on financial assets. For instance, during the 1980s and the 1990s, Krippner (2011: 37–40) found that the ratio of portfolio income to corporate cash flows among US non-financial firms ranged between three and five times the levels of the 1950s and the 1960s. Much of this massive growth in portfolio income comes from interest income on financial assets rather than dividends (declining) or capital gains (constant). Compared with their counterparts in the non-manufacturing sector, US firms in the manufacturing sector led this trend towards financialization. These manufacturing lead firms did not just increase their offer of financial services to expand their product lines, but also directly engaged in managing financial assets through mergers and acquisitions.[42] More importantly, they retained far less after-tax profits for industrial investment, and increasingly used a greater proportion of these profits for dividends payments and share buybacks in order to raise their stock prices and shareholder returns. Measuring dividends and share buybacks as a percentage of internal funds (cash flows), Milberg (2008: 437) and Milberg and Winkler (2013: 220–1) found that the ratio among US non-financial firms surged from a low of 15 per cent in 1984 to historical peaks of 55 per cent in 1990, 65 per cent in 2000, and a staggering 140 per cent in 2007, just before the onset of the 2008 global financial crisis.

This financial transformation of corporate America has put immense pressures on non-financial lead firms to engage in global production. First, the pressure on cost was intensified in the early 1980s when the Federal Reserve's high interest rate policy created much higher and more volatile interest rates and increased borrowing costs to lead firms. This monetary policy also led to a high US dollar that exerted intense cost pressure on American manufacturing firms to increase their international outsourcing. As the cost–capability ratios of their international suppliers increased over time, these lead firms began to realize that development of global production networks allowed for increased profits and permitted a shift of corporate resources from long-term industrial investment in firm growth to the more strategic manœuvres of financial asset management. By reducing production costs and the need to reinvest profits at home through international outsourcing, these lead firms could leave a greater share of their profits for distribution to shareholders, and this greater share-holder return would lead to higher stock prices and greater executive compensation through stock options. By the 1990s, inflation in the USA was under control, and prices of durable goods and services could not be raised further, creating another set of cost pressures on US manufacturing firms to seek lower cost–capability ratios through international outsourcing. Divestment of high cost manufacturing operations to increasingly capable international suppliers allowed lead firms to increase their shareholder values and yet maintain their dominant market positions.[43] These strategic partners and suppliers shouldered the financial investment necessary to supply to global lead firms so that the latter could focus on extraction of financial value from their proprietary assets (for example, branding, technology, and knowhow) and financial assets (for example, newly acquired or merged businesses).[44]

Second, the emphasis on shareholder returns puts serious pressure on lead firms through the rise of finance-driven performance measurement systems of corporate performance. One such system is represented by the use of Economic Value Added (EVA), which includes the level of expected shareholder returns in its calculation. Instead of being the residual claim on corporate profits, shareholder returns are now imputed a priori into the measurement of corporate performance (for example, Apple Inc.'s business model). As noted by Palpacuer (2008: 395), the use of EVA promotes a transfer of risk from shareholders to their invested firms that in turn encourages outsourcing production and transferring investment risks to their employees and independent suppliers. Similarly, Gibbon (2008: 39) argues that '"financialized" corporations prioritize delivering growing returns on invested capital, with the result that an increasing share of risk is transferred from shareholders to the firm, its employees and its suppliers'. Financialization of lead firms has now come full circle, transforming the strategic intent of lead firms towards capitalizing on financial assets and putting much greater pressures on their domestic and foreign suppliers to deliver goods and services at ever lower cost–capability ratios. The causal effect of financialization on expanding global production networks is clearly transmitted through lead firms and their international suppliers, albeit within a favourable institutional context supported by extra-firm actors (for example, state incentives, lower labour and environmental standards, and so on).

Disciplining Suppliers

As these suppliers strive to reduce their cost–capability ratios and take on more value activity in lead firms' global production over time, they inadvertently are subject to the same ruthless financial discipline as their lead firm customers. To begin, the sheer financial costs to suppliers increase exponentially when they

upgrade from subcontractors to full package producers and contract manufacturers. Under the disguise of supply chain rationalization, lead firms driven by
financial considerations are inclined to source from fewer, but larger, suppliers
in order to achieve greater economies of scale and lower unit purchase prices.
Lead firms also tend to adopt more aggressive price-reduction policies with
these suppliers. In the apparel industry, for example, full package producers
bundle value activity and take over all dimensions of the production process,
including logistics, organization, and sourcing of all inputs required for the
manufacture of garments. As noted by Dussel Peters (2008: 17), this type of
contract manufacturing allows for more learning and linkage development than
traditional assembly subcontracting arrangements. But its financing costs can
be ten times greater and substantially increase the investment risk on these
producers.

A significant proportion of these financing costs go into inventory management. Via model stock replenishment programmes, suppliers must now
finance cloth and fabric inventory for a certain period, typically six to twelve
months, and hold their manufacturing capacity open for minimum guaran-
teed volumes in their contracts with lead firm buyers.[45] In the electronics and
automobile industries, the phenomenon of lead firms passing on as much, if
not most, financial exposure to their suppliers is also pervasive. Through what
is termed vendor-managed inventory, suppliers are financially liable for holding the parts and modules required until they are assembled into final products on the factory floor.[46] The costs of engaging in a greater range of
production activities are much higher in the capital-intensive segments of
these industries (for example, semiconductors). It can cost contract manufacturers hundreds of millions of dollars to build new plants or to acquire existing
production lines from their lead firm customers. Only suppliers with the
ability to raise capital cheaply can afford such a form of functional upgrading
in their articulation into global production networks.[47]

Moreover, financial pressures on international suppliers can be transmitted
through trade finance, comprising a number of financial instruments such as
letters of credit, pre-export financing, factoring and forfeiting, advance pay-
ment guarantees, export credit insurance and guarantees, and so on. While
these instruments existed long before the financialization of lead firms, their
role in spreading the cascading effects of financial shocks becomes much
greater because of the heightened sensitivity of lead firms to financial volatility
and the closely interconnected organization of their global production networks. Milberg and Winkler (2010: 38; 2013: 56) found that, during the 2008
global financial crisis, credit market problems experienced by lead firms
(importers) in advanced economies were rapidly transmitted to their suppliers
(exporters) in developing economies through the freezing up of lines of credit
for undertaking international trade transactions. This cascading effect of
financial bottlenecks can paralyze entire global production networks, shutting

down production lines and factories in different locations and tiers of suppliers.

To address this severe credit shortage and to sustain their global production networks, some lead firms and trade intermediaries had to rely on their internal funds to provide an alternative to the traditional means of financing in these suppliers.[48] In the apparel sector, a number of retailers and buyers offered direct financial support to their suppliers. For example, Kohl's from the USA offered a Supply Chain Finance programme to 41 per cent of its suppliers. Under this programme, Kohl's promised to pay suppliers quickly upon approval of their invoice payments. Wal-Mart launched a similar Supplier Alliance Program for expediting payments within 10–15 days of receipt of goods to about 1,000 suppliers. As an intermediary between these large retailers and apparel contractors, Hong Kong's Li & Fung served as a lender of last resort to factories and small importers suffering from the credit crunch during the 2008 crisis. In such a crisis situation, finance became absolutely pivotal in shaping the mutually constituted relationships between global buyers and their struggling suppliers. In short, financialization on a global scale has a significant causal impact on the development and sustainability of suppliers and their articulation into global production networks.

MANAGING UNCERTAINTY AND RISK

Driven by the competitive dynamics of cost–capability ratios, market development, and financialization, global lead firms and their suppliers are confronted with a greater sense of uncertainty and unpredictability in a global economy characterized by rapid technological shifts, massive production fragmentation and international outsourcing, and the rise of new markets and competitors. Managing these challenges successfully requires the entire spectrum of firm and extra-firm actors in global production networks to develop a fuller understanding of changing risk circumstances and to create corresponding coping strategies and platforms. In this penultimate section, we examine how specific elements of this uncertainty and unpredictability can be translated into different forms of risk that can be mitigated through appropriate (re)configurations of global production networks. Our conceptualization internalizes this causal importance of risk and its management in understanding the dynamics of actor-specific strategies in these networks.[49] Here, we present briefly these different forms of risk and leave their mitigation strategies to the next chapter. Clearly the impact of risk on different firm and extra-firm actors varies. The geography of this impact is also highly variable across the different locations and regions articulated into specific global production networks.

Our conceptualization of the causal dynamics of managing uncertainty through global production networks invokes the crucial distinction between economic risk and uncertainty. Following Frank Knight (1921: 19–20) in his classic *Risk, Uncertainty, and Profit*, we argue that uncertainty refers to conditions leading to unknown and random outcomes not amenable to *ex ante* calculations and predictions. But, once these unknown outcomes can be predictable subject to probability distributions, they are no longer uncertain conditions; rather, they can be measured as risk, and management strategies can be developed accordingly. The existence of uncertainty thus fundamentally allows for profit to be made by economic actors because only *some* of them—lucky ones—may take advantage of unknown and incalculable outcomes. When an actor takes a risk, as often understood in the conventional wisdom, its calculability and measurability mean other actors can follow suit, and such competition will eventually dissipate economic profit. To cope with uncertainty in economic life, actors create institutionalized mechanisms such as firms and networks to mitigate only those measurable outcomes—that is, risk. Uncertainty, however, is not amenable to such mitigation strategies and their institutional solutions. It is, therefore, not manageable by economic actors.

In this sense, global production networks are fundamentally an organizational platform for economic actors to mitigate the different forms of *risk* inherent in the competitive dynamics of cost reduction, capability building, market growth, and financial discipline. As hinted at various points in the above sections, risk can primarily take five forms: economic, product, regulatory, labour, and environmental. Table 3.4 summarizes the nature and causal effects of these risks on actors in global production networks. Four points require further elaboration. First, risk is generally produced beyond an individual actor and is therefore a collective dynamic. While an economic actor (for example, a lead firm) can actively participate in the creation of the initial condition underpinning a particular form of risk (for example, new technology or industrial pollution), the translation of this initial condition into a risk requires the enrolment of other economic and non-economic actors in the same global production network. For a lead firm's new technology to be market-transformative and 'risky' to other lead firms in the same industry, it must be well supported by its strategic partners (for example, contract manufacturers or service providers) and key customers. Similarly, for an environmental risk to be efficacious, the initial condition (for example, industrial pollution by a lead firm) must be identified and taken up by one or more social actors (for example, environmental groups) and state institutions (for example, environmental protection agency). On the other hand, structural dynamics may increase or decrease such economic or environmental risks. Regulatory changes at the national or international levels, for example, may substantially increase the economic risk posed by a new technology (for

Table 3.4. Different forms of risk in global production networks

Form	Nature	Causal effects on actors	Recent examples
Economic risk	Systemic shifts in markets—new technologies and innovations, changing demand, financial disruptions, exchange rate fluctuations, and so on	Loss of competitive position in cost and/or market leadership; reduction in financial returns and profitability; lower income and structural volatility to localities and regions	Decline of Canada's RIM (BlackBerry) and Finland's Nokia in smartphone devices, 2013
Product risk	Quality, safety, branding, and efficiency considerations	Negative views of goods or services by consumers and customers; greater demand for corporate social responsibility	The demise of Arthur Anderson LLP in 2002 because of its criminal involvement in the Enron fiasco; Toyota's quality issues with its 'sticky pedals' in the USA, 2009–11
Regulatory risk	Political, public-to-private governance, and changing standards and norms	Disruption or termination of global production, existing industrial practices, and organizational arrangements	EU's tough regulation of genetically modified organisms (GMOs) since 2003 and impact on GM crop-growers (e.g. Monsanto's MON810 maize)
Labour risk	Struggles over working conditions and employment practices	Resistance and industrial action by employees; disruptions to global production and employment prospects; and potentially greater reputational risk	Strikes in Foxconn's plants in China, maker of Apple's iPhones, owing to workers demanding for better terms and working conditions, 2012–13
Environmental risk	Natural hazards or human-made disasters	Accentuating the above four forms of risk and their causal effects	Japan's 2011 Fukushima earthquake and production stoppage in automobile manufacturing owing to parts shortage

Source: Yeung and Coe (2015: table 2). © 2014 Clark University.

example, the Internet) to existing incumbents not receptive to such technology. Exchange rate fluctuations can fundamentally reshape the calculation of cost–capability ratios by all economic actors in any global production network. More stringent pollution regulation can also accentuate the environmental risk of 'dirty' production processes. Identifying the causal effects of risk in global production networks thus requires both actor- and structural-level analyses.

Second, the qualitative nature and causal effects of risk play out differently in the context of global production networks such that we can term it *GPN risk*. While all five risk forms existed in the earlier era of vertically integrated mass production, their nature and effects have a much broader geographical scope and temporal dimension in global production networks. To Gereffi and Luo (2014: 6), participation in global production networks necessarily entails 'higher risk because international standards for price, quality, standards and delivery schedules are much less forgiving'. Geographically, these risks can spread across the entire range of geographically dispersed actors articulated into a particular global production network. For example, while a lead firm in one location is susceptible to rapid shifts in end market demand in another location, its suppliers in other locations are also exposed to the same financial risk taken on between receiving orders and final payments from this lead firm. Because of their tightly interlocked network connections and the tendency of value chain actors to exhibit what Lee et al. (1997a, b) call the 'bullwhip effect' of information distortion and over-amplification, market risk can occur and be transmitted very quickly, and its negative ramifications for value activity can be very serious. The same amplification effect can apply to regulatory risk when trade barriers (for example, tariffs on intermediate inputs) faced by suppliers of goods can substantially escalate the final costs of lead firms.[50] Better management of this expanding spatial–temporal scope of the GPN risk allows a lead firm and its related network partners/suppliers to capture more value from the initial shift in market conditions.[51]

Third, mitigating risk is not necessarily a zero-sum process whereby the gain by one economic actor must entail the loss to another actor—firm or extra-firm. In some circumstances (for example, demand shift or technological change in market conditions), such a zero-sum scenario is possible among different lead firms or their suppliers. But in many other cases (for example, financial crisis or 'race to the bottom' cost competition), most, if not all, economic actors can suffer from negative consequences of economic risk. In this scenario, local firms, workers, and state institutions often lose out in this disadvantaged articulation into global production networks, and, as we will detail in Chapter 5, the 'dark sides' of this articulation tend to prevail. Similarly, regulatory and environmental risks often affect all actors in the same industry. For example, post-9/11 counter-terrorism measures in the USA require more stringent checks on cross-border movements of all goods (for example, the mandatory inspection of all seaborne containers by the US Customs and Border Protection agency; see Gattorna 2013: 236). This differential effect of risk under changing circumstances in turn explains why some risks are more causally efficacious in shaping firm-specific strategies because more value can be captured or losses can be minimized through the mitigation of these risks.

A final point is that different forms of risk can be industry-specific. In more globalizing industries such as apparel, electronics, and automobiles, economic risk associated with changing demand, new technologies, financial crises, and so on can be very substantial precisely because of the geographically dispersed nature of these industries. But, even among these three industries, the automobile industry is generally much more susceptible to regulatory risk such as industrial policy and protectionist interventions by nation states and other extra-firm actors. For example, Van Biesebroeck and Sturgeon (2010: 214) point out

> the political sensitivity to high levels of imports, especially of finished vehicles, in places where local lead firms are present, as they are in the United States and Europe. In our view, the willingness of governments to prop up or otherwise protect local automotive firms is comparable to that of industries such as agriculture, energy, steel, utilities, military equipment, and commercial aircraft.

Meanwhile, labour and environmental risks are more potent and damaging respectively in labour-intensive industries (for example, apparel) and in resource extractive industries (for example, mining and oil and gas).[52] A complete analysis of risk in global production networks must incorporate these industry-specificities in the identification of its causal effects.

CONCLUSION

As an important first step in developing the explanatory apparatus of GPN theory, this chapter has argued that global lead firms and their suppliers are increasingly confronted with the competitive challenges of optimizing their cost–capability ratios, sustaining market development through, for example, shortening their time-to-market, and working with the immensely disciplining pressures of global finance. These three dynamic forces compel firms and extra-firm actors to develop active strategies in order to thrive in today's highly competitive global economy. More specifically, we have identified and elucidated the causal mechanisms through which these dynamic forces impinge on firm-specific actors in different global production networks. To sustain or further their competitive positions, lead firms and their network partners need to optimize cost–capability ratios in recursive ways that reduce costs over time and/or enhance firm-specific capabilities. These co-evolutionary dynamics are at the forefront of globalizing industries such as apparel, electronics, and automobiles.

Over time, optimizing cost–capability ratios allow lead firms to succeed only in existing markets. In delimiting the market development imperative, we postulate that, irrespective of their cost–capability ratios, global lead firms and their network partners must continually develop new markets for their products and services, whether in advanced economies or in newly emerging economies in the Global South. This market-making approach to reframing the evolutionary dynamics of global production networks moves away from the 'productionist' focus that characterizes much of the existing literature. It throws into sharp relief the causal importance of the intermediate and final consumption of goods and services in the geographical dispersion of their production and distribution. In short, this market-making imperative affords greater analytical weight to customers and their consumption in shaping how economic and non-economic actors orchestrate or participate in different global production networks.

As global financial integration takes place in tandem with global production, a third dynamic of financial discipline, often missing in the existing literature, originates from the shareholder revolution that places far greater emphasis on short-term returns to shareholders and corporate restructuring and downsizing to increase shareholder value. While unintended by the political and economic institutions underwriting the rise of global finance, particularly in the USA and the UK, this process of financializing lead firms in manufacturing and non-financial service industries has profound impacts on the corporate organization and governance of global production networks. Iteratively coupled with the first two dynamic forces, financialization exerts enormous pressures on lead firms to optimize cost–capability ratios and to capture more value from new markets. More importantly, it incentivizes these lead firms to seek greater shareholder returns through investment not in new plants and equipment, but in financial assets that may not be related to these firms' core products or services. Investment decisions by most lead firms are often trumped by short-term financial returns rather than longer-term synergies in production and market development arising from product and/or technological complementarities.

Taken together in the sequence of their evolving importance over time, these capitalist dynamics constitute the three-pronged causal explanation of *why* global production networks emerge and evolve. But this GPN analysis is incomplete without a nuanced consideration of the diverse and substantial risks associated with global production. As global lead firms engage more in international outsourcing and as their foreign partners and suppliers actively develop their own firm-specific capabilities, these economic actors from drastically different territorial formations are confronted with an operating environment that is much less certain and predictable than their home economies and domestic markets. Some of these uncertainties can be calculated and translated into different forms of risk specific to global production networks. Mitigating these GPN risks not only forces firms to develop actor-specific strategies, but also necessitates the involvement of other non-economic actors in these global production networks. In the next chapter, we will continue with this theory development and conceptualize *how* these economic and non-economic actors develop, organize, and govern their global production networks in order to respond effectively to the continuous challenges of these competitive dynamics.

NOTES

1. Our approach to theory development is based on a critical realist epistemology that seeks to uncover the necessary and causal mechanisms shaping empirically observable events or patterns such as global production networks. Context and contingency matter in this approach to theory because they provide the relevant condition (s) in which these mechanisms can be efficacious. See Bhaskar (1979, 1997) and Sayer (1992, 2000) for their pioneering work on critical realism and its application to social science.

2. Exceptions are few and relatively recent. See Hamilton et al. (2011) and Ouma (2015) for the role of market development in the emergence of GVCs, and Gibbon (2002), Milberg (2008), and Milberg and Winkler (2013) on financial considerations in GVCs.

3. In her attempt to invigorate a second generation of commodity chain research, Bair (2005: 154) has made a plea for 'research focusing on the broader political-economic environment in which chains operate, including the institutional and systemic factors that shape commodity chains and condition the outcomes associated with them'. Our conceptual efforts here not only respond to this call, but also go further in developing an integrated theory of how these broader institutional and systemic factors (we term them dynamic forces) causally shape actor-specific strategies and their (re)organization of global production networks.

4. As noted in Chapter 1, in perhaps the most influential conceptual work so far in the GVC literature, Gereffi et al. (2005) provide a theoretical explanation of the role of the complexity and codifiability of inter-firm transactions and supplier capabilities in determining the governance of GVCs in different industries. More recently, Ponte and Sturgeon (2014) further argue for the modularization of theory development in GVC studies.

5. In this epistemological sense (see also Yeung and Coe 2015), we differ from Gereffi et al.'s view (2005: 82) that, 'if a theory of global value chain governance is to be useful to policymakers, it should be parsimonious. It has to simplify and abstract from an extremely heterogeneous body of evidence, identifying the variables that play a large role in determining patterns of value chain governance while holding others at bay, at least initially'. For examples of such parsimonious models in economic studies of international outsourcing and trading of production tasks, see Jones and Kierzkowski (1990, 2001), Grossman and Helpman (2002), Antràs and Helpman (2004), Grossman and Rossi-Hansberg (2008), and Milberg and Winkler (2013).

6. It is useful to note that risk considerations have been examined more in the supply chain management literature (see Sheffi 2005; Simchi-Levi 2010; Lessard 2013;

Asia-Pacific Economic Cooperation 2014). But this literature tends to focus on the impact of supply chain risks—e.g. demand variations and supply disruptions—on brand name lead firms, rather than on the dynamics of the entire global production network.

7. Neoclassical economic models of international outsourcing tend to attribute causal effects to falling costs associated with improvements in communications and transportation technologies (e.g. Jones and Kierzkowski 1990; Arndt and Kierzkowski 2001; Grossman and Rossi-Hansberg 2008) and specification of property rights (e.g. Antràs and Helpman 2004; Antràs 2005; Antràs and Chor 2013; Baldwin and Venables 2013). Extra-firm institutions do play a significant role in reducing these costs—e.g. through better regulation and enforcement of rules. In GPN thinking, however, these cost improvements are conceptualized as *enabling* factors rather than causal conditions for the emergence of global production networks because they do not generally accrue to particular firms and actors. These costs are generally shared among all economic actors inside particular jurisdictions.

8. This is the phenomenon first identified as the New International Division of Labour (NIDL) in the seminal work of Fröbel et al. (1980). Their analysis was based on detailed empirical work on the international relocation of German-owned textile and garment production over the period 1960–75 both within Europe and beyond to North Africa and Asia.

9. The resource-based view of the firm is a major strand of theoretical and empirical literature in strategic management. For some of the most influential studies, see Barney (1991, 2001), Teece and Pisano (1994), and Teece (2009).

10. As noted in Chapter 1, Kaplinsky and Morris (2001) offer a typology of four forms of industrial upgrading: functional upgrading, process upgrading, product upgrading, and inter-sectoral upgrading. We will analyze these upgrading trajectories in Chapter 5. It is important, nevertheless, to distinguish cause and effect in upgrading processes. Increasing firm-specific capability is one of its most important causes, and industrial upgrading is often the outcome, contingent on other necessary conditions such as strategic choices made by lead firms (e.g. technology transfer and production outsourcing) in response to cost pressures, market development, and financial considerations.

11. To be clear, this is not a deterministic argument. Both lead firms and suppliers face considerable organizational and competitive challenges in enacting these strategies, some of which are innately geographical in nature and shaped by a variety of extra-firm actors—e.g. forging relationships across different national regulatory and institutional contexts. Nonetheless, instances where these transitions have occurred are crucial to understanding shifting patterns of development in the global economy, as we shall see in Chapter 5.

12. In this chapter, we will not delve into firm-specific strategies in resolving these competitive dilemmas. The next chapter will explain *how* lead firms, suppliers, and other extra-firm actors in global production networks strategize and respond to these competitive dynamics. The dyadic approach in Figure 3.1 is also illustrative of the complex reality within which firms experience a continuum of these opposing forces.

13. As argued by Winter (2008: 60), some of these capabilities are of a 'higher order', and are known as 'dynamic capabilities' that involve long-term commitments to specialized resources (e.g. dedicated personnel and continuity in facilities and equipment) and thus higher costs to the firm.

14. There are exceptions though. Lead firms with high capabilities and high costs may remain competitive if their products or services are highly proprietary, unique, or regulated, meaning they can enjoy a virtually monopolistic position in their domestic end markets. Examples are industries fulfilling government procurement contracts (e.g. sophisticated military equipment) and captive markets (e.g. fine foods and software systems).

15. See Cattaneo et al. (2010a), Staritz et al. (2011a), Lüthje et al. (2013), and Pickles and Smith (2015) for nuanced analyses of these three global industries.

16. See the pioneering work on the modularization of industrial production in Baldwin and Clark (2000) and its application to the American electronics industry in Sturgeon (2002).

17. Prime empirical examples are apparel (Fröbel et al. 1980; Bonacich et al. 1994; Abernathy et al. 1999; Pickles 2006; Lane and Probert 2009; Pickles and Smith 2011, 2015) and electronics (Morgan and Sayer 1988; Henderson 1989; Angel 1994; Hobday 1995; Dedrick and Kraemer 1998; Lüthje et al. 2013). The internationalization of automobile production was driven more by market access than by cost considerations. We will discuss the role of the market in the next section of this chapter.

18. Lazonick and O'Sullivan (2000) offer an influential analysis of this general shift in corporate strategy and governance in response to pressures of maximizing shareholder value since the early 1980s.

19. This relentless drive towards a lower cost–capability ratio is also confirmed in Gibbon and Ponte's study (2008: 371–2) of the business considerations of purchasing managers in US manufacturing. They found that, prior to 1985, purchasing agents and supply chain managers of US manufacturing firms focused primarily on securing a smooth and uninterrupted flow of buying-firm operations in terms of the availability of raw materials and inputs and increased capacity utilization and economies of scale. Between 1993 and 1998, the issue of maximizing cost savings began to emerge as one of the most important rationales for supply management. By 2001, it had become the second most important vector of corporate profit.

20. For contemporary studies of IT outsourcing to India and the Philippines, see Dossani (2013), Parthasarathy (2013), and Kleibert (2014). Gereffi and Fernandez-Stark (2010) offer a general analysis of service outsourcing.

21. The term 'demand-responsive economies' comes from Feenstra and Hamilton (2006), Hamilton and Gereffi (2009), and Hamilton and Kao (2011).

22. For classic work on these developmental states and their initiatives up to the late 1980s, see Amsden (1989), Wade (1990), Evans (1995), Mathews and Cho (2000), and Amsden and Chu (2003). For a more recent reprise of this literature from the perspective of GPN thinking, see Yeung (2009d, 2014) and Whittaker et al. (2010).

23. While for brevity's sake we have concentrated here on three highly globalizing manufacturing industries, similar arguments can be applied to a range of service

sector global production networks. In food retailing, for instance, large retailers act as lead firms across a plethora of agro-food and food-processing sectors and seek to reduce their costs through benefiting from the enhanced capabilities (e.g. in terms of selection, processing, packaging, labelling, and standards enforcement) of a range of specialized suppliers and wholesalers (see, e.g., Reardon et al. 2003; Coe and Hess 2005). In logistics, lead firm third- and fourth-party providers increasingly use extensive subcontracting networks of transport, storage, and supply chain service firms to provide a seamless global service to their clients (see, e.g., Dicken 2011; Coe 2014). In tourism, global tour operators capture value by coordinating complex webs of national and local tour operators, travel agents, and tourism service providers (see, e.g., Dörry 2008; Christian and Nathan 2013). Interestingly, in such sectors the formation of global production networks often blends the rationales of cost–capability ratio minimization and market access/control.

24. The role of market access in shaping the internationalization of production has been identified much earlier in studies of transnational corporations seeking entry into foreign markets protected by host country state policies or other trade barriers—e.g. automobiles and extractive industries (Dunning and Lundan 2008; Dicken 2015). For example, Ford established its first overseas production facility in Manchester, the UK, as early as 1911 because of market access and trade barriers (see Dunning 1958; Dicken and Lloyd 1976). This market-seeking motive, however, is served through multi-domestic operations by local subsidiaries or affiliates of lead firms, rather than the international outsourcing to, and development of, independent suppliers that characterize the rise of global production networks analyzed in this book.

25. For a concise narrative of such a causal link between American retailers and Asian manufacturers between 1965 and 2005, see Hamilton's (2005) testimony to the US–China Economic and Security Review Commission and his further work in Feenstra and Hamilton (2006) and Hamilton et al. (2011).

26. A methodological note is useful here. Even at the finest level (e.g. four-digit), the use of international trade data to analyze market linkages in global production networks remains cursory because only broad trends in tradable goods and/or services can be analyzed. The causal mechanisms of network dynamics and actor-specific value activities cannot be adequately addressed via this methodology.

27. For a detailed empirical analysis of such market-making processes in the context of agro-food global production networks, see Ouma (2015).

28. Knickerbocker (1973) offers an influential analysis of how oligopolistic competition leads to internationalization and the emergence of transnational corporations. An earlier interpretation of this market power approach to internationalization of production is found in Hymer's 1960 MIT doctoral dissertation, which was published posthumously as Hymer (1976).

29. See Fine's *Clockspeed* (1998) for a pioneering discussion of the critical importance of understanding temporality in value capture.

30. Given the scale of its international sourcing, US retailer Wal-Mart often plays a central role in these accounts (see Brunn 2006 and Lichtenstein 2006, for excellent overviews). It is important to note, however, that leading European transnational

retailers such as Ahold, Carrefour, IKEA, Lidl, Metro, and Tesco are also significant global buyers of durable goods.

31. See Petrovic (2011) for a detailed analysis of this transformation in US retailing and its internationalization between 1970 and 2010. Reardon et al. (2005, 2007) chart four waves of global retail transformation in emerging markets from the early 1990s to the late 2000s.

32. Global retailers are a pivotal part of this story, as their globalization involves the formation of global production networks both through the establishment of international sourcing operations and through the international expansion of store activities (which occurs later in most cases). These twin, interlinked dynamics are the defining characteristic of the leading retail transnational corporations, and there are important functional connections between the globalization of sourcing and stores. For more conceptual work on retail globalization, see Coe (2004), Wrigley et al. (2005), and Coe and Wrigley (2007, 2009).

33. Dedrick and Kraemer (2011) offer a fascinating analysis of such market making in the personal computer industry.

34. Anti-Nike campaigns are perhaps one of the best-known cases. Through such campaigns, consumers have asserted their power over Nike's outsourcing practices and the working conditions in its suppliers (see Locke et al. 2007). For more theoretically informed analyses of ethical consumption, see Hughes (2001, 2012), Hughes et al. (2008), and Barnett et al. (2011).

35. For a general analysis of this market shift to the Global South, see Cattaneo et al. (2010a), Staritz et al. (2011a, b), and Gereffi and Luo (2014). More specific studies of new markets in GVCs have focused on China and India (Kaplinsky and Farooki, 2010, 2011; Yang 2014) and, more generally, Asia (Ferrarini and Hummels 2014).

36. Compared to cost factors and governance structures, the role of financialization in shaping lead firm strategies and their global production organization has received far less attention in the GCC–GVC literature. For a few exceptions, see Gibbon (2002), Gibbon and Ponte (2005), Milberg (2008), Palpacuer (2008), and Milberg and Winkler (2013). See Coe et al. (2014) for an overview of GPN analysis and financialization.

37. See also earlier work on the rise of global finance in Frieden (1991), Helleiner (1994), Cohen (1996), Epstein (2005), and Glyn (2006).

38. More specifically, these elements of financialization were manifested in the Depository Institutions Deregulation and Monetary Control Act passed in spring 1980 to deregulate interest rates on consumer savings deposits, the massive inflows of foreign capital from the early 1980s owing to the high interest rate policy pursued by the Federal Reserve to curb inflation, and the radical change to US monetary policy with the Volcker Shock of October 1979 and the subsequent abdication of the Fed's control over credit to the financial market.

39. Although the USA and in turn the UK are usually seen as the originators of financialized capitalism, the processes have much wider resonance and import, for two interrelated reasons. First, there have been convergence tendencies between financial regimes associated with different varieties of capitalism. Clark and Wojcik (2007), for example, profile changes within the German financial system (and associated modes of corporate governance) in response to the growing

dominance of Anglo-American norms within global finance. Second, the formation of global production networks means that firms are increasingly exposed to
this global finance system, even if institutions in their home market seek to limit
the impacts of financialization. Johal and Leaver (2007), for instance, undertook a
comparative analysis of the financial performance of leading French, British, and
American firms over the period 1987–2005. They found that the French firms
were relatively unprofitable in terms of return on sales measures, in part owing to
the nature of the national social settlement in France. During the study period,
however, French firms were also using funds raised in global capital markets to
internationalize vigorously, consolidating sales and profits in liberal economies
such as the UK and USA in order to cross-subsidize the social settlement in their
home market.

40. For an in-depth analysis of saving and borrowing in the realm of consumer
finance, see Langley's (2008) excellent book *The Everyday Life of Global Finance*.

41. We thank John Pickles for this last point on changing corporate governance
forms. See O'Sullivan (2000), DiMaggio (2001), and Whitley (2007) for general
accounts, Yeung (2004, 2007b) and Witt and Redding (2014) for examples in Asia,
and Pickles (2007, 2008) for examples in Eastern Europe.

42. One well-known example is General Electric, which started its wholly owned
financial arm, GE Capital, during the Great Depression to support its sales of
goods and services. By the 1980s, GE Capital had begun to focus on helping
external customers to purchase, lease, and distribute equipment, and to provide
the capital for their real estate and corporate acquisitions, refinancing, and
restructurings. GE Capital takes pride in providing 'more than just financing: we
bring insight, knowledge, and expertise to every loan. And as a result, businesses
that finance with GE Capital benefit from the global know-how and expertise of
GE' <http://www.gecapital.com> (accessed 5 June 2014). For several years prior to
2008, GE Capital contributed about half of General Electric's group profit, and its
GE-related financing accounted for less than 5% of its overall lending.

43. This financial discipline varies quite substantially among lead firms from different
political economies, and also takes on varying forms in different sectors. In
apparel, for example, Palpacuer et al. (2005) and Gibbon (2008) found that
financial pressures led to different sourcing practices between US/UK and European lead firms. But Lane and Probert's (2009) study shows some convergence in
these practices, with more German buyers beginning to impose financial discipline
on their suppliers. Palpacuer (2008: 396–8) also reports substantial difference in
the distribution of corporate cash flows to fund dividends and share buybacks
(and thus less for reinvestment) between European and American lead firms in the
food sector between 1996 and 2000—respectively 33.9% and 89.2%. The largest
European food lead firms, including Nestlé, Unilever, and Danone, began to
engage in US-style financialization, however, from the late 1990s onwards, primarily to support their international expansion and growth strategy. For other
sectoral windows onto these dynamics, on automobiles see Froud et al. (2002), on
pharmaceuticals see Vitols (2002), on legal firms see Faulconbridge and Muzio
(2009), and on retailers see Baud and Durand (2012).

44. Apple Inc.'s business model of complete outsourcing in a context of financialization is instructive here. See studies by Froud et al. (2012) and Haslam et al. (2013), which show how Apple's profitability is critically dependent on its exercise of lead firm power over its suppliers, which in turn allows Apple to extract financial 'point values' from its global production networks.

45. For more details of such programmes in the context of apparel suppliers, see Gibbon's (2008) study of African clothing exports and Pickles and Smith's (2011, 2015) studies of suppliers in Eastern and Central Europe.

46. See Sturgeon and Kawakami (2010, 2011a).

47. See the case of Taiwan's Hon Hai Precision (trade name Foxconn) described in Yeung (2014).

48. See Gereffi and Frederick (2010) and Frederick and Gereffi (2011) for more.

49. See Power's (2009) work on the emergence of risk management in a corporate world of greater uncertainty.

50. A recent report by OECD-WTO-UNCTAD (2013: 14) estimates that trade facilitation alone can yield potential cost reductions of between 10% and 16% for producers in economies at different income levels.

51. This GPN risk is particularly visible in the global electronics industry (see Sturgeon and Kawakami 2010, 2011a; Milberg and Winkler 2013). For example, a fire in SK Hynix's DRAM production plant in China's Wuxi on 4 September 2013 led to substantial disruption in the global supply chain of memory chips for electronics devices. Chip prices increased by 19% within days of the fire. With a third of the global market share in memory chips, SK Hynix is the world's second largest producer, after Samsung Electronics. Its Wuxi plant produces about half of SK Hynix's total production <http://blogs.wsj.com/digits/2013/09/09/chip-supply-concerns-linger-after-hynix-factory-fire> (accessed 12 June 2014).

52. A very good example is the 2010 BP oil spill off the Gulf of Mexico in the USA that led to over 50% drop in its market capitalization within weeks and over US$40 billion of subsequent damage liabilities and government fines.

4

Strategies

In arguably the most influential theoretical 'model' of global value chains (GVCs) to date, Gereffi et al. (2005) explain how the governance structure of such chains is determined by three supply chain variables—the complexity of transactions, the ability to codify transactions, and the capabilities within the supply base. They conclude that these key GVC variables, in turn, are determined by the technological characteristics of the products and processes involved. Crucially, these variables 'often depend on the effectiveness of industry actors and the social processes surrounding the development, dissemination, and adoption of standards and other codification schemes. It is the latter set of determinants, in particular, that opens the door for policy interventions and corporate strategy' (Gereffi et al. 2005: 98). In this chapter, we further conceptualize these industry actors and their corporate strategies in order to develop a complete set of *causal mechanisms* for analyzing global production networks. As we have made clear in this book, production networks are merely organizational devices, providing different windows of opportunity for actor-specific learning, practice, and upgrading. Their empirical efficacy, therefore, depends critically on the strategic choices made by the various actors—both economic and non-economic—that constitute, and, in turn, are embedded in, these networks.

This chapter extends our explanatory thread connecting the competitive dynamics of global production networks to the strategies of the actors constituting these networks. We argue that these actor-specific strategies are an indispensable part of GPN 2.0 because they 'translate' the causal power of the competitive dynamics conceptualized in Chapter 3 into differential value activities that in turn produce diverse developmental outcomes (as we shall see in the next chapter). As noted in Figure 1.3, this 'translation' of causal power through strategies is recursive in nature such that, over time, developmental outcomes can feedback into, and influence, competitive dynamics and actor strategies. While our earlier conceptualization of dynamics provides answers to the question of *why* global production networks form, this chapter's conceptual exposition on actor-level strategies offers answers to the question of *how* these networks work and operate in different organizational fields and industrial sectors. In Figure 4.1, we briefly summarize these causal mechanisms of global production networks. In a theoretical sense, competitive dynamics in the global economy provide the structural properties of causality and emergence that are mediated through firms. Actor-specific strategies serve as the corresponding mechanisms for firms organizing their networks. Taken together, these dynamics and strategies co-constitute the *causal mechanisms* of global production networks, explaining empirical outcomes in terms of economic development—for example, firm growth, technological acquisition and innovation, industrial upgrading and sectoral transformation, local and regional development, and so on.

After a brief reprise of the importance of strategy in the next section, the four strategies in Figure 4.1 are explicitly developed in this chapter. At the intra-firm level, we conceive of *coordination* through internalization and consolidation as a firm-specific strategy in organizing global production networks driven by a particular set of competitive dynamics. At the inter-firm level, two strategies are particularly prominent in the contemporary organization of global production networks—*control* and *partnership*. The actor-specific choice to adopt these strategies is determined by different configurations of competitive dynamics that are described in greater detail in respective sections. Last but not least, *extra-firm bargaining* refers to the strategic interface through which capitalist firms interact with extra-firm actors in different global production networks in ways that can lead to institutional capture, cooperation, and collaboration. In rethinking these four strategies, we bring firm-specific *variability* to the forefront of discussion. In each case, our analytical approach is to start with generic conceptualization by defining the strategy and explaining why it is deployed in relation to the structural dynamics identified in Chapter 3. We will then analyze

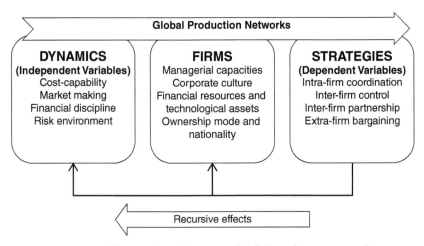

Figure 4.1. The causal mechanisms of global production networks

which actors are involved in this strategy and why it matters to the configuration of particular global production networks. Finally, we will move onto more specific and empirical discussion and illustration of how the strategy works— in variable ways—in relation to selected examples or cases. In doing so, we build on the conceptual arguments and empirical findings in the emerging literature identified in Chapter 1.[1]

STRATEGY MATTERS!

Why does actor strategy matter in GPN analysis? In identifying the causal properties of strategy, we argue for the analytical importance of *intentionality* and *agency* in accounting for empirical outcomes. While recognizing the crucial role of historical contingencies (for example, episodic shifts in Chapter 1) and structural imperatives (for example, capitalist dynamics in Chapter 3), GPN theory places actors and their choices centrally in its conceptual model and identifies explicitly the causal mechanisms of concrete outcomes, which range from organizational structures to industrial transformation and developmental impacts. It postulates that actor-specific strategic choices lead to diverse modes of organizing global production networks. Without such an explicit rethinking of strategy, any exclusive analytical focus on governance modes *per se* may fall into the trap of putting the cart (governance) before the horse (strategy). Moreover, strategy matters because it represents the purposeful response of actors to the challenges of competitive dynamics in the face of the real world uncertainty outlined in Chapter 3.[2] It underscores the critical importance of opening the 'black box' of firms in global production networks. Conceived as such, strategy provides the crucial bridge between economic actors and structural dynamics in GPN thinking.

Though relatively under-theorized, the importance of strategy has been partly reaffirmed in existing approaches to global value chains. While focusing primarily on inter-firm relationships as modes of governance, the GVC literature does recognize that the dynamics of these relationships are not spontaneous, automatic, or even systematic. Instead, Ponte and Sturgeon (2014: 6) argue that 'these [governance] processes are "driven" by the strategies and decisions of specific actors. The relevance of GVC [global value chain] governance is that it examines the concrete practices, power dynamics, and organizational forms that give character and structure to cross-border business networks'. In this bid to develop a broad brush and descriptive tool for characterizing an entire global value chain or even a global industry, however, concrete practices and power dynamics are frequently subsumed under different modes of chain governance. The strategic thrust in these practices and dynamics becomes invisible or assumed, giving way to broader chain-level characterizations such as modular, relational, and captive inter-firm relationships.

Going beyond this top-down characterization of chain characteristics and actor-specific practices, this chapter rebuilds the analytical causality in favour of the four types of firm strategy that shape the particular configurations of global production networks in specific historical and geographical contexts. Our analytical focus on actor-specific strategies in global production networks provides a partial solution to the risk of *methodological nationalism* that is inherent to any country-level GVC analysis that uses input–output data to explain the global reorganization of value added trade activity—for example, in international economics and international business studies. As noted in UNCTAD's *World Investment Report 2013*: 'While the link between FDI [foreign direct investment] and TNC [transnational corporation] activities, on the one hand, and value added trade patterns, on the other, can thus be established *at the macro level*, determining how TNCs and their networks of affiliates and contractual partners shape value added trade patterns through *firm-level evidence* remains challenging' (UNCTAD 2013b: 137; emphasis in original). One crucial missing link in this macro-economic approach to analyzing value added trade activity in global production networks is the actor-specific view of competitive strategy and organizational practice.

The key challenge for GPN 2.0, then, is to incorporate a broader consideration of firm-specific strategies. This is where *variability* becomes one of the most critical attributes of strategizing by actors in global production networks. The intentional acts of strategy formulation (planning) and implementation (practice) are highly dependent on the knowledge and judgement of these actors in their engagement with the value creation, retention, and capture processes made possible by emerging global production networks. Their strategic choices are likely to vary substantially across different networks, sectors, and geographical contexts. No single strategy can adequately characterize all the actors in one production network, let alone an entire industry. The same actor (for example, a lead firm, a strategic partner, or a state regulator) is also likely to adopt and implement multiple strategies over time in order to cope with different or changing competitive dynamics. The strategic choices of lead firms (mostly TNCs) range from intra-firm flows to inter-firm trade between lead firms and contract partners or independent suppliers (arm's length transactions). While strategizing on how to engage with external partners and suppliers, these lead firms may well be concomitantly rethinking how they should best coordinate and operate value activity within their own affiliates. Our approach thus improves on prevailing characterizations in the GVC and GPN literature because we allow for the possibility of actors in the *same* global production networks exercising multiple or all four types of firm-level strategy. The precise combination of these strategies can be ascertained only through empirical investigations.

To account for this variability in strategies and to eschew a one-size-fits-all approach to configuring global production networks, we attempt to incorporate firm- and industry-specificities. At the *firm* level (see middle box of Figure 4.1), the different types of corporate cultures, ownership forms, and national origins described in Chapter 2 can significantly influence the strategic predisposition of all the economic actors involved in global production networks. First, firms are collective social actors rather than production functions or cost minimization devices.[3] A firm is made up of social beings, whether they are executives, managers, technologists, engineers, specialists, shopfloor workers, sales representatives, and so on. Through internally coordinated and differentiated organizational structures and processes, these individuals can build a strong corporate culture that shapes the core competencies of the firm as a whole. These competencies can be expressed in the form of firm-specific knowledge (for example, technology and patents), social capital (for example, trust relationships and routines), and organizational innovations (for example, strategic business units). These social beings form specific communities of practice and socialize others into their groups on the basis of shared representations, motivations, norms, and values.[4] Schoenberger (1999: 211) argues for the importance of 'not only where "the firm" (conceived as unitary agent) meets the world (competitors, markets, suppliers), but also internally as competing subcultures strive for validation and expression'. As illustrated later in our analysis, the importance of corporate culture is predicated on the empirical reality that firms from the same industry and of the same national origin often pursue significantly different strategies to create and capture value through global production networks.

Second, ownership plays a major role in firm behaviour. Publicly traded firms are much more susceptible to the pressures of financial discipline, whether they are lead firms, strategic partners, or independent suppliers in any given global production network. They are less likely to engage in the strategy of vertical integration and cross-subsidization across different affiliates. Instead, they are more driven by financial incentives to focus on core capabilities in value-adding processes and to externalize non-core activity to other actors in their global production networks. Third, the national origins of firms in global production networks are also significant in their strategy formulation and implementation. Extra-firm actors are particularly influential in shaping these national and regional institutional contexts. Firms from national business systems characterized by corporatist and developmental states tend to experience greater incentives for sustaining long-term institutional support and employment relations. Their strategic response to cost pressures and financial discipline is likely to be different from those embedded in neoliberal market economies, which are more dominated by financial considerations in economic transactions.[5]

At the *industry* level, technological change, common standards, and market shifts are highly important specificities that influence corporate strategies in global production networks. These specificities can vary within and between different industries such that strategic responses by actors may differ within the same industry or may converge between different industries. As argued earlier in Chapter 3, unpredictable technological change and market shifts can constitute serious uncertainty for economic actors. Those who negotiate this uncertainty successfully through their firm-specific practices are likely to reap exceptional economic rents. In many instances, these changes and shifts are calculable in the sense that some actors are forward-looking enough to identify future possibilities and to make the necessary organizational arrangements and corporate investments. In so doing, they turn uncertainty into quantifiable risks that can be mitigated through appropriate corporate strategies and action. In particular, to create or capture more value from the unique nature and speed of technological change, firms develop different strategies to improve their cost–capability ratios and time-to-market. Standard industrial practices such as flexible production technologies and the modularization of design and products allow firms in *some* industries to adopt much more rigorous inter-firm control and partnership strategies. Lead firms and their collaborative partners can take advantage of these flexibilities in design and production technologies to increase the resilience and robustness of their global production networks, and can thereby mitigate the economic and environmental risks associated with production disruptions and natural disasters, for instance.[6]

In other industries dominated by new and evolving technologies or in markets characterized by highly unpredictable trajectories and a lack of industry-wide standards and codification schemes, lead firms regularly deploy the strategy of intra-firm coordination to capture more value under conditions of uncertainty. Rapid market shifts in specific segments of an industry or in an entire industry can impinge seriously on both incumbents and innovative firms in different global production networks. Again, their strategic responses tend to differ in relation to these shifts. The most market-sensitive firms may adopt the strategy of intra-firm coordination or inter-firm partnership in order to reduce their time-to-market and to ensure the quality consistency and standards of their products or services. Meanwhile, other incumbents in the same industry may be locked into a more myopic strategy limited to controlling their independent suppliers and therefore may miss major market shifts. In the following four sections, we will put to work these crucial considerations of strategy and variability in global production networks.

INTRA-FIRM COORDINATION

As the first strategy we will consider here, *intra*-firm coordination is particularly important because the existing GVC and international outsourcing literatures tend to focus exclusively on *inter*-firm relationships. We know far less about how firms in global production networks reorganize their internal value activity in order to meet the competitive challenges of the structural dynamics identified in Chapter 3.[7] In general, we can define this strategy of intra-firm coordination as the *internalization* and *consolidation* of value activity within the lead firm, the strategic partner, and/or the supplier firm in order to achieve greater firm-specific system efficiencies such as lower inventories and better cost control, greater market responsiveness, and higher-quality products or services. As described by Kaplinsky and Morris (2001: 29), this coordination goes beyond a firm's strategic (re)positioning in a global production network to incorporate its production and logistics management, its integration of design and R&D into supply networks, and its monitoring of quality standards and production outcomes. Through greater attention to intra-firm coordination, a firm can identify and capture more value from its bundles of firm-specific resources and organizational capabilities.

More specifically, internalization takes place when a firm engages in horizontal specialization, a strategy of expanding into adjacent markets and/or products or services by fully exploiting its firm-specific proprietary assets—for instance, in terms of branding, knowhow, and technology. This strategy of internalization often entails the articulation of a firm into multiple industries, producing the three types of inter-industry intersections identified in Figure 2.3(c). Internalization thus allows for the exploitation of economies of scope by a firm. Consolidation of value activity, on the other hand, goes hand in hand with internalization because it requires a firm to integrate much more explicitly its diverse resources and capabilities in order to support its expansionary efforts through internalization. Consolidation can be achieved through tightening internal procurement and supply processes, exploiting cross-functional capabilities (for example, design, marketing, and production), and integrating resources across affiliates in different industries and geographical locations. Overall, the strategy of intra-firm coordination through internalization and consolidation enables firms to respond effectively to competitive dynamics in ways that produce particular configurations of global production networks.

In Table 4.1, we summarize how the varying magnitude of the three competitive dynamics and risks interact with, and shape, the adoption of intra-firm coordination strategy by *different* firm actors, and how these actors in turn pursue different organizational configurations of global production networks. We will address the strategies of extra-firm actors and development

Table 4.1. The strategy of intra-firm coordination in organizing global production networks

Actors	Competitive dynamics			Risks	Global production network structures
	Cost–capability ratio	Market imperative	Financial discipline		
Lead firm	Low	High	Low	High	Domestic expansion and/or FDI-driven internationalization
Strategic partner	Low	High	Low	High	Mergers and acquisitions of existing capacities
Independent supplier	Low	High	Moderate	High	Specialization and in-house capacity building and integration
Non-firm actors (e.g. labour and state institutions)	Enhancement of value capture	Facilitation of value creation	Regulation of value destruction	Reduction	Supportive

outcomes in the next chapter. But, before we unpack the strategic responses of these different firm actors, let us work through the analytical logic of this causality. In general, firms with efficient internal cost control and high proprietary capabilities are likely to engage in intra-firm coordination to capitalize on their *low* cost–capability ratios. Outsourcing to third-party suppliers is unnecessary because it may not significantly lower the cost of producing goods or services, but instead may increase the firm's risk of capability reduction owing to the potential leakage of highly proprietary knowledge and codifiable technology to these independent suppliers. Through adopting intra-firm coordination, these firms are also more driven by a *high* market imperative, since product cycles stay dynamic, the industry remains unsaturated, and new market segments continue to emerge. Internalization provides the best organizational platform for creating, enhancing, and capturing value in these market conditions. As most of these firms are not subject to intense short-term financial discipline (*low* financial pressure), they are not compelled to externalize their value activity to third-party suppliers or to generate large ongoing financial returns for their shareholders. In an environment of *high* risks, intra-firm coordination is effective in helping firms navigate risky technological and/or market environments. It allows the firm to internalize critical technological or marketing resources in the face of such environments. Under these causal conditions of varying competitive dynamics and risks, the strategy of intra-firm coordination is likely to produce highly integrated global production networks in which corporate headquarters exercise tight control over their subsidiaries and affiliates. As indicated in Table 4.1 and illustrated below, it may be adopted by firms performing different roles in a global production network. The coupling, decoupling, and recoupling dynamics of these networks in different regions and places will have profound implications for their developmental trajectories.[8]

For a *lead firm* exercising control of its market or product definition, intra-firm coordination entails an investment-led configuration of its global production network. To internalize new markets and to expand into adjacent products (for example, from semiconductors to automobile electronics) or services (for example, from retail to financial products), a lead firm can invest in existing or new affiliates and integrate them into new market or product initiatives. When these markets are located outside its home country, the lead firm can engage in foreign direct investment (FDI) and establish greenfield operations to serve these markets. Its capacity for investment is also facilitated by the longer-term horizon of its financial backing. While it may source some of its production inputs and services from third-party suppliers, this external sourcing is likely to be limited to highly specialized materials (for example, components) or services (for example, information technology (IT) systems or legal services). As such, its global production network is constituted mostly by its domestic and foreign affiliates and by some specialized suppliers. This network resembles the lead firm-centric model illustrated in Figure 2.2(b). Through horizontal specialization, affiliates of this lead firm can supply to multiple production or service platforms that in turn allow for stronger market control and product definition. Lead firms in extractive industries such as mining and oil and gas, for example, tend to adopt this strategy in configuring their global production networks.[9]

Under similar competitive dynamic and risk conditions described in Table 4.1, other economic actors, such as strategic partners and independent suppliers to lead firms, may also adopt this strategy of intra-firm coordination. As a *strategic partner* to a lead firm, a manufacturing firm can take advantage of its relatively low cost–capability ratio and low financial pressure to expand its production capacity through mergers and acquisitions. Some of these merged or acquired capacities may belong to its lead firm customers or their competitors. This strategy of intra-firm coordination requires the strategic partner to possess strong firm-specific resources and capabilities in order to integrate these previously excess or inefficient capacities into its own facilities. Internalizing a customer's production capacities and consolidating them into a more efficient operation can therefore enable the strategic partner to achieve greater economies of scale in production capacity and economies of scope through offering full package services to diverse customers. Adding to the existing literature, we believe this strategic approach tends to be pursued by partner firms engaging with multiple production networks within the same industry, leading to the sophisticated intra-industry intersections in global production networks described in Figure 2.3 B1. Our approach accounts for *both* intra- and inter-firm relationships in these intersections of global production networks. A good example is the dominance of some very large electronics manufacturing service providers and semiconductor foundries in today's global electronics industry (see examples of Hon Hai and TSMC later in this chapter under the heading of inter-firm partnerships).

As an *independent supplier* to different lead firms and their strategic partners, a firm can also implement this strategy of intra-firm coordination. If efficiency in production and economies of scale underscore a strategic partner's low cost–capability ratio, the possession of superior knowhow or technology tends to buttress a specialized supplier's competitive advantage and market positioning in global production networks. Because of the high risks associated with technological or knowledge leakage and the erosion of firm-specific reputational capital, externalization of this core expertise is generally not an option if the independent supplier aims to expand into new markets and to consolidate its current market share. Instead, it can adopt the strategy of intra-firm coordination to meet this market imperative. This strategy entails continual or greater specialization on the part of the supplier through in-house R&D and marketing initiatives. It can also expand its production or service capacity through intra-firm investment in order to cater to new market opportunities. All these expansion and investment efforts require significant intra-firm integration of resources and capabilities. Overall, successful intra-firm coordination allows these independent suppliers (for example, ABB, Intel, or Microsoft) to serve multiple customers in the same industry (Figure 2.3 B2) or in different industries (Figure 2.3 C2). As noted by Sturgeon (2013: 20), while global sourcing is often channelled through affiliates of lead firms, the rise of specialized global suppliers means that intra-firm coordination through FDI has become commonplace at every nexus of global production networks, and international sourcing from these suppliers may well connect one lead firm to another.

Finally, non-economic actors are not auxiliary in our conceptualization— they can play a significant role in the enhancement, facilitation, and regulation of the intra-firm coordination strategies pursued by lead firms, strategic partners, and independent suppliers. Through productivity-enhancing policies and practices, for example, labour and state institutions can increase value capture by workers in these global production networks wherein the cost–capability ratios of these firms are relatively low. The potential and scope for skill upgrading and wage increases among workers in these firms is also high in relation to their significant role in value creation, enhancement, and capture. Moreover, to facilitate value creation in the market imperative of these firms, extra-firm actors can provide stronger regimes of trade and investment promotion and intellectual property rights that enable intra-firm coordination and protect value in firms' innovation activities. To avoid value destruction owing to excessive financial market manipulation and to provide longer-term financial stability to industrial firms, extra-firm institutions can establish and enforce a more prudent regulatory regime. This requires careful monitoring of the discrete and complex relationships between financial-sector actors and industrial firms. While high risks tend to characterize the firm's impulse to adopt this strategy, extra-firm actors can potentially galvanize different firms and institutions to develop a collective order among these industry players and to socialize such risks through industrial consortiums and joint business initiatives. Such consortiums and initiatives, for example, are particularly prevalent in high-tech and knowledge-intensive industries such as biotechnology, pharmaceuticals, semiconductors, banking, and tele-communications. Taken together, extra-firm actors can play a significant and supportive role in the pursuit of intra-firm coordination by economic actors who seek to reconfigure their global production networks within and across different industrial intersections.

Before we move on to the next strategy, it is useful to illustrate briefly how intra-firm coordination works in a particular empirical context. Here, we have chosen the global retail industry.[10] Leading transnational retailers such as Wal-Mart (USA), Carrefour (France), Metro (Germany), and Tesco (UK) all pursue intra-firm coordination with respect to their global store operations, which often number several thousands of stores across tens of countries. This strategy allows for greater value creation and capture. In their global retail operations, these giants tend to internalize most, if not all, of their own outlets, in order to achieve economies of scale in dealing with suppliers, brand and quality consistency, and efficiency in logistical support. This pattern of intra-firm coordination applies also to their increasing presence in new and emerging markets outside their home countries. They have also sought to enhance value capture by expanding their private label business, both at home and abroad, at the expense of branded good suppliers. As estimated by Appelbaum (2008: 71), private label products account for as much as one-third of all retail apparel sales in the United States, rising to 80 per cent for Wal-Mart and its domestic competitor, Target. These retail giants are also increasingly engaged in horizontal specialization by offering financial services such as credit cards and insurance policies.

These transnational retailers require significant inputs from intermediaries in order to pursue this intra-firm coordination strategy. As illustrated in detail in Gibbon and Ponte's *Trading Down* (2005), many of these retailers have relied on network intermediaries to handle their logistics, inventory management, and even placement on shelves—taking ownership of products only when they are in their depots. Even in their private label business, large retailers tend to internalize only branding, not production and delivery. These retailers put pressure on agro-food processors to reorganize their operations and to acquire additional roles (for example, inventory management), in response to increased demands on lead time, quality and safety standards, sustainability, volume, product portfolios, and so on.[11]

Meanwhile, these transnational retailers work closely with a large number of brand name suppliers that are lead firms in their respective industries such as healthcare products (for example, Johnson & Johnson and Unilever), food (for example, Kraft Foods and Nestlé), and beverages (for example, Coca-Cola and Diageo). To safeguard the quality and standards of their products, these brand name producers themselves tend to engage in intra-firm coordination of their global production networks, establishing production facilities near to major markets. This strategy also allows them to be responsive to market demand and consumption patterns. When their distribution channels articulate into the expanding networks of global retailers, these lead firm consumer goods producers perform a crucial role as independent suppliers. Through technological platforms (for example, real-time sales data interchange) and joint marketing activity (for example, cross-firm promotion), their highly internalized production networks are integrated with those coordinated by global retailers. In these inter-industry intersections (see Figure 2.3 C2), power relations are often balanced between brand name suppliers and global retailers.[12] Both groups also share the various risks inherent in their intertwined global production networks. A major product recall because of safety or quality defects, for example, will harm the brand name supplier as much as the global retailer. Intra-firm coordination becomes the most effective strategy for them to mitigate these 'GPN risks'.

While we can generalize to a degree about the strategies of leading global retailers, such an account would conceal significant variations in their implementation of intra-firm coordination and organizational relationships with non-brand name or generic suppliers in different markets. Here we can usefully compare Wal-Mart and Tesco. Building on its success and dominance in the home market—the USA—Wal-Mart is known for rolling out its *sui generis* business model at all costs.[13] In this model, Wal-Mart insists on buying from generic suppliers offering the lowest price and establishing retail outlets wherever possible in non-unionized locations. By pushing input and wage costs to the lowest level possible, Wal-Mart captures value through massive throughput and economies of scale in its retail sales. Abernathy et al. (1999: 3) observe that, through its lean retailing, Wal-Mart has brought generic suppliers under more direct control and required them to 'implement information technologies for exchanging sales data, adopt standards for product labelling, and use modern methods of material handling that assured customers a variety of products at low prices'. Tesco, on the other hand, comes from a much smaller home country, the United Kingdom. It does not have Wal-Mart's large home market to cross-subsidize its global operations. Tesco thus adopts a much more flexible and communicative strategy towards its intra-firm coordination. Unlike Wal-Mart, it does not insist on replicating its home-base model in its foreign subsidiaries and joint ventures. In South Korea, for example, Tesco works with its strategic partner, Samsung, to penetrate into an otherwise difficult retail market characterized by highly competitive conditions, distinctive and demanding consumer preferences, and a strong local supply base. Overall, these two contrasting examples help us understand why and how intra-firm coordination is often adopted as a key strategy to organize global production networks in the retail industry.[14]

INTER-FIRM CONTROL

Compared to the strategy of intra-firm coordination, where a firm—lead firm, strategic partner, or specialized supplier—attempts to internalize and consolidate a high level of value activity within its highly integrated global production network, inter-firm control represents a highly managed *externalization* strategy through which a lead firm outsources a very significant portion of its value activity to independent suppliers and contractors, and exercises strong control over their production processes and product/service quality.[15] This outsourcing can apply to key components or services, complete modules or service packages, and systems and subsystems. The high levels of explicit control of its suppliers and contractors are deemed necessary by a lead firm in order to gain collective competitiveness across its entire global production network. The GVC literature terms this a captive form of chain governance (Gereffi et al. 2005), but it tends to generalize at the level of the entire industry (for example, automobiles or apparel). While equity investment in external suppliers is generally not necessary for such organizational control to be effective, a lead firm may sometimes choose to invest in suppliers to shore up their financial strength and/or to secure long-term supply of key materials or services.

To account for the strategic choice of externalization through tight inter-organizational control, it is useful to revisit the peculiar configuration of competitive dynamics and risk environments impinging on a lead firm. This causal explanation is essential in GPN 2.0 because, as argued by Mahutga (2012: 6), 'a complete theory of global value chain governance should therefore explain how lead firms determine which activities to exclude from within their formal boundaries, and where to locate externalized activities globally'. For Mahutga, the concept of 'the height of entry barriers'—such as labour skills, capital requirements, and industrial experience—can help us understand why a lead firm keeps value activities with the greatest perceived competitive advantage in-house and externalizes those with the greatest perceived comparative advantage to other firms. As shown in Table 4.2, however, the strategy of inter-firm control is influenced by competitive dynamics well beyond these entry barriers, which tend to relate primarily to cost–capability ratios. Instead,

Table 4.2. The strategy of inter-firm control in organizing global production networks

Actors	Competitive dynamics			Risks	Global production network structures
	Cost-capability ratio	Market imperative	Financial discipline		
Lead firm	High	Low	High	Moderate	Outsourcing to and developing domestic and international suppliers
Independent supplier	Low	High	Low	Moderate	Dependent integration into production systems
Non-firm actors (e.g. labour and state institutions)	Training and industrial upgrading initiatives	Developing new markets	Provision of grants and investment incentives	Reduction through collective bargaining	Cautiously supportive

we take into account the market imperative, financial discipline, and risk mitigation in explaining a firm's strategic choice of how to organize its global production network.

Before we explain how the strategy of inter-firm control operates in relation to different actors, it is important for us to understand the analytical logic of how this strategy relates to different competitive dynamics and risk environments in Table 4.2. In general, *high* cost–capability ratios tend to prompt firms to engage external suppliers in order to regain their cost advantage in different industries. In some cases, this process of externalization entails strategic business exits from lower-value activities so that a firm can focus on building and sustaining its higher-order and more costly dynamic capabilities.[16] As explained in the previous section, firms experiencing low cost–capability ratios are much more likely to internalize their production of goods or services through intra-firm coordination, which in turn allows them to maximize their value capture. Externalizing value activity to third-party suppliers, however, may reduce the amount of value captured by a lead firm. In some instances, these suppliers may even develop sufficient in-house capabilities (for example, branding and marketing) over time to compete against its customer—that is, the lead firm. As such, external sourcing makes sense only when a lead firm suffers from higher costs in relation to its existing capabilities, and its suppliers enjoy substantial cost advantages through, for instance, access to cheaper production inputs (for example, labour, land, and material costs) and less stringent regulatory regimes (for example, labour standards and environmental constraints).

On the other hand, externalization may be feasible if the market for a product or service is generally mature and saturated (that is, a *low* market imperative). The lack of significantly new market opportunities hinders a lead firm's desire to compete solely on the basis of its higher cost–capability ratio and to engage in intra-firm coordination with more capital investment. The existence of other major competitors in the same markets also tends to push a lead firm to adopt externalization as a means to protect its market share through cost competitiveness. In addition, greater reliance on capital markets can lead to *high* financial discipline, which induces firms to focus on their core competencies. This discipline imposes serious pressures on firms to extract greater financial returns from their current assets or investments in order to satisfy their shareholders. Finally, the risk environment matters for externalization through inter-firm control. Risks associated with technological change and market shifts cannot be too high for outsourcing to take place because suppliers and contractors are less likely or willing to take on these risks. Without the availability of these external actors, a lead firm's outsourcing strategy will not work. At the same time, a certain level of risk may actually promote outsourcing, as a lead firm can use greater organizational flexibility to mitigate these risks.

Given the above generic explanation of how outsourcing works in tandem with competitive dynamics and risk mitigation, we can now explore how different actors in a global production network articulate with the strategy of inter-firm control in Table 4.2. To begin, the power relation in a global production network characterized by a high degree of externalization is likely to be highly asymmetrical in favour of the *lead firm* at its apex. For it to exercise greater inter-firm control, a lead firm such as an original equipment manufacturer (OEM) or a brand name firm normally retains key assets, technologies, and proprietary knowhow, in areas such as branding and marketing, R&D, and distribution. Suffering from a high cost–capability ratio or strict financial discipline, however, a lead firm may outsource part of or the entire production of goods or services to independent suppliers. By controlling crucial market knowledge (for example, demand forecasts and customer information), engineering or management processes (for example, just-in-time systems), core designs and technologies (for example, patents and copyrights), and proprietary standards (for example, production platforms), a lead firm can then exercise effective control over its suppliers, even if it does not own any equity stake in them. The sheer quantity of orders from a lead firm may constitute a sufficiently large chunk of the suppliers' production capacity or business volume and underscore these asymmetrical power relations. In such a lead firm-centric model of global production networks, independent suppliers are often subservient to the needs and requirements of the lead firm.[17] Despite its explicit desire to control and lock-in suppliers, a lead firm may also be keen to develop supplier capability because of the potential for improving collective efficiency at the level of the global production network.

A global production network dominated by a lead firm's strong strategic desire to exercise inter-firm control, however, is unlikely to create favourable conditions for any *strategic partner* to emerge. In general, tight control and cooperative partnership do not go hand in hand in a lead firm's strategic predisposition. The tighter a lead firm controls its suppliers and contractors, the less likely it is that any of them will be involved in joint product, process, or market development with the lead firm—a transactional relationship characterizing the strategy of inter-firm partnership that we will consider in the next section. Without this potential for joint collaboration and co-development, suppliers and contractors are also unlikely to invest in customer-specific assets and capabilities over and above those necessary to secure orders from the lead firm. As indicated in Table 4.2, *independent suppliers* are compelled by a high market imperative to take on these outsourcing demands from the lead firm. Lacking brand presence, complete products or services, and independent distribution channels, these suppliers can survive only through insertion into global production networks tightly controlled by OEM or brand name lead firms. In this organizational context, a high level of inter-firm control by a lead firm results in the dependent integration of suppliers into its global production network. But, without the involvement of strategic partners, this network is unlikely to achieve the synergistic effects of externalization, described by Sturgeon (2013: 5) as 'external international sourcing arrangements [that] imbue inter-enterprise trade with characteristics similar to intra-group trade: better control from the center, higher levels of bi-lateral information flow, tolerance of asset specificity, and a harmonization and immediate integration of business processes that increase the potential for foreign activities to substitute for activities performed at home'. In fact, dependent suppliers are more likely to be controlled and kept at a distance by a lead firm so that the latter can capture more value from the reduced claims on rents from lower-tier contractors and the lower accountability for standards through externalization to independent suppliers. As low-cost suppliers to global lead firms, these economic actors are mostly market followers in tightly controlled global production networks. Only a limited number of such independent suppliers can break out of this dependent relationship through limiting their exposure to individual lead firms and acquiring stronger backing from extra-firm actors.

As such, the role of *extra-firm actors* in shaping this strategy of inter-firm control can be significant and causal in nature. As optimizing cost–capability ratios is a critical dynamic underscoring lead firms' adoption of this strategy of inter-firm control, state institutions and labour organizations are normally actively involved. This involvement can vary significantly across different national regimes and policy contexts.[18] In the home economy of a lead firm, these extra-firm actors tend to be resistant to the partial or wholesale offshoring of production to its own affiliates or external suppliers located in developing countries because of the serious negative impacts on employment prospects, industrial linkages, and regional growth trajectories. To mitigate some of these impacts, state and labour institutions may provide stronger support for worker training, skills upgrading, and industrial development in order to retain *in situ* higher-value production activity (functional upgrading) or to shift employment towards a more productive sector (inter-sectoral upgrading). In developing countries, similar extra-firm actors are keen to attract these outsourced jobs to kick-start or to boost further their local or national development. Even though they may be aware of the possibilities of regional lock-in from this dependent mode of industrial development (see more in Chapter 5), extra-firm actors may still implement various policies and initiatives to increase labour availability (for example, inter-regional migration), to connect local suppliers to global lead firms (for example, trade shows and market information activities), or to reduce financial constraints on these low-cost suppliers (for example, government grants and incentives). While broadly supportive, this relationship between extra-firm actors and global lead firms and their suppliers is often tenuous and can be subject to serious 'GPN risks' such as labour unrest and violations of safety and environmental standards. As such, the consistent implementation of inter-firm control by a lead firm can be realized and viewed only in relation to the initiatives and policies of these non-economic actors.[19]

This analysis of the causal role of market imperatives, financial discipline, and risk in engendering inter-firm control strategies allows us to provide a more nuanced analysis of the role of different actors (lead firms, strategic partners, suppliers, and so on) and their power relations in evolving global production networks. Our approach not only deepens the existing GVC analysis of the captive *form* of governance. More importantly, it goes beyond the identification of this governance form and provides a crucial explanation of *why* these actors are causally shaped by dynamic imperatives that cannot be elucidated by focusing on industry-specific transactional and technological conditions. More specifically, we can examine this difference in conceptual efficacy through revisiting the global automobile industry. The strategy of inter-firm control is frequently deployed in this industry by global lead firms, defined as brand name assemblers, to ensure cost competitiveness, rapid time-to-market, and quality consistency.[20] Lead firms in this industry not only outsource significant levels of component, module, and subsystem manufacturing to independent auto suppliers, but also increasingly pressurize them to establish production and supply facilities near to lead firms' final assembly plants in different locations. These first-tier suppliers, in turn, compel second- or third-tier suppliers to follow suit or to make the appropriate locational adjustments. Defined spatially as a nested structure in Sturgeon et al. (2008), this cascading hierarchy of organizational control radiating from the lead firm assembler to different tiers of suppliers represents one of the most vivid forms of this strategy for organizing global production networks.

In particular, the desire of an automobile lead firm for inter-firm control can be understood in relation to the various dynamics explained in Table 4.2. First, intense cost pressures owing to an excessive number of global assemblers have pushed lead firms to exercise stronger control over their different tiers of suppliers in order to achieve collective efficiency and cost competitiveness at the network level. This inter-firm control is necessary to implement highly coordinated production systems, such as just-in-time inventory management, in order for the lead firm to leverage on common production platforms in one location for different products and markets. The non-existence of common industrial standards across different lead firms, a consequence of the sophisticated technical challenges of automobile design and engineering and the complex balance between system integration and product performance, also requires different lead firms to exercise stronger control over their production platforms and demand extensive customization of parts and components from their suppliers. When first-tier suppliers are under similar cost pressures, they too transmit the pressures of optimizing cost–capability ratios to their lower-tier suppliers that are generally located in developing countries. General Motors, for example, is well known for its search for the lowest price suppliers for its components and modules and for controlling these suppliers through large orders. Suppliers unable to produce for GM in different regions are also less likely to be considered. In the 1990s, another American assembler, Chrysler, developed its SCORE programme into a formalized mechanism for its suppliers to suggest ideas on product or process modifications and to meet a cost-reduction suggestion target of 5 per cent per year. While the suggested ideas had to be implementable, the assembler reserved the right not to adopt them (Whitford 2005: 77).

Second, the peculiar market structure of the automobile industry tends to facilitate inter-firm control in the global production networks coordinated by different lead firms. Virtually all of today's lead firms in this industry have grown out of their initial market position as lead firm assemblers at birth. While the largest suppliers may gain technological competence and greater locational presence over time, none of them can eventually evolve into a full-scale lead firm assembler. In short, there is limited upward mobility or potential for functional upgrading within the industry. Unlike other global industries such as apparel and electronics, this lack of functional upgrading from a supplier to a lead firm tends to exacerbate inter-firm control and allow lead firms free rein to control tightly their suppliers through interlocking global production networks. This strategic outcome owes less to the inter-firm transactional conditions specified in the existing literature and more to oligopolistic market competition. In an industry characterized by fairly mature technologies and an oversupply of products, lead firms place a higher strategic priority on intense price-based competition and become less compelled by the market-making imperative (except perhaps the top premium brands). These market dynamics mean that most lead firm assemblers can potentially capture more value from optimizing cost–capability ratios through tighter inter-firm control than from developing new technologies, products, and markets.

Third, financial discipline tends to work against brand name assemblers because of the high cost of developing new models, the large capital investment outlay on production platforms, and the global glut in the automobile market. Automobiles are often seen by the global financial market as an 'old' economy product to be bypassed by the 'new' economy of the digital revolution and knowledge-intensive services. The weakening financial position of most brand name assemblers has forced them to externalize more production and functions to different tiers of suppliers, exposing these suppliers to the same ruthless discipline of the global financial market. This pressure has particularly been the case since the 2008 global financial crisis. As argued in Van Biesebroeck and Sturgeon (2010: 229): 'Starved of funds for vehicle development, Western lead firms have relied on more global suppliers to tailor vehicles to local tastes. The need for cost savings has intensified the quest to utilize lower cost second- and third-tier suppliers in China as well'. The strategic predisposition of most lead firms towards exercising stronger inter-firm control is therefore closely tied to short-term shareholder demands in major capital markets. This strategic positioning is further encouraged by the modest risk environment. Unlike in some high-tech industries such as bio-medical sciences, nanotechnology, or digital media, automobile technologies generally do not experience radical and transformative innovations; the industry also lacks the major product innovations that lead to breakout products. For example, although electric cars have gained some traction after over a decade of R&D and market launches, they are still some way from being a full replacement for cars with petrol-based internal combustion engines. The regulatory and exchange rate risks, however, can be quite substantial for the automakers. Monetary union in the European Union since the late 1990s, for example, has provided enormous exchange-rate stability for lead firm assemblers from France, Germany, and Italy. Their competitors in the UK, however, experience much greater exchange rate risks associated with British sterling.

This brief case of inter-firm control in the automobile industry, nevertheless, is further complicated by substantial variations in the national origins and corporate cultures of different lead firm assemblers.[21] Lead firms from the USA, for example, are much more dependent on market-based price mechanisms for controlling their different tiers of suppliers. Japanese automobile firms, on the other hand, are more likely to co-invest in their suppliers and develop closer interlocking relationships in these production networks that approximate the inter-firm partnerships to be explained in the next section. With intermediaries keeping network actors together, the presence of dense business networks (for example, *keiretsu* or groups) and industry associations in Japan also reinforces the promulgation of common standards and dispute resolution between lead firm assemblers and their tiers of suppliers. In terms of global production network configurations, lead firms from different national origins may develop production platforms in the same geographical location but with drastically different market orientation. This market difference can seriously alter their relationships with local suppliers. In South Africa, for example, German assemblers have made a strategic choice to use their assembly production facilities to serve their customers worldwide, enabling local suppliers in their production networks to gain ready access to the global market. American, Japanese, and French assemblers, however, tend to develop production facilities in South Africa only for the macro-regional market in Africa, denying the access of local suppliers to the wider global market. In other emerging economies, some lead firms sell final products only in very large markets such as Brazil, China, or India. In China, American and European assemblers are more likely to engage in localization through local design, engineering, and regional headquarters facilities.[22] Partly because of their relationship-based corporate cultures, Japanese and South Korean automakers are much more cautious in taking this localization approach for fear of losing control over their local suppliers and thus risking poor product quality and brand damage. In short, the strategy of inter-firm control can help lead firms cope with intense competitive pressures, but its operationalization can vary substantially in relation to firm-specific and country-of-origin attributes.

INTER-FIRM PARTNERSHIP

In a complex world economy interwoven by global production networks, not all inter-firm relationships are characterized by lead firms tightly controlling their suppliers and contractors. As alluded to earlier in the example of Japanese and South Korean automobile assemblers, cooperative relationships can also be formed between lead firms and their strategic partners and specialized suppliers. In this section, we describe this cooperative strategy as one of *inter-firm partnership*, defined as the collaboration, co-evolution, and joint development of a lead firm and its strategic partner(s) or key suppliers in the *same* global production network in order to compete against other lead firms and their network partners.[23] This partnership strategy is generally underpinned by two necessary conditions. First, there must be complementarities between a lead firm and its partners in terms of assets, technologies, knowledge, or market expertise. These capabilities are unique to each firm in the network and can be developed and accumulated through firm-specific initiatives (for example, learning-by-doing or acquisitions) and/or external interventions (for example, technology transfer). Because of a certain degree of mutual dependency, these complementarities can produce the positive network synergy that allows all firms in the same network to increase their competitiveness.

Second, the existence of open and transparent industrial standards and codification schemes, supported by technical innovations and institutional backing, is critical because overly tacit or proprietary standards will tend to reduce trust and confidence between collaborating firms. Intermediated through other firms (for example, service specialists) and extra-firm actors (for example, professional associations), these standards and schemes reduce inter-firm behavioural uncertainty and allow firms to make credible commitments to each other through extensive information-sharing and relationship-building. While the pursuit of inter-firm partnership does not necessarily entail equity investment, it does require substantial resource commitment from the lead firm and its network partners. The flow of knowledge and information among these actors in the same global production network can be enhanced by these common standards, without which the synergistic potential of their complementarities cannot be fully realized.[24]

In the presence of complementarities and common standards, what then prompts firms to enter into inter-firm partnership to compete as a global production network? This necessarily brings us back to the generic logics of the competitive dynamics and risk environments summarized in Table 4.3. While differential cost–capability ratios can partially account for the externalization of production of goods or services from a lead firm (high ratio) to its strategic partner (low ratio) and independent suppliers (low ratios), it is the *simultaneous presence* of all three remaining competitive pressures—high market imperative, high levels of financial discipline, and high risk environment—that turns this externalization strategy from the strong inter-firm control discussed above into cooperative partnership. In the first place, the market imperative is clearly very significant for all firms in a cooperative global production network. The prospect of an expanding and unsaturated market assures a lead firm and its partners and suppliers that they can collectively benefit from their cooperative value creation and enhancement process. Even though the value capture is unlikely to be evenly distributed among these network actors, partnership provides a more mutually beneficial competitive strategy in the expanding global marketplace.

Moreover, the financial environment can be punishing for the lead firm, so much so that it is unable or unwilling to risk its working capital to pursue the intra-firm coordination strategy described in Table 4.1. In manufacturing industries, high financial discipline compels the lead firm to externalize

Table 4.3. The strategy of inter-firm partnership in organizing global production networks

Actors	Competitive dynamics			Risks	Global production network structures
	Cost–capability ratio	Market imperative	Financial discipline		
Lead firm	High	High	High	High	Outsourcing all production to partners
Strategic partner	Low	High	Low	High	Joint product development with lead firm customers
Specialized supplier	High	High	High	High	Platform leaders
Independent supplier	Low	High	Low	Moderate	Dependent integration into production systems
Non-firm actors (e.g. state and labour institutions, standards and research institutes)	Industry collaboration and consortiums, and increasing collective efficiency	Deregulate related industries and markets	Strategic financing	Managing through technical and market solutions	Strongly supportive

more, if not all, of its manufacturing activity to strategic partners because much of this activity tends to involve high sunk costs and long investment horizons. In service industries, a lead firm under severe financial discipline can extract greater returns to its investment by offloading lower value and more standardized service activities to its strategic partners. This complete outsourcing is feasible if these partners, often located outside the lead firm's country of origin, are less subject to high financial discipline and therefore are able to secure the necessary capital to invest in production facilities and firm-specific capabilities (for example, product or service design and process technology). By a similar token, specialized suppliers are also subject to the same sort of financial discipline as the lead firm. In some high-tech industries (for example, ICT), these specialized suppliers of key modules (for example, processors) or solutions (for example, software) focus only on developing specific technological platforms as the product interface for inter-firm partnership, leaving much of the market definition and final production to the lead firm and its strategic partners, respectively. Further to these competitive dynamics, the risk environment in which all cooperative partners operate tends to be high. These risks range from market volatility to rapid technological shifts and potential supply chain disruptions. To reduce their exposure to these risks and to capitalize quickly on rapid market changes, the lead firm and its partners enter into cooperative arrangements underpinned by finely organized divisions of labour and mutual dependency in market success.

To understand fully the peculiar configurations of a cooperative global production network, we analyze how each of these firm actors adopts the strategy of inter-firm partnership (see Table 4.3). Because of the cooperative nature of their inter-firm divisions of labour, the power relations among these actors are not as hierarchical as in the case of a lead firm pursuing an inter-firm control strategy. As argued by Whitford (2005: 17; emphasis in original), 'needing to improve interfirm cooperation and information transfer, OEMs [lead firms] give more business to fewer suppliers, and forge closer relationships with a core strategic group that they hope to align with their own goals. Importantly, these key suppliers are *not* envisioned as mere satellites orbiting a dominant but benevolent patron, dependent and beholden'. While a *lead firm* in an inter-firm partnership retains its effective control over market and production definition (for example, through marketing and R&D capabilities), it cannot fulfil market demand without the cost-effective production support from its strategic partners and the provision of platform-leading components or modules by its specialized suppliers. Specializing in the highest value added activities, a lead firm invests continuously in the design and marketing of products or services. Because of the tacit nature of firm-specific knowhow related to design and marketing, some of these investments (for example, new in-house R&D facilities or design centres) are internalized and therefore take place through the intra-firm coordination strategy described earlier.

Depending on the capabilities of its strategic partners, a lead firm may also outsource some of these business services/solutions and design and R&D activities, particularly those process technologies that can be optimized at the production stage undertaken by the partners. As shown in Figure 2.2(a), a *strategic partner* can take on significant value added functions in a global production network. There are two mechanisms for inter-firm partnership. In both instances, a strategic partner is likely to capture more value from its partnership with the lead firm, and its firm-specific capabilities are likely to co-evolve within a deepening collaborative relationship. On the one hand, a strategic partner can add value to the lead firm's original design and product specifications by offering process knowhow and production expertise (in terms of improvements in yield and quality). This joint product development often underpins the highly strategic and co-evolutionary nature of their partnership because it requires dedicated assets and resources from the partner beyond just production facilities (for example, engineering manpower, patents for process technologies, and alignment of strategic planning). In manufacturing, a strategic partner needs to have facilities near to the lead firm's R&D centres to work out the production details of new product designs in collaboration with the lead firm's design teams. It also has to develop high-volume production facilities in low-cost locations or near to important or new markets. In advanced producer services, strategic service providers work closely on team-based projects with personnel from the headquarters of these global lead firms.

On the other hand, a strategic partner can provide full package services to a lead firm. These services range from complete product manufacturing to inventory management, logistical support, and distribution to end users. Sturgeon et al. (2011: 235) call these firms 'global suppliers', who take over many of the most complex and difficult tasks in global production, including FDI, global purchasing and inventory control, capacity planning, fixed asset management, and logistics: 'Global suppliers now have capabilities—accumulated through internal development and acquisition—to provide "one-stop stopping" for lead firms seeking regional and global supply solutions. This new class of suppliers has internalized many of the most difficult and costly aspects of cross-border integration such as logistics, inventory management, and the day-to-day management of factories, call-centers, and engineering centers'. During market downturns (for example, the 2008 global financial crisis), this full-scale capability tends to allow globally operating first-tier suppliers to retain their role as strategic partners, who are then poised for further expansion during market upswings. Global lead firms are more likely to maintain suppliers with whom they have already invested in technology, capital, or cooperation, and these tend to be the larger and more capable strategic partners. As observed by Cattaneo et al. (2010a: 17), 'the elimination and shutdown of marginal suppliers during the crisis could exacerbate asymmetric buying patterns when demand recovers. Because large orders give them an advantage in credit markets, global suppliers will be in a better position to expand when the market rebounds, further reinforcing the consolidation of GVCs at the firm level'.

In terms of suppliers, some high-tech industries are characterized by the existence of highly specialized suppliers of intermediate goods or advanced producer services necessary for the production of major products (for example, computers, smartphones, and automobiles) or services (for example, transportation and consumer services). In these industries, a *specialized supplier* provides the core components or modules, such as microprocessors and operating systems in computers and smartphones, or transmissions and steering systems in automobiles, or intermediate services (for example, IT solutions, financial and accounting services, logistics, and so on). While they are technological leaders in these intermediate goods or services and capture fairly substantial value from their product/service specialization, these specialized suppliers (for example, Microsoft, SAP, Intel, Qualcomm, Brembo, Graziano, and ZF) are not necessarily lead firms in their own right because they do not necessarily define the final market or the finished product. Instead, they often work collaboratively with global lead firms and their strategic partners to develop cutting-edge intermediate goods or services that enhance the market appeal of these lead firms' final products. Unlike the strategic partners of a lead firm, a specialized supplier performs a much narrower range of roles, albeit high-value ones, in a global production network. In addition to its partnership with a lead firm, a specialized supplier tends also to pursue the strategy of intra-firm coordination to internalize and consolidate its technological development and core expertise. In some instances, a specialized supplier may enter into inter-firm partnership with its own strategic partner, which takes charge of manufacturing its intermediate goods. In the global semiconductor industry, for example, this cooperative relationship is quite common between fabless suppliers (for example, chip design by Qualcomm or Broadcom) and their foundry partners (for example, chip manufacturing by TSMC or GlobalFoundries).

Meanwhile, *independent suppliers* in these cooperative global production networks remain dependent on lead firms and their strategic partners. While their roles are not fundamentally different from those in the strategy of inter-firm control (see also Table 4.2), because of the highly intense competitive dynamics and risk environment in these markets, independent suppliers may benefit from their initial dependent relationships with less established lead firms and accumulate or develop further firm-specific capabilities over time to become strategic partners of these emerging lead firms. This process of functional upgrading is more likely to occur if *extra-firm actors* play a supportive role in these global production networks. Some of these actors, such as state institutions, business associations, and labour organizations, can promote industry collaboration through skill upgrading initiatives, building common technical platforms, and organizing technological consortiums. Other actors, such as universities and research institutes, may create greater knowledge spillovers between fundamental and applied research by collaborating with firms or by spinning off new technologies and innovations to form private initiatives. All these efforts bode well for developing firm capabilities and enhancing value capture in a highly competitive and risk-prone market environment. Extra-firm actors, particularly state institutions, can also undertake market deregulation in order to encourage greater inter-firm partnership in an expanding market. In a rather challenging financial market, these actors may participate in the strategic financing of, and joint equity investment in, collaborative initiatives led by lead firms and their strategic partners.

Empirically, some or most elements of these inter-firm partnerships can be found in two global industries—electronics and apparel.[25] In the first instance, the world of global electronics is characterized by an increasing separation between the design and manufacturing of electronics products owing to immense pressures from the three competitive dynamics. This firm-specific specialization in the electronics division of labour is rendered particularly effective by the strategy of inter-firm partnership. For example, the inter-firm partnership between Apple Inc. (a brand name lead firm without manufacturing facilities) and Taiwan's Hon Hai Precision (the world's largest provider of electronics manufacturing services) contains many of the elements described above. In its successive generations of iPhones, Apple has retained full control of its branding, product innovation, and marketing, and has left virtually the entire task of assembly to Foxconn, Hon Hai's subsidiary in China. As a strategic partner of Apple, Foxconn benefits from the immense scale of its manufacturing operations and supply chain flexibility few in the world can match. Apple's own executives have conceded that switching from Foxconn would be very time-consuming and costly.[26] Foxconn's competitive advantages embedded in its lower cost–capability ratios are predicated on its ability to combine discretion with a solid record of quality control and competitive pricing. Established in China's southern city Shenzhen in 1988, its 'Foxconn City' is well known for guarding the identities of Hon Hai's key customers (for example, Apple, Dell, Hewlett-Packard, Motorola, Nokia, Sony, and Toshiba) and strategic partners, at the same time as its optimal production operation and in-house manufacturing of many parts for its electronics products have significantly reduced its per unit costs.

Meanwhile, US-based Qualcomm is a major supplier of Apple iPhone's baseband chips, which are responsible for transmitting simultaneous voice and data transfer. As a highly specialized supplier of, and a platform leader in, wireless telecommunication processors, Qualcomm is a fabless firm designing chipsets for mobile communications equipment such as the iPhone. Lacking manufacturing capacity, it has entered into long-term partnership contracts with semiconductor foundries in Taiwan (TSMC) and Singapore (Global-Foundries) to produce its chipsets and other semiconductor devices. Since its inception in 1985, Qualcomm has eschewed the vertically integrated model of global production networks adopted by other platform leaders such as Intel and AMD (until 2009), and developed a horizontal production network leveraging on the core competencies of its foundry suppliers (for example, TSMC) and downstream customers (for example, Apple and other smartphone lead firms). Interestingly, specialized foundries such as TSMC also manufacture Apple-designed A-series system-on-a-chip (SoC) microprocessors for the iPhone. In short, TSMC has become a specialized manufacturing supplier to Apple and Qualcomm, both of which are also in a lead firm-specialized supplier relationship.

As a technology leader in its field (semiconductor foundry), TSMC does not serve as a strategic partner to either Qualcomm or Apple. It wants to retain control over its production flexibility and choice of customers in order to prevent being locked into a dependent relationship. In August 2012, Apple and Qualcomm made separate but failed attempts to invest more than US$1 billion each in TSMC in order to try and ensure that TSMC's fabrication facility was dedicated exclusively to producing their chipsets.[27] Apple wanted to diversify the supply of its core A-series chips used in iPhones and iPads away from South Korea's Samsung Electronics, its major chip supplier since the launch of the first iPhone in June 2007 and yet also a fierce competitor in the smartphone market. Qualcomm was already relying on TSMC to manufacture most of its chipsets. To maintain its organizational autonomy as a 'pure play' foundry, TSMC refused to dedicate its facilities to a single customer and preferred the organizational flexibility of switching customers and products. If TSMC acceded to the advances of Apple and Qualcomm, it would have had to drop long-term customers such as Nvidia, another leading fabless chipset firm. Its preference for fostering innovation among fabless firms, particularly new start-ups, also led to its rebuff of two industry giants— Apple and Qualcomm. This case study of the iconic iPhone brings together several intersecting global production networks comprising one of the world's leading brand name lead firms (Apple), its manufacturing partner and the world's largest provider of electronics manufacturing services (Hon Hai), and three specialized suppliers that are the world's leading semiconductor manufacturer and another lead firm competitor (Samsung), fabless semiconductor firm (Qualcomm), and semiconductor foundry (TSMC). In this rather complex intersection of multiple production networks, we witness the significance of inter-firm partnership in creating the unprecedented market success of a breakout consumer product—the iPhone.

However, corporate culture and national origin continue to matter even in this segment of the highly globalizing industry. As noted above, one of Apple's key competitors in smartphones is South Korea's Samsung Electronics. Unlike Apple and the general tendency for American lead firms to externalize component sourcing and manufacturing activity, Samsung has historically been a family-controlled business conglomerate (known as a *chaebol* in South Korea).[28] It has rigorously pursued an intra-firm coordination strategy to organize the global production network of its smartphones. By developing a home-based and export-oriented production system, it has benefited from several key competitive advantages, such as faster time-to-market and better control of production costs and technological knowhow. In particular, Samsung not only develops in-house a significant share of its smartphone technology (including applications processors and the SoC chips supplied to Apple's iPhones), but also internalizes most of the production activity through its world-leading semiconductor division (processing and memory chips) and Samsung SDI (battery and display panels).

In the global apparel industry, inter-firm partnership has profoundly transformed the buyer-driven relationship between large retailers in developed countries and apparel producers in developing economies observed in much of the literature. The rise of large contract manufacturers and intermediary traders as strategic partners of lead firm retailers has complicated the dichotomous view of retailers as lead firms and their suppliers as mere followers. First, large contract manufacturers have emerged in apparel production to capitalize on economies of scale and scope and to squeeze more value from lower-tier suppliers. Appelbaum (2008: 71) considers this phenomenon of what he calls 'giant transnational contractors . . . a largely unexpected development' (see also Appelbaum 2011). Pursuing the strategy of intra-firm coordination, these global suppliers have taken over important value activity from their lead firm customers, such as inventory management, sales forecasting, and pre- and post-production functions, including design, warehousing, and control over logistics. In so doing, these large suppliers have become strategic partners of brand name buyers who have to rely on their management and logistics expertise. In the case of Taiwan's Luen Thai Holdings and its supply chain city in China's Dongguan, for example, its technicians work closely in one single location with designers from one of its brand name buyers, Liz Claiborne, to cut production costs and market response times. In another example, Hong Kong's TAL performs inventory management for its American buyer, JCPenney, to increase production flexibility and to reduce time-to-market. Their inter-firm partnership is evident in JCPenney granting TAL access to its point-of-sale data through its proprietary software.

Second, the rise of intermediary traders as strategic partners of brand name lead firms in global apparel is quite phenomenal. Pooling different orders from brand name customers, some of these traders have even more buying power than a single brand name buyer. Milberg and Winkler (2013: 127), for example, found that Hong Kong's Li & Fung is not only an intermediary trader for major apparel brands (for example, Tommy Hilfiger) and retailers (for example, Wal-Mart and Target). It also has such power as a buyer, mainly because of the magnitude of its orders, that it is able to charge a 5 per cent fee to suppliers desperate to maintain Li & Fung contracts. Tommy Hilfiger's CEO Fred Gehring once quipped that 'Li & Fung has an incredible amount of buying power. When they go to a factory and place orders, they get better clout than if we went on our own'. To Liz Claiborne's CEO William McComb: 'They are the Wal-Mart of purchasing. There isn't even a close No. 2'.[29] In short, through their inter-firm cooperative relationships with key customers, large apparel producers and intermediaries have increasingly mediated the buying relationship between brand name lead firms (apparel brands and retailers) and their manufacturing suppliers. As we shall see in the next section, this emerging mediating role in conventional buyer-driven global value chains can also involve extra-firm actors through the strategy of extra-firm bargaining.

EXTRA-FIRM BARGAINING

The role of extra-firm actors in the above three firm-specific strategies for configuring global production networks has so far been conceived as generally supportive and cooperative in Tables 4.1 to 4.3. For the purpose of our conceptual development, this role is viewed mostly from the lens of firm actors—lead firms, strategic partners, and independent suppliers. In practice, this group of extra-firm actors is highly diverse and driven by a large number of possible rationalities that go beyond any simple classification. In this section, we attempt to introduce more autonomy and causal power to these extra-firm actors and explain how they interact with lead firms, strategic partners, specialized suppliers, and independent suppliers and contractors in such ways as to benefit their core constituencies. This strategy of extra-firm bargaining is critical because it provides the crucial analytical nexus for understanding how economic processes, embodied in firms, intersect with non-economic issues (for example, political reforms, social justice and security, environmental sustainability, and so on). In other words, it takes place in all of the above three firm-specific strategies. As such, we define the strategy as a contested two-way process of *negotiation* and *accommodation* between firms and extra-firm actors in order to reach, as far as is possible, a mutually satisfactory outcome in relation to the creation, enhancement, and capture of value through global production networks.

We argue that this concept of extra-firm bargaining enriches our analysis of global production networks because actor-specific interaction in these networks represents more than a set of inter-firm power relations *along* the value chain, as commonly conceived in the existing literature.[30] The existing GVC frameworks offer little explanatory power to these extra-firm actors in shaping inter-firm governance; they are often seen as outside the analytical parameters of industry-specific value chains. Our conception here also sheds crucial light on the institutional underpinnings of the strategic coupling of regional economies with global production networks identified in the GPN 1.0 framework.

Influenced by the competitive dynamics and risk environments described in the previous chapter, firm and extra-firm actors pursue bargaining strategies to achieve three interrelated objectives: (1) market power; (2) proprietary rights; and (3) social and political legitimacy.[31] The first objective stipulates that global lead firms shaped by a strong market imperative are likely to be more interested in gaining *market power* from extra-firm bargaining relations with state actors who, for the most part, remain the key regulator of uneven market access even in an interconnected world economy. This market power-oriented motive is often found in the intense negotiations and bargaining between lead firms and state authorities in different national markets. Securing this dimension of extra-firm relations can enable lead firms (see Tables 4.1 and 4.3) to achieve market definition and thereby dominate through inter-firm networks as well. State actors can also benefit from the economic and social outcomes through more productive articulations into different global production networks. These intense bargaining relationships between foreign lead firms and domestic state institutions for market access are particularly evident in industries subject to strong state regulation such as resource extraction, automobiles, petrochemicals, retail, telecommunications, and finance. Network outcomes in these industries are often mediated by (geo) political imperatives.[32]

Specifically, extra-firm bargaining relations are manifested in discretionary state regulations that may be applicable to some, but not other, firms. Nationality and ownership of these firms often become important considerations in these bargaining processes. For example, domestic lead firms—particularly state-owned and government-linked enterprises—in highly regulated and large markets tend to receive more favourable policy treatment from protectionist home states that seek to increase value capture in their domestic economies. These markets range from advanced economies such as Japan to emerging economies such as Brazil and China. Differential regulatory regimes in areas such as equity ownership, technology transfer, and local employment requirements provide a potential source of market empowerment for domestic lead firms and their strategic partners. To gain access to these regulated markets, foreign lead firms and suppliers endeavour to develop favourable extra-firm bargaining relationships with state authorities. In some instances, foreign firms are willing to reduce their pursuit of inter-firm control strategies in order to strengthen their case in extra-firm bargaining with host state institutions.[33] In other cases, foreign firms seek institutional support from their home states, which take on the task of inter-governmental negotiations.[34] When this inter-state bargaining on behalf of national firms breaks down or fails to reach a satisfactory conclusion, the issue may be referred to the relevant international organizations, particularly the World Trade Organization, for arbitration and mediation. Extra-firm bargaining can thus become a multi-scalar process incorporating actors at different scales of governance and authority.[35]

The second motive prompting firms to adopt an extra-firm bargaining strategy is related to the quest for *proprietary rights* in the context of technological and market innovation. This bargaining process is prominent in industrial segments characterized by high levels of financial discipline and high risk of technological or market shifts (see, for example, Table 4.3). In this competitive environment, domestic firms tend to seek strong regulatory regimes and codification of standards in order to protect their firm-specific R&D investments and intangible assets (for example, brand names, patents, and trademarks). These lead firms enter into robust negotiations with relevant domestic extra-firm actors such as state authorities, standards organizations, and industry associations. These extra-firm negotiations, however, may not yield positive outcomes if there are substantial differences in the economic priorities (for example, pressing unemployment issues), political ideologies (for example, a neoliberal approach to non-market intervention), and institutional capacities (for example, weak bureaucratic rationality) of these extra-firm actors. As argued earlier in the chapter, the absence of such extra-firm bargaining relations can accentuate the internalization of relations by lead firms. Without sufficient assurance of institutional support from extra-firm actors, domestic lead firms may also seek to reorganize their global production networks by internationalizing their core R&D activity to locations endowed with more favourable institutional support. As foreign lead firms in these locations, they have to negotiate with host institutions for preferential access to resources (for example, specialized training institutes and scientific laboratories) and fiscal incentives (for example, financial grants and tax benefits).

Extra-firm actors in these host locations, particularly territorially based organizations (for example, regional development agencies), are often keen to attract higher-value activities from foreign lead firms because they may induce local technological innovation, industrial upgrading, and, possibly, the development of stronger inter-firm partnership between foreign lead firms and local suppliers. Geographical proximity between the R&D activity of foreign lead firms and local firms can facilitate the possibility of joint product development and market innovation. Host state institutions may also socialize the high risk of technological and market shifts by co-funding such joint development with foreign lead firms and transferring technologies and blueprints to local firms when they can be commercialized. As local firms acquire or develop greater technological and market capabilities, they may bargain with home institutions for the same sort of preferential access to resources and fiscal incentives given to foreign lead firms. Over time, successful technological and market innovations are underpinned by strong extra-firm bargaining between lead firms and extra-firm actors in different geographical locations.[36]

While market power and proprietary rights are important strategic considerations for firms organizing their global production networks, the *non-economic goals* of firms and extra-firm actors can be a powerful imperative for pursuing extra-firm bargaining strategies. Even though all capitalist firms seek to create and capture value through their profit-oriented activity, not all of them view profit-making as their only *raison d'être*. In fact, a number of today's global lead firms have non-economic social and political goals embedded in their corporate mantra. One specific way for these firms to attain non-economic goals is to gain broad social and political legitimacy through developing continuous extra-firm relations with social or political actors. This strategy is particularly relevant to firms with multinational operations. Confronted with a much more diverse global economy constituted by different political–economic systems and sociocultural practices, many transnational corporations realize that their economic goals cannot be achieved unless they are legitimized as responsible actors in different markets and territories. They are also under immense market pressure because their firm-specific assets (for example, brand names and major products or services) are subject to higher risk potential of reputational damage and other unexpected possibilities of devaluation. In consumer-oriented industries, many of the world's most famous lead firms are increasingly dependent on their brand value in creating financial returns to their shareholders.[37] Subject to high levels of financial discipline, these lead firms are concerned with protecting their brand names and trademarks through developing and implementing extra-firm bargaining strategies.

In a context of competitive dynamics and risk pressures, many global lead firms voluntarily engage in a diverse range of non-economic value activity to seek social and political legitimacy for their global operations. Most, if not all, of these activities are mediated through extra-firm bargaining relations. Corporate social responsibility (CSR) programmes, for example, are one of the most visible ways through which these firms engage with extra-firm actors and social communities in different locations.[38] CSR programmes range from financial and technical assistance at the local and regional level to codes of conduct, corporate philanthropy, and environmental sponsorship at the global level. Indeed, many of these programmes are targeted at labour issues such as worker conditions and rights throughout the entire global production network.[39] Labour codes of conduct, for example, shape firm behaviour through their specificity of coverage and compliance through monitoring (often through intermediaries). Lead firms are thus compelled to reorganize their inter-firm relationships with their domestic and foreign suppliers in order to meet these codes and standards (for example, the Global Alliance for Workers and Communities and the UN Global Compact). By enrolling extra-firm actors such as international agencies, state institutions, and non-governmental organizations into their production networks, global lead firms can cooperate in exchange for reciprocal returns on their investments—for instance, through good corporate citizen awards or certification sanctioned by these institutions and organizations.

On the other hand, the pursuit of non-economic goals is clearly more pronounced in the bargaining strategy of extra-firm actors in their engagement with firms in global production networks. As noted in Table 2.4, these extra-firm actors can play fundamentally different roles in influencing value activity and firm behaviour. The state, for example, is responsible for the wellbeing and security of its electorates. Its political and social legitimacy are largely dependent on the extent to which the benefits of value creation, enhancement, and capture in global production networks can be accrued to its citizens. But not all states behave in the same manner when they engage with global production networks (see more in the next chapter). Some state authorities are much more aggressive in promoting value activity through the aforementioned means of bargaining with firms in global production networks for market power and proprietary rights. Driven by dire concerns such as massive unemployment or underdevelopment, other more vulnerable states may be placed in a much weaker bargaining position in relation to foreign and domestic firms seeking market opening or preferential treatment. These weak states regularly suffer from institutional capture when they have to sacrifice local and/or national interests in favour of firm-specific demands (for example, resistance to minimum wage efforts or labour standards). Moreover, a relatively small number of states may become predatory when its self-interested elites collude with domestic or foreign firms and engage in embezzlement. In short, the extra-firm bargaining relations between firms and state actors are significantly dependent on firm-specific interests and pressures as well as the institutional capacity and priorities of these state actors.

Other extra-firm actors such as labour and consumer groups and civil society organizations are also actively involved in bargaining relationships with firms and states. Representing their vastly different constituents, these groups and organizations may put collective pressure on firms by staging strikes, protests, and awareness programmes. Their bargaining power with firms in global production networks depends largely on their organizational capability and the effectiveness of their social activity. Sometimes, the bargaining goals and strategy of these organizations towards firms may be at odds with those of the state. For example, a firm-specific strike proposed by the local chapter of a labour union may not be welcomed by the state because it fears the imminent closure of all plants by this firm at other locations within the same country. To resolve this impasse, a tripartite bargaining process may occur that brings together labour, the firm, and the state. This multi-stakeholder negotiation may lead to partial fulfilment of the original goal (for example, wage increase) set by the union's local chapter, representing a more amenable solution at the national scale (for example, no plant closure) within the wider global production network. A multi-actor approach is therefore vital in helping us reconcile the diverse economic and non-economic outcomes of extra-firm bargaining relationships in global production networks.

In a highly interconnected global economy, locally or nationally based extra-firm actors are often on the losing end of these bargaining processes because firms are relatively mobile across national boundaries and can use their threat to exit, whether real or imaginary, during negotiations. Lead firms can generally reconfigure their global production networks to bypass national regulation by state institutions and social demands from different groups and organizations. This institutional asymmetry in bargaining relationships between lead firms in global production networks and territorially based extra-firm actors can nevertheless be rebalanced by the emergence of standards and conventions established by international organizations. These standards and conventions serve as extra-firm mechanisms—or intermediaries (see Chapter 2)—for governing firm behaviour in global production networks. In many industries, state institutions and international organizations seek to establish conventions, regulations, and standards as extra-firm actors in governing bargaining and negotiation relations in global production networks. As defined by Ponte et al. (2011b: 1), this extra-firm governance refers to 'the shaping of the conduct of others through network forms of organization involving a wide range of non-state actors but also government, mainly through exchange and negotiation rather than through traditional state-led regulation'. This shaping of firm behaviour takes places through the establishment of standards and conventions enforced by intermediaries in global production networks. Here, we distinguish between regulatory and voluntary standards. The former involves the state and its formal institutions and enforcement mechanisms such as legal means and penalties for non-compliance. Voluntary standards, however, are dependent on moral claims and come with weaker enforcement capacity.

Global lead firms, meanwhile, are actively involved in extra-firm bargaining in order to lobby for, and shape the nature of, public regulation. However, the most effective governance through standards tends to come from business-to-business modes. In the agro-food industry, for example, large retailers are able to impose Global-GAP certification on their fresh food suppliers. This form of private regulation of inter-firm relations tends to dominate in food retailing, a sector in which all sorts of public and private certification schemes are available for lead firms to govern their supply chains. Moreover, standards are critical to how firm-specific actors participate in different global production networks (see also Table 2.6). This is the arena in which international organizations can play a significant role in shaping extra-firm bargaining strategy through such standards as ISO9000 (quality), ISO14000 (environment), SA8000 (labour standards), and other industry-specific standards such as HACCP (hazard analysis and critical control point) in the food-processing industry (Kaplinsky and Morris 2001: 30). In other cases, extra-firm actors play a critical role in private formal and informal initiatives such as advocacy for codes of conduct and corporate social responsibility. For example, environmental sustainability issues are critical in the agro-food and forestry sectors in developing country contexts where formal regulation by the state often fails to achieve effective governance owing to the lack of political will and/or weak institutional capacity. While private and voluntary in nature, the Roundtable on Sustainable Palm Oil, for instance, is an international organization and certification scheme established through the participation of multi-stakeholders such as firms, advocacy groups, and local communities.[40] Under certain circumstances, notably where there is active local participation and a strong collective sense of ownership, actors in local communities in the Global South can benefit from these governance initiatives in the sense that their value creation, enhancement, and capture activities are not driven entirely by the capitalist imperative of global lead firms located elsewhere.

CONCLUSION: MULTIPLE ACTORS,
MULTIPLE STRATEGIES

This chapter has emphasized the conceptual significance of strategy in GPN theory. It extends our conceptualization of competitive dynamics and risks in the previous chapter and connects their structural properties with actor-specific strategies in order to enhance our understanding of the causal mechanisms of global production network formation and operation (see Figure 4.1). Extending beyond the lead firm focus that prevails in the existing literature, we argue that strategy matters in analyzing *diverse* actor practices and network configurations. Considering strategy reveals actor intentionality and agency, in turn helping to counter the analytical tendency towards structural determinism in dominant conceptions that view global value chains as outcomes of industry specificities or declining transaction costs. This chapter has illustrated why and how multiple actors tend to adopt multiple strategies to cope with different configurations of competitive dynamics and risk environments. By mapping the dynamics and risks of global production networks onto these four strategic choices by different network actors, we have demonstrated that not only are there diverse possible trajectories for competitive success in global industries, but also that this multiplicity of strategic choices and network configurations defies simple characterization via the parsimonious modelling commonly found in the existing literature.

In particular, this chapter has introduced firm- and industry-specificities in the operationalization of four strategies, in singular or combinatorial forms: intra-firm coordination, inter-firm control, inter-firm partnership, and extra-firm bargaining. In Table 4.4, we summarize the aggregate interaction of these four firm-specific strategies and the corresponding competitive dynamics and risks within the global economy. Intra-firm coordination tends to be deployed by firms subject to strong market imperatives and high levels of risk. Their network configurations are likely to be internalized through domestic expansion, FDI, and M&As. On the contrary, firms under pressure from high cost–capability ratios and financial discipline are likely to engage in inter-firm control through production outsourcing and dependent integration of suppliers into their global production networks. In this mode of externalization, an inter-firm partnership relationship can be developed if firms enjoy significant complementarities and mutual dependency in the context of highly competitive market dynamics and risky environments. Similar competitive and risk environments may also compel firms to enter into bargaining relationships with extra-firm actors in order to extract greater value from their global production networks. While for analytical purposes we have necessarily tended to separate out the four types of strategy, the reality for many firms in global production networks is that they are usually actively combining two or

Table 4.4. Firm-specific strategies and organizational outcomes in global production networks

Strategy as actor practice	Competitive dynamics			Risks	Global production network structure as organizational outcome
	Cost–capability ratio	Market imperative	Financial discipline		
Intra-firm coordination (e.g. pharmaceuticals and retail)	Low	High	Low	High	Domestic expansion and/or FDI and M&As; high level of network integration
Inter-firm control (e.g. automobiles and IT services)	High	Low	High	Moderate	Outsourcing but dependent integration of suppliers
Inter-firm partnership (e.g. electronics and logistics)	High	High	High	High	Outsourcing, joint development with partners and platform leaders
Extra-firm bargaining (e.g. resources and agrofood)	Medium	High	High	High	Differentiated integration into global production systems

Source: Yeung and Coe 2015: Table 4. © 2014 Clark University.

more such strategies across their various operations and activities. The global retailers discussed earlier in the chapter, for instance, in different ways combine internalized store operations with strong control over myriad small and medium-sized suppliers, partnership-style arrangements with large brand suppliers and logistics providers, and the ongoing management of multi-stranded extra-firm relations—for instance, with planners and regulators in local and national government.

Of course, at face value this theoretical mapping may appear to be abstract and categorical. But in this book, we explicitly conceptualize the importance of variability in understanding how firms, originating from different home economies and endowed with different ownership structures and corporate cultures, might respond differently to competitive dynamics and risks, thereby pursuing contrasting firm-specific strategies in configuring their global production networks. The variable strategic choices made by intentional actors offer strong support for our arguably more nuanced analysis of a highly complex and interdependent global economy characterized by a diverse range of firms and extra-firm actors operating at different geographical scales, from the global to the local. They shed critical analytical light on the much discussed governance modes in global value chains and global production networks. By conceptually linking actors, dynamics, strategies, and the organizational modes of global production networks into one coherent theory, GPN 2.0 represents, we argue, an important advancement over the earlier GPN conceptual framework reviewed in Chapter 1. This theory is more robust in explaining the effects of global production networks on the ultimate dependent variable—development outcomes. In the next and penultimate chapter, we will take this final analytical step to explain how and why the above diversity of actors and their varied strategic choices shape developmental outcomes at different geographical scales.

NOTES

1. In the next two chapters, we will explicitly revisit and engage with this literature in order to outline our distinctive contributions.

2. The causal importance given to the competitive dynamics in Chapter 3 differentiates our work from the strategic management literature, which tends to focus more narrowly on the strategy–structure–performance of firms in global competition. In this literature, which can be traced back to Alfred Chandler's *Strategy and Structure* (1962) and Porter's *Competitive Strategy* (1980), the structural environment of firms is often underdeveloped, giving overwhelming theoretical weight to firm strategy in determining competitive outcomes. See Burgelman and Grove (2002), Mathews (2006), and Spender (2014) for in-depth discussions of actor-specific strategizing under uncertain circumstances in the business strategy literature. McGrath-Champ (1999: 244; emphasis in original) offers one of the few explicit reviews of strategy in economic geography, usefully observing that strategy exists on a spectrum between '*deliberate* strategies (where intentions that existed previously are realized) and *emergent* strategies (where patterns of action develop in the absence of intentions, or despite them)'. Our reading of strategy in the context of global production networks places more emphasis on the former aspect.

3. See Yeung (2005b) for a more in-depth discussion of this relational conception of the firm as social networks in which individuals are embedded in ongoing power relations and discursive processes. Relatedly, O'Neill and Gibson-Graham (1999) offer a case study of how a major TNC can be understood as a constellation of competing discourses.

4. The study of corporate culture in shaping firm performance has been well developed in strategic management (e.g. Nohria and Ghoshal 1997; Doz and Hamel 1998), economic geography (e.g. Schoenberger 1994, 1997; Storper and Salais 1997; Shackleton 1998; Amin and Cohendet 2004), and allied social sciences.

5. These theoretical arguments are generally validated in the varieties of capitalism (VoC) literature discussed in Chapter 1.

6. For more detail on these mitigation strategies through the reduction, pooling, and transfer of risk, see Lessard (2013: 204–12).

7. In international business studies and strategic management, there is a very large literature explaining firm strategy and internationalization (see reviews in Rugman 2005; Gulati 2007; Dunning and Lundan 2008; Dicken 2015). But few of these studies engage directly with the nature and organization of global production networks (e.g. Buckley and Ghauri 2004; Levy 2008; Buckley, 2009, 2011). See De Marchi et al. (2014) for a more recent reprise.

8. See Mackinnon (2012) for an analysis of these coupling dynamics in the light of the pursuit by lead firms of intra-firm coordination through foreign direct investment (FDI). In Chapter 5, we will offer a full analysis of these developmental trajectories that goes well beyond the FDI mode of strategic coupling. See Phelps and Fuller (2000) for earlier discussion on the nature of the intra-TNC competition for investment and regional development.

9. For a pioneering study of the extractive industries using the GPN 1.0 approach, see Bridge (2008). Other related analyses of natural resource-based sectors are found in Murphy and Schindler (2011), Murphy (2012), Sovacool (2012), and J. D. Wilson (2013).

10. For a review of contemporary global strategies in retailing, see Dawson and Mukoyama (2014).

11. We thank Stefano Ponte for this important point.

12. This pattern of mutual dependency between brand name suppliers and global retailers is often overlooked in the existing literature, where the emphasis is often on giant retailers as the powerful actor governing non-brand name suppliers in so-called buyer-driven chains. See, for example, Coe and Lee (2006, 2013) on the influence of large brand name manufacturers on retail TNCs in South Korea.

13. This intransigence has led to several high-profile exits from host markets, most notably Germany and South Korea, both in 2006 (see Christopherson 2007). See also Aoyama (2007) for an analysis of Wal-Mart's competitive predicament in Japan.

14. This observation, however, does not mean that all actors in the retail industry must necessarily pursue this strategy of intra-firm coordination. Empirical complexity may possibly compel *some* of these actors to adopt other strategies conceptualized in the next three sections. For instance, for certain kinds of retailing, most notably fast food and convenience stores, franchising is often the preferred mode of securing rapid expansion, particularly abroad.

15. In his *The New Old Economy*, Whitford (2005: 3; emphasis in original) argues that this externalization process represents 'a qualitative break with the recent past, the emergence of a *new old economy* in which most of what matters to manufacturing firms no longer happens under roofs they own or control. This has made the quality of relationships between firms much more important and their structure much more complex'.

16. See Winter (2008) for a discussion of these higher-order dynamic capabilities.

17. In Gereffi et al.'s terminology (2005), this strategy of inter-firm control is likely to produce market and captive configurations of governing global production networks.

18. Our conceptualization goes beyond the institutionalist approach in GPN 1.0, which views firm actors as embedded in broader institutional contexts. We specify

the mechanisms through which these extra-firm actors causally shape firm-specific strategy. Our position thus sits between a GVC analysis of a limited number of dependent variables such as chain governance types and an institutionalist approach that takes on board a wide variety of institutions and actors. We thank John Pickles for pointing this out.

19. A very relevant example is China's 'Going West' policy since the early 2000s. See Zhu and Pickles (2014) for the case of the apparel industry.

20. In the existing literature, these brand name assemblers are commonly known as producers because of their capability of producing an entire automobile. However, in today's highly globalizing automobile industry, all producers require very substantial inputs from external and multiple tiers of suppliers. These lead firms are really assemblers of different components, modules, and subsystems into a finished product. In terms of value activity, their R&D, marketing, distribution, and sales are often as significant as their assembly facilities in different geographical locations.

21. See Sturgeon et al. (2008) and Sturgeon and Van Biesebroeck (2011) for more in-depth analyses of these variations in inter-firm governance in the global automobile industry.

22. See empirical details in Liu and Dicken (2006) and Van Biesebroeck and Sturgeon (2010: 227–8).

23. In Gereffi et al. (2005: 86), this cooperative form of industrial governance is known as relational or modular chains, but our conception goes beyond these broad governance relationships within the same industry. In addition to these intra-industry relationships, firms may also enter into inter-industry partnership relationships with other firms, most notably with advanced producer service firms providing financial, legal, accountancy, information technology, management consultancy, advertising, and logistics services, among others. The level of inter-dependency in these relations, however, is not as intense as with firms in the same global production network or sector—producer service firms tend to be multi-industry players—and we focus primarily on the intra-industry forms of partnership here. This is also an opportune moment to reassert our observation from Chapter 2 that dominant firms in producer service sectors (e.g. a large transnational bank or logistics provider) may also be conceptualized as lead firms in their own global production networks.

24. Although we do not adopt the terminology here, clearly these ideas chime with the pioneering work of Tim Sturgeon (2002, 2003) on modular production networks, wherein manufacturing capacity is outsourced by lead firms to globally operating turnkey suppliers. Gereffi et al. (2005: 86) suggested that value chain modularity is likely to develop 'when product architecture is modular and technical standards simplify interactions by reducing component variation and by unifying component, product, and process specifications, and also when suppliers have the competence to supply full packages and modules'.

25. See Chapter 3 for a discussion of the competitive dynamics in these two global industries and references to empirical studies.

26. Reported in Duhigg and Barboza (2012). See also two analyses of Apple's business model and inter-firm relationship with Foxconn in Froud et al. (2012) and Haslam et al. (2013).

27. Reported in King et al. (2012).
28. For more firm-specific detail on Samsung Electronics, see Sea-Jin Chang's fascinating book *Sony versus Samsung* (2008), which profiles its rise into a formidable global lead firm in the electronics industry.
29. These quotations are reported in Kapner (2009).
30. A growing body of empirical evidence suggests that extra-firm actors have significant influence on global production network dynamics. For example, ethical and fair trade initiatives in developed countries, strongly advocated by the state and civil society organizations, are generally seen as effective in influencing sourcing strategies of certain kinds of lead firms, such as major retailers and their domestic and foreign suppliers in the agro-food and apparel industries (Freidberg 2004; Hughes et al. 2008; Barnett et al. 2011). In other industries such as electronics and automobiles, these initiatives have much less purchase in shaping how lead firms configure their global production networks.
31. These broader objectives are over and above cost-specific gains derived from bargaining with state and non-state institutions—e.g. maximizing financial returns through tax concessions, externalizing the costs of labour training to state agencies, avoiding environmental costs through lower regulatory enforcement, and so on. See Dicken (2015) for in-depth elaboration on these domains of firm–state bargaining, some of which have become hugely controversial nationally and internationally (e.g. tax-avoidance structures and the associated issue of transfer pricing pursued by lead firms such as Apple, Starbucks, Google, and others). We will take up this issue in relation to value capture in the next chapter.
32. See Glassman (2011), Smith (2014), and Yeung (2014).
33. In China's automobile industry, for example, Liu and Dicken (2006) argue that the willingness of foreign lead firm assemblers to enter into joint ventures with domestic Chinese firms and to reduce their control of network configurations is largely determined by the host state's regulatory capacity. Foreign lead firms thus engage in what they call 'obligated embeddedness' in order to bargain with the Chinese state and to fulfil their own market development strategy.
34. In *Rival States, Rival Firms*, Stopford and Strange (1991) characterize these complex firm–state relationships in terms of 'triangular diplomacy', constituted by firm–firm, firm–state, and state–state bargaining relationships. In his successive editions of *Global Shift*, Dicken (2011, 2015) argues too that the tensions confronting global lead firms and nation states should be understood as differentiated power relations in global production networks. For lead firms, competitive pressures are generating dual tendencies—namely, to globalize operations in order to achieve greater efficiencies, while also localizing operations in order to ensure a degree of autonomy and responsiveness. For nation states, conditions of accelerating globalization have been associated with far-reaching forms of institutional and functional reorganization, as 'the pressures towards certain kinds of putative supranational organization at one extreme are counterpoised against a pressure toward greater degrees of local political autonomy at the other' (Dicken 1994: 122). The bargaining relationships between global lead firms and nation states are therefore situated within these complex global–local tensions (see also Yeung 2015b). Azmeh (2014b) provides a fascinating example through the analysis of

what he terms a 'GPN-driven trade agreement' in respect of the Qualifying Industrial Zones (QIZs) of Egypt and Jordan.

35. Classic examples of extra-firm bargaining issues in relation to market access at the WTO level are anti-dumping litigation, infringements of intellectual property rights, and the removal of non-tariff trade barriers previously initiated by state authorities on behalf of their national firms.

36. The rapid growth of industrial and technological capabilities in Taiwan's ICT sector is a clear example of extra-firm bargaining between global lead firms and extra-firm actors such as state institutions and business associations (see Amsden and Chu 2003; Breznitz 2007). See Wong (2011) and Weiss (2014) for two thorough analyses of different state roles in technological innovation in contrasting national economies.

37. For a good source on the brand value of the world's largest lead firms, see <http://www.interbrand.com> (accessed 8 September 2014).

38. See Van Tulder et al. (2009) and Dicken (2015: ch. 11) for a full elaboration of the significance of these CSR programmes for understanding global production networks.

39. See Barrientos et al. (2011) for an authoritative analysis of this topic in relation to social upgrading in global production networks.

40. For further examples, see Stringer (2006) on forestry standards, Ouma (2010, 2015) on agro-foods, and Baird and Quastel (2011) on dolphin-friendly tuna. Dicken's *Global Shift* (2015) remains the definitive source for detailed industry studies across all sectors.

5

Development

The preceding two chapters have identified the causal dynamics *driving* the formation and evolution of global production networks (GPN) and mapped those dynamics onto the different organizational strategies that constituent firms and extra-firm actors may pursue. Our challenge in this chapter is to theorize further the relationships between these dynamics and strategies, collectively known as the causal mechanisms of global production networks, and patterns and outcomes of on-the-ground economic development. As outlined in Chapter 1, one of the key tenets of GPN 2.0 (in order to improve over the earlier conceptual framework) must be to enhance its explanatory power in relation to processes and impacts of economic development. It is perhaps too heroic to expect one approach to explain entirely the full complexities of value generation and capture and resultant patterns of uneven development within the contemporary global economy. At the same time, it should already be clear by this stage that GPN analysis offers significant analytical traction for tackling this issue in the context of the ongoing global and organizational fragmentation of production.

By directly connecting the causal drivers and strategies within global production networks to economic development outcomes, our goal is to develop an integrated GPN approach that is able to shine more light on the key question of why global production networks matter for the people, organizations, and territories that are enrolled into them. Without such conceptual integration, any theory of global production will ultimately have only limited utility in addressing the economic development challenges experienced by the myriad places that constitute the global economy just as much as global production networks do. As Dicken (2011: 430; emphasis in original) describes, global production networks 'not only integrate *firms* (and parts of firms) into structures which blur traditional organizational boundaries ... but also integrate *places* (national and local economies) in ways that have enormous implications for their economic development'. The central tenet of our argument is that, while processes of value creation and enhancement are important, it is ultimately the dynamics of value *capture*—themselves intricately connected to the wider structures and strategies at play within global production networks—that shape economic development in particular territories.

In this chapter, we will unfold the above argument across four sections. First, we seek to 'frame' our understanding of economic development in the contemporary global economy. This is important not only to outline how economic development is best conceived from a relational and multi-scalar perspective, but also to draw some necessary boundaries around what we can realistically cover in this chapter. Extending our conception of regions in Chapter 2, we will also justify our main focus on the sub-national region as the key territorial unit for understanding economic development processes in the world economy. Second, we seek to move beyond the inherent limits of the prevailing upgrading approach in the existing literature and focus on what we call the *value capture trajectories* of individual firms embedded within global production networks. Such trajectories are much more varied, contingent, and multi-directional than is seemingly implied in the common notion of economic upgrading. From our actor-based perspective, it is the presence of firms that are able to achieve significant levels of value capture within a particular territory that is at the heart of economic development processes.

Third, we conceptualize how these individual firm trajectories coalesce at the regional scale through the concept of *strategic coupling*. Introduced in Chapter 1 as part of the analytical toolkit of GPN 1.0, this concept has already achieved some prominence in the literature with its focus on the dynamic and multi-scalar interface between regional economic actors and institutions with those in global production networks. Here, we seek to deepen the utility of this concept by connecting it to the different value capture trajectories achieved by actors in global production networks, and by delimiting the various modes and types of couplings that integrate different regional economies and global production networks. Fourth, we will consider the wider political–economic forces that ultimately underpin regional development, both within and between regions. This involves looking at who actually gains from value capture dynamics within a global production network, and in turn considering the extent to which those gains benefit the regional economy more widely—that is, beyond those actors and institutions that have a direct stake in global production networks.

FRAMING ECONOMIC DEVELOPMENT IN THE CONTEMPORARY GLOBAL ECONOMY

The myriad processes of transnational economic integration that go under the shorthand of globalization pose profound conceptual challenges to the understanding of economic development in the contemporary era. Put simply, understanding the forces that drive economic development is more challenging than it was just two decades ago. The global fragmentation and dispersal of production mean that the traditional lens of the bounded national economy has long been outmoded, while the organizational fragmentation of production demands that we look beyond hierarchically organized transnational corporations (TNCs) and the uneven developmental impacts of their foreign subsidiaries. While these aspects remain of considerable importance, global production networks also shape economic development from outside particular territories without there being substantial direct relations of equity ownership to firms located therein. Domestic firms can plug into global production networks through a wide range of non-equity modes of economic organization such as industrial subcontracting and outsourcing arrangements. This section starts our challenging task of theorizing economic development in an interconnected world by delimiting some key analytic parameters for our ensuing discussion.

We start by highlighting that our focus here is on *economic* development, rather than development more generally. This is not to deny the importance of the social, cultural, and environmental dimensions of human existence that the latter term implies, but rather to note that they are beyond the scope of this book (although we will touch on some elements in the final section to the chapter).[1] Nor do we frame development in terms of what Hart (2001) calls 'big D' Development—namely, a post-war project of state-sponsored intervention in the developing world set against a backdrop of decolonization. Rather, we are operating with 'little d' development and the outcomes of 'the development of capitalism as a geographically uneven, profoundly contradictory set of historical processes' (Hart 2001: 650). We are concerned with grounded material processes, rather than discursive projects. In so doing, we do not aim to downplay the wider geopolitical and neo-imperial dimensions to contemporary economic globalization, but rather to foreground uneven development and its production as the key feature of capitalism we are seeking to understand here.[2] The notion of economic development that we mobilize is a relative one, rather than something that can necessarily be collapsed into a checklist of quantifiable indicators of economic performance. In its simplest terms, we see economic development as a process that results in the improvement of economic conditions within a particular territorial unit.

This leads us to the issue of the relevant spatial scale at which economic development is best understood. While the above notion of economic development could be deployed at the national or supra-national (macro-regional) scale, we argue that the functional realities of the global economy mean that it is best employed at the level of the sub-national *region*. Since the late 1980s years a vast literature has been developed on the importance of regional economies as the basic functional building block of the global economy.[3]

We also subscribe to this view, although we contend that the literature has tended to prioritize endogenous, territorial attributes at the expense of wider network relations beyond the regional or even national economy. We use the term 'region' as a taken-for-granted scale of economic space—the wide range of cultural, political, and historical forces behind the forging of regional spaces is not our primary consideration here. Some flexibility of definition is required—encompassing city states, city regions, states/provinces or parts thereof—but we are generally referring to a sub-national space with some kind of coherence to its economic relationships and, importantly, some kind of territorial governance apparatus. If we refer back to Figure 2.4 and our discussion of the territoriality of global production networks in Chapter 2, the region can be thought of as the key horizontal territorial interface in which global production network activities are grounded (that is, are taking place) and their implications felt and materialized. The operations themselves may be located in particular localities or urban areas—the local scale in Figure 2.4—but they are always embedded and integrated into some kind of wider regional economic entity.

Regional development, as the on-the-ground manifestation of economic development processes, is an inherently territorial phenomenon. Again keeping Figure 2.4 in view, in the preceding two chapters we have largely focused on the *vertical* dimension of global production networks—that is, the transnational inter-organizational relationships that tie together actors with different spatial extents and responsibilities. Understanding regional economic development, however, requires us to invoke the *horizontal* dimension, and the territorial interfaces of global production networks. This does not mean to say, however, that the central drivers of economic development necessarily reside within a particular region—far from it. In an interconnected global economy, regional development is, by definition, an interdependent or relational process. The fortunes of regions are shaped not only by what is going on within them, but also through wider sets of relations of control and dependency, of competition and market access.[4] Economic development is driven by the intersection of vertical and horizontal forces, or, put another way, by the articulation of the network and territorial relationships that co-constitute global production networks. It is thus not a matter of considering either global networks or regional territories—both dimensions need to be mobilized at the same time to capture fully the multi-scalar nature of regional economic development.[5] The relational nature of regional economic development also means that it is a path-dependent process in the way alluded to by Hudson (2007: 1158): 'Without falling into the trap of equating path dependency with a deterministic iron law of history, it is important to recognize that historical legacies are important and that path dependency constrains—if not determines—the future developmental possibilities of regions'. In other words, the manner in which regions have coupled with global production networks will have an important but not determining bearing on subsequent forms of coupling.[6]

The notion of regional economic development that we employ here also seeks to shed any remaining legacies of the world-systems theory that may linger in the literature on global production.[7] We aim to cover the development of all kinds of firms and regions enrolled into global production networks. The complexity and multi-polar nature of the contemporary global economy is such that simple distinctions between core, semi-peripheral, and peripheral regions are now being stretched to breaking point.[8] Lead firms and globally significant suppliers come from an ever-increasing range of economies. Similarly, binaries such as home/domestic versus host/foreign, production versus market, and developing/emerging/latecomer versus developed are also losing analytical purchase as meaningful categories for analyzing regional and national economies. As discussed in Chapter 3, one of the chief characteristics of the global economy today is that economies previously understood as production spaces for developed world consumption (for example, East Asia for consumption in North America and Western Europe) are rapidly developing into significant consumption markets in their own right. This reconfiguration of global markets adds new complexity to the causal links between global production networks and regional development. We similarly seek to move beyond simple readings of the development implications of the ownership of firms—that is, whether they are domestic or foreign firms. As argued in Chapter 2, we recognize that this distinction matters analytically in terms of home country effects and how firms construct and control global production networks. However, we do not want to argue that there is a deterministic relationship with development—that is, to suggest that domestic firms necessarily drive growth more effectively than foreign firms.[9] To us that is an empirical question. Analytically, we suggest that the kinds of firms located within a particular territory, the roles they perform within wider global production networks, and the possibilities those roles afford for value capture are of prime importance.

Finally, it is important to state clearly that our approach does not celebrate uncritically the developmental implications of integrating regional economies with global production networks. Our initial formulation of strategic coupling as part of GPN 1.0 was usefully critiqued for not being clear in this regard. There are, of course, numerous potential 'dark sides' to coupling with global production networks, and they will be given fuller consideration in what follows. These may take the form of significant *ruptures* in which connections between global production networks and regional economies are severed, perhaps quickly or with little warning, owing to the shifting strategic priorities of lead firms or changing global market conditions.[10] Equally, however, they may take the form of *frictions* between global production networks actors and local firms and institutions.[11] These more ongoing and everyday tensions of course reflect the wider politics of economic development and the fact that actors in global production networks do not operate in isolation from broader societal relations and constraints. For us, therefore, the developmental outcomes of regions coupling with global production networks are almost always contingent, and require empirical investigation in particular industries and localities. Nonetheless, as more and more localities become enrolled into global production networks in different ways, we remain convinced of the potential of the GPN approach for illuminating the causal relationships between regional coupling with global production networks and their consequential uneven developmental outcomes.

Building upon these basic tenets and conceptual clarifications, the next three sections seek to demonstrate that GPN 2.0 can help to explain patterns of economic development by working through three levels of analysis. First, as befits an actor-focused approach, the starting point must be the firm-level dynamics of value creation, enhancement, and capture within and across individual global production networks. Value capture from coupling with global production network actors is seen as a necessary condition for regional economic development. Second, the intersections and aggregations of global production networks should be conceptualized at the level of the regional economy. Many regional economies connect to multiple global production networks, often in different industries, and as such it is critical to find ways of characterizing this collective interface. Third, the wider processes of economic development within and between regional economies have to be revealed by stepping back from the global production networks themselves to consider the macro political–economic structures in which they are embedded. Put another way, we need to think about how economic development *in* a region via global production networks may, or may not, lead to development *of* a region. This is by no means a novel question in regional development debates, but takes on new saliency in an era of highly fragmented and dispersed global production.

BEYOND UPGRADING: CHARTING VALUE CAPTURE TRAJECTORIES

The starting point for our analysis is that the key mechanism that ultimately drives economic development in the contemporary era is the insertion or plugging-in of firms into global production networks. As Dicken (2011: 448) argues, the fact that global production networks 'have become the predominant mode within which production is organized means that it is very difficult indeed for local firms/economies to prosper outside them. Being there—as an insider— is virtually a prerequisite for development'. Importantly, this plugging-in can occur in two ways. From an outside–in perspective, key firms in a global production network may be inward investors into a particular territory, allowing for local firms to forge economic relationships that tie them into the wider transnational production system. This is the model considered in the huge literature on TNCs and the developmental implications of their subsidiaries. Alternatively, an inside–out mode of incorporation may see a firm in a particular territory reaching out to establish transactional relationships with global production network actors based outside their home patch. These connections could be in different directions; backwards links to suppliers, forwards links to customers, or lateral links to partners or specialized service providers. Once a firm has established reasonably stable transactional relationships with other actors in a global production network, as described in Chapter 1, we characterize this as the firm having *strategically coupled* with the wider production system. This notion highlights the intentionality of the connections from the perspective of the actors involved and the fact that the relationships involved are time–place specific rather than generic and deterministic connections that can be read off from broad notions of governance within particular industries or production networks.

Assuming a firm has strategically coupled in this way, like every corporate actor in a global production network—be it an independent firm or branch of a multi-plant organization—it is by definition a site of value creation. As outlined in Chapter 2, value creation refers to the generation of a surplus over and above the costs of undertaking a given economic activity through the application of labour, capital, technology, and organizational knowledge of different kinds. Value, though, needs to be seen in dynamic terms, and value enhancement, in turn, highlights the ways in which firms strive over time to maximize the surplus generated, again through using the various forms of labour, capital, technology, and knowledge at their disposal. It is value *capture*, however, that we argue is the most important dimension in developmental terms. This refers to the ability of firms to retain the surplus within their organizational boundaries in the context of the wider power dynamics within a global production network. It is perfectly possible for a firm (for example, a fresh food supplier) to undertake significant value creation (for example, growing produce) and enhancement (for example, taking on more of the preparing, packaging, and labelling of that produce over time), and yet to capture less or little value from those activities, owing to the contractual obligations imposed by a major customer and/or lead firm (for example, price concessions and slotting fees imposed for selling through a dominant retailer). As argued strongly by Tokatli (2013: 1000), 'simply entering into a higher value-added activity does not guarantee the capture of additional value, as this often happens due to a shift of responsibility (in part or in whole) for this activity from the buyers to the manufacturing suppliers'. Therefore the extent to which a firm is able to stop the leakage of the surplus value it generates becomes key. Moreover, as introduced in Chapter 2, there is also a significant territorial component to this value capture. For the purposes of economic development, value must be retained within firms, or the parts of firms, based in the territory under question. In other words, value needs to be retained and redeployed in a particular region and not transferred to other regions via the intra-firm networks of multi-plant firms (for example, through the internal movement of profits, or transfer pricing).

Importantly, the level of value capture that a firm accrues from involvement in a global production network is a dynamic rather than static variable. Here we posit the notion of *value capture trajectories* for charting the evolutionary aspects of a firm's value capture position. As outlined in Chapter 1, these trends are often characterized in the literature through different forms of industrial or economic upgrading. The literature outlines an ideal-type, and often linear, path starting with product upgrading, moving through process and functional upgrading to, in some cases, chain upgrading, wherein firms move into a different sector altogether. In making this 'upward' journey, firms move from supplying to original equipment manufacturers (OEMs) through engaging in original design manufacture (ODM) to eventually developing own-brand manufacture (OBM), with value capture increasing at each step up the value chain at the same time as the disembodied knowledge content of that value also increases.[12] Moving from product and process to functional upgrading is seen as particularly challenging as it often means that firms are starting to encroach on the core competences of their customers who therefore may increasingly resist such moves. Increasingly, the upgrading discourse is coming under greater scrutiny in the GVC and GPN literatures.[13] There are several elements to this critique, some of which—for instance, the extent to which it can be scaled up to understand regional and national development patterns, and the relative neglect of the social dimensions of upgrading—will be considered later in the chapter. Here, we draw attention to its limitations in capturing firm-level value dynamics.

First, the standard upgrading account is too developmental and deterministic. Upgrading is just one possible outcome of many from a firm's incorporation into global production networks, and indeed in some contexts the upgrading potential may be stronger from national- or regional-based production networks. As Pickles et al. (2006: 2319) describe:

> Some firms are literally sliding backwards (losing capital and capacity, suffering workforce depletion and weakening management skills). But other firms may be increasing their workforce skills, levels of capitalization, and production and still experience 'downgrading' as their relative position in the supply chain becomes precarious because of changes in regulatory policies . . . or shifts in the competitive 'field' within which they are situated.

Second, the upgrading concept tends to be applied to certain kinds of firms—namely, suppliers—within certain kinds of regional and national economies—namely, emerging and latecomer contexts—rather than being tailored to all global production network participants. The upgrading literature thus tells us a lot about low-end suppliers undergoing those four types of upgrading and yet remains fairly silent on the upgrading trajectories of global lead firms (for example, sectoral shifts or even downgrading) and strategic partners.[14] Third, at the industry scale, there is likely to be a zero-sum element to upgrading processes. If all firms in all locations upgrade simultaneously, competition will probably be enhanced and value capture eroded.[15] Upgrading processes are geographically variegated, and the key question then becomes why are certain firms in certain places (at certain times) successful in following some kind of upgrading process? In short, the upgrading thesis underplays the extent to which the potential for upgrading is shaped by local institutional conditions as much as wider chain and network dynamics.[16]

Fourth, upgrading studies often confuse the means of upgrading—that is, the range of strategies that firms may pursue in order to enhance their functional position within a global production network—and the purported ends—that is, the capture of greater value added. As noted above, these two dynamics need not automatically coincide and may indeed work in opposite directions. The flipside of this is that, in some circumstances, downgrading may actually make economic sense for certain firms, if, for instance, such a move secures greater volumes of lower-risk sales or reduces the need for new capital investment in a constrained financial environment. Hence, and fifth, the upgrading concept obscures a wide range of value capture trajectories that firms may follow owing to a combination of their own actions and wider pressures. In reality, this may often result from the fact that many firms are operating across several global production networks simultaneously and adopt multiple strategies accordingly. One of the best studies of these complexities is the work of Ponte and Ewert (2009: 1648) on South Africa's wine industry. Their conclusions are worth quoting at length here:

> analysis should break away from normative views of upgrading as 'moving up the value chain' or as always producing 'value added-products', and embrace a view that a 'better deal'... may entail sometimes processes of functional downgrading and periods in which even product downgrading may be the best option available... if a 'better deal' for developing country firms entails more than just 'moving up' the value chain or embedding higher value into products, and is indeed characterized by a complex mixture of upgrading and trading down, does it still make sense to use the term upgrading...? If not, a new effort is needed to re-shape the conceptual and heuristic discussion on the matter.

To us, the heuristic device of value capture trajectories can offer a useful way of moving beyond this seeming impasse. Firms may move along a wide range of value capture trajectories, and will not necessarily follow a deterministic upgrading path. As depicted in Figure 5.1, for a single firm in a given locality that has strategically coupled with a global production network (at time zero) there is a wide range of ways in which the level of value captured by the firm may unfold over time. Although clearly highly schematic, in Figure 5.1a we can see that the standard upgrading narrative—namely, of an increasing degree of value capture over time, whether in terms of increasingly rapid (curve A) or steady (B), growth is but one of several possible trajectories. Firms may equally occupy a static value capture position (C), or see a steady (D) or rapid (E) decline over time in their level of value capture.[17]

In Figure 5.1b we extend the time horizon to rethink how each of these value capture trajectories may, over time, take a dynamic and multi-directional path. This reworking enables us to break out of the linearity of value capture conception in the upgrading literature. For instance, steady decline may bottom out and be translated into gradual growth (F) or, conversely, rapid initial gains in value capture may peak and then wane as competitive conditions change (G). Importantly, the strategic coupling of a firm with a global production network is clearly not a permanent arrangement; over time a firm suffering a declining degree of value capture may decouple from the global production network, either voluntarily, because it is going out of business, or because other network participants choose to end relationships with the firm (H). That firm may also hypothetically recouple with the same global production network at a later point in time, for instance, because it is able to adjust favourably its cost–capability ratio (I). Finally, by extending our analysis to multiple global production networks (Figure 5.1c), we can conceptualize how a firm faced with declining value capture from a given global production network (J) may instead decouple from one network and recouple with another in the same industry that offers enhanced value capture trajectories (K). Hypothetically, this could also be with a global production network in a different industry (similar to the idea of chain upgrading in the literature).

Our reframing of value capture trajectories in this way offers four important advantages over existing conceptions in the upgrading literature. First, by focusing on the individual firm, we are able to think about how firms may offer multiple products and services within a given global production network. Following Ponte and Ewert (2009), we conceptualize the degree of value capture as the overall, aggregate value capture position resulting from the activities of a firm in a single global production network (which may encompass different roles with different value capture characteristics). Focusing on the intersection of an individual firm with a single global production network as the basic unit of analysis is also an important first step in seeking to mitigate the analytical slippage across firms, value chains, and different territorial units that characterizes much of the wider upgrading debate. Second, the explicit focus on value capture helps to ameliorate another important limitation of the

(a) Fixed trajectories

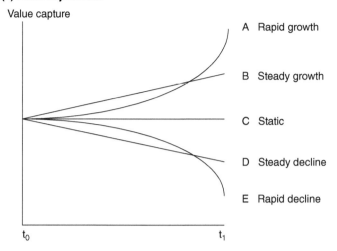

Value capture

A Rapid growth

B Steady growth

C Static

D Steady decline

E Rapid decline

t_0 t_1

(b) Multi-directional paths

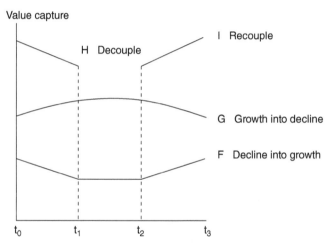

Value capture

I Recouple

H Decouple

G Growth into decline

F Decline into growth

t_0 t_1 t_2 t_3

(c) Shifts between global production networks

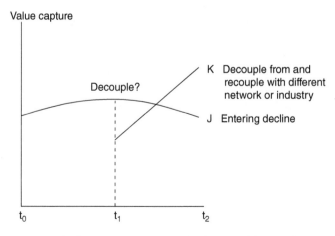

Value capture

K Decouple from and recouple with different network or industry

Decouple?

J Entering decline

t_0 t_1 t_2

Figure 5.1. Varieties of value capture trajectories for firms in global production networks

upgrading discourse, mentioned earlier—namely, that it prioritizes the means of upgrading over the ends. Here, value capture is seen as the ends, given its centrality in territorial economic development.

Third, strategic coupling is not a static equilibrium concept, as has been misunderstood by some critical commentators on GPN 1.0. As argued in Coe et al. (2004: n. 1), the strategic coupling process is not automatic and always successful, but rather it evolves over time. There is no inherent assumption that strategic coupling will improve the relative position of a firm. Moreover, a dynamic notion of value capture trajectories allows us to incorporate the sequential processes of coupling, decoupling, and recoupling between a particular corporate actor and specific global production networks. It also lets us profile the different starting points from which firms strategically couple with global production networks, which is very important when considering development outcomes. Fourth, this perspective enables us to chart the movements of firms between different global production networks. Such interglobal production network shifts are arguably underplayed in the existing literature. Schrank (2004: 145) describes this lacuna in the context of the apparel industry:

> While failure to pursue upgrading would lead to exclusion from the apparel trade and is therefore not a viable option, a more realistic . . . strategy would encourage lateral movement into sparsely populated chains rather than upward movement in densely populated chains. After all, the returns to a given economic activity are a function of the number of suppliers available as well as their positions in the relevant chains, and the 'choice' of chain is therefore no less important than the 'choice' of position in the chain.

Firm-level value capture trajectories can be thought of, then, as the basic building blocks of evolutionary economic development processes. How, though, do we explain these trajectories? In GPN 2.0, they are conceived as the empirical outcome of the strategies pursued by individual firms and other extra-firm actors in specific global production networks, which in turn represent their collective responses to the dynamic drivers delimited in Chapter 3— namely, the need to optimize costs and capabilities, to create and sustain a market for goods and services produced, to manage the wider imperatives of financial discipline, and to mitigate the risks inherent to the global economy (see Figure 5.2, a development and extension of Figure 4.1). These structural forces will directly drive the ways in which firms seek to manipulate their meshes of intra-firm coordination, inter-firm control, inter-firm partnership, and extra-firm bargaining networks to maximize the level of capture.[18] Their ability to do so effectively will depend on a number of broader influences: firm-level capabilities (for example, managerial expertise, capacity to raise financial capital), global production network-level influences (for example, the configuration of power relations between network members, the ease with

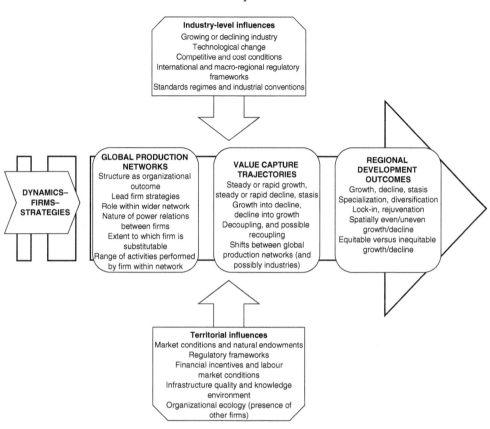

Figure 5.2. Multiple influences on firm-level value capture trajectories

which the role of the firm can be substituted), industry specificities (for example, growing or stagnant market, level of cost competition), but also territorialized conditions (for example, the extent to which activities are supported and facilitated by local policy and incentive structures).

Importantly, given our analytical emphasis on intra- and inter-global production network variation, we are wary of attributing particular value capture trajectories to particular types of firms occupying specific positions within those networks. As Pickles et al. (2006: 2319) point out, 'it remains an empirical issue as to whether . . . relative changes in position in international value chains reflect significantly on the financial position . . . of specific firms'. In Table 2.1 we identified five key types of corporate actors in global production networks—namely, lead firms, strategic partners, specialized suppliers (industry-specific), specialized suppliers (multi-industrial), and generic suppliers. Hypothetically, any of these types of firms can follow any of the value capture trajectories depicted in Figure 5.1. It is not only lead firms, for instance, that can benefit from the rapid growth scenario, nor is it only generic suppliers that are squeezed over time, sometimes to the point where they are forced to decouple. Simple attempts to map rigidly developed value capture trajectories onto firm types and roles within global production networks in a hierarchical manner do an injustice to the complex and dynamic realities of firms juggling multiple roles across multiple networks.

Implicit in many upgrading accounts is an inherent linearity; firms move away from basic manufacturing in the direction of design, branding, and sales, securing an increasing level of value capture as they do so. Relatedly, in some high-technology industries, analysts have identified a so-called smile curve, in which value capture is lowest at the assembly stage, but higher in both the preceding design and component manufacture stage and subsequent distribution phase. There are at least two issues with such portrayals, however. First, they tend to focus on sequential value chain activities, rather than looking at the range of activities undertaken by particular corporate actors, which may, for example, encompass both pre-manufacture design, and post-manufacture branding and sales.[19] Second, the linear, activity-based perspective tends to efface the role of a range of cross-industry suppliers who may be capturing significant value at the firm level from global production network involvement. Advanced business service firms (for example, financial services, legal services) and logistics providers are two prime examples.[20]

Notwithstanding our earlier point about firm specificities, we are now ready to connect conceptually back to Figure 2.2 and consider the potential differences in levels of value capture across the two ideal-type global production network configurations—namely, the lead firm-centric and strategic partnership models. In very general terms, in the former (Figure 2.2(b)) we would expect high levels of value capture for lead firms in relation to specialized and generic suppliers, while in the latter (Figure 2.2(a)) strategic partners can accrue significant value capture, though usually still not on a par with lead firms. In addition, however, even in this most schematic and basic form we start to see the merits of the network metaphor for profiling the value capture landscape of global production networks. For instance, we can think about different forms of suppliers, such as manufacturers of entire modules and specialized business service providers, in addition to intermediaries such as logistics operators and finance providers, who may be able to capture significant value from involvement in strategic partnership type configurations. And, of course, these are dynamic relationships; over time, strategic partners may become lead firms in their own right, specialized suppliers may become strategic partners, and so on, with concomitant implications for the overall value capture trajectory of the firm.

Useful though such general overviews may be, ultimately, as we have argued, the precise value capture trajectories of firms will be global production network-specific. Another limitation of these schematic representations of chains and networks is that they are 'flat' representations. As illustrated in

Figure 2.4, they reside in the vertical realm of network relations linking places together across the global economy. As argued earlier, however, value capture trajectories and economic development are also territorialized dynamics that are mutually constituted with the particular institutional and regulatory formations in which they are embedded. Value capture trajectories are inherently dynamic and must be seen in evolutionary terms, while those trajectories are in turn heavily shaped by territorialized institutions and social relations. In the next section, we turn to the regional economy as the key territorial unit for considering how firm value capture trajectories can aggregate up into distinctive regional modes of economic development in an interdependent global economy.

COUPLING LOCAL AND REGIONAL DEVELOPMENT WITH GLOBAL PRODUCTION NETWORK DYNAMICS AND STRATEGIES

'Aggregating up' is probably one of the most profound conceptual challenges in work on global production networks and global value chains. As we have seen, the prevailing upgrading literature suffers from significant slippage across firms, chains, industries, regions, and national economies in terms of *who* is being seen to upgrade, and *who* is being seen to accrue the developmental benefits. Greater analytical clarity is urgently required to advance this genre of research in the social sciences and international policy communities. As Brewer (2011: 312; emphasis in original) puts it:

> developmental progress at larger scales hinges not just on successful upgrading at the level of the firm, but indeed successful upgrading *across* firms and commodity chains within a given territory. In both cases, the temporal dimension is equally important—after all, comparatively short-term gains in value-added generated by seemingly successful upgrading strategies might, in the longer run, diminish in the face of growing competition brought on by the earlier success of the strategy itself.[21]

A necessary first step, we have argued above, is to chart the value capture trajectories of the individual firms that have strategically coupled with global production networks. In its most basic sense, regional development is then understood as the dynamic aggregate effect of the value capture trajectories of the various firms located in a particular territory.

We borrow from Dicken (2011) the notion of a region's organizational ecology for thinking about the intersection of global production networks and particular regional territories (cf. Figure 2.4). This can be thought of as a region's 'mix of firms and parts of firms, large and small, old and new, foreign and domestically owned, connected together through geographically extensive production circuits and networks' (Dicken 2011: 430). At its most basic, we can first consider the intersection of a single global production network with a region—in other words, which of the corporate actors are located in the region in question. In some cases just one kind of firm—say, a generic supplier—will be present, in others there may be more than one—for instance, a lead firm and specialized business service providers. Importantly, moving beyond the linear logic of value chain analysis allows us to consider a wide range of firm types and value activities that can connect into global production networks, in turn with developmental outcomes. As noted in the previous section, multi-industry service providers such as advanced business services and logistics firms are often overlooked. Equally, connections to the global production network may be through distribution functions or through final consumption, activities that are often simply assumed in the existing literature to take place in the home market of the lead firm.

We can then map on the size and ownership structure of the different firms present, be that in terms of, for example, a small, locally owned firm or a large subsidiary of an externally owned firm. Importantly, this will reflect different modes of incorporation into global production networks. In some cases, regions will be connected via the local investments of externally owned firms, most commonly in terms of the subsidiaries of transnational corporations or multi-location national firms based in other regions, who may then forge connections and linkages with local firms to a greater or lesser extent. In others, however, there may be no externally owned firms present, but rather only local firms connecting into the network through trading (for example, outward processing) or contractual inter-firm relation-ships (for example, industrial subcontracting or service provision). Other local firms, in turn, may be enrolled into the global production network through relations with these plugged-in domestic firms. This is an important distinction, as much of the literature still implicitly assumes that connection to global production networks requires inward direct investment from foreign transnationals, which is categorically not the case and has important policy implications (as we will see in the next chapter). In reality, of course, external investment leading to global production network incorporation may, from a regional perspective, also come from domestic firms headquar-tered elsewhere in the same country.

Another issue with existing accounts is that they tend to assume a host region context in which firms are looking to connect into global production networks that are controlled from elsewhere. Equally important in develop-mental terms, however, is to look at the home regions of large lead firms, strategic partners, specialized suppliers, and so on. This matters analytically in two regards as we endeavour to scale up to the regional level. First, in dynamic terms it allows us to think about how regional economies may shift role, moving, for example, from being simply a dependent supply base to a site of indigenous innovation and control of external networks. Second, such a view allows us to consider how a regional economy may perform very different roles in different global production networks simultaneously. It may be a site of leadership and control in one network, and a site of dependency and basic service provision in another.

This in turn speaks to the considerable challenges of profiling the overall organizational ecology of a region, which is produced by the aggregation of the multiple global production networks to which it is connected. Some regions might effectively be connected to or locked into only one global production network—for instance, a peripheral region that attracts external investment from foreign or national firms in an automobile assembly plant. Others will intersect with a range of global production networks in a particular industry—for example, an agricultural region that provides horticultural products for a variety of externally controlled retailers in different countries. Most regions, however, will be enrolled into multiple global production networks across a range of industries. There may be inter-global production network and inter-industry similarities in how local and external firms in the region plug in. Firms may be fulfilling similar roles and following similar value capture trajectories, making the task of bridging between firm and regional level developmental outcomes relatively straightforward. Domestic firms and subsidiaries of external firms in export processing zones, for example, may be fulfilling the needs of global production networks for labour-intensive manufacturing in several different industries (for example, apparel, household goods, and toys). In other contexts, there may be highly varied patterns both within and across industries. From a regional perspective, positive value capture trajectories in some networks and industries may be cancelled out by worsening positions in others. And there will be different on-the-ground horizontal territorial patterns that result (cf. Figure 2.4). In some cases, firms connected to global production networks will be confined to clearly defined zones or enclaves, such as industrial estates or science parks. In others they will be dispersed more evenly across the territory—for instance, in the case of retailing and distribution activities.[22]

Once the overall organizational ecology of a region is profiled and connections to global production networks are aggregated, we can analyze how value capture at the firm level (and their trajectories) can be translated to developmental outcomes at the regional and national levels. Table 5.1 helps us to conceptualize four important types of indicators of these regional economic development outcomes that accrue from insertion into global production networks, all of which ultimately underpin the regional dynamics of value capture.[23] These indicators reflect the intersections of global production network structures and the territorial assets of the regional economy. In general, we expect greater or more positive development outcomes *if* firms

Table 5.1. The development impacts of global production networks on regional economies

Nature of global production network operation		Nature of the regional economy		Indicators of global production network impact
Mode of connection				**Capital flows**
Inward investment by external firms:				Inflows/outflows of capital
establishment of new unit or acquisition of				Revenues from exports/costs of imports
existing firm				Profits held locally/profits transferred out
Joint ventures with external firms				Reinvestment/leakage to financial sector
Outward contractual connections	→			State subsidies/enhanced taxes
Function		**Level of economic development**		**Organizational ecology**
To utilize local resources (including knowledge		Size of the economy		Firm growth/decline
and skills)		Resource endowment		New firm formation/firm displacement
To serve regional or national market	→	Knowledge and skill base		Deep or shallow connections to subsidiaries of
To serve export markets (export platform)		Composition of labour supply		externally owned firms
		Infrastructure		Clustering economies/diseconomies
		Social, political, cultural attributes	→	
				Knowledge/technology
				Access to new technology/knowledge
				Loss of benefits from new technology/knowledge
Attributes				**Employment**
Industry type				Net jobs created/displaced
Technology				Types of jobs created/displaced
Scale of operations				Changes in wage levels
Degree of integration into network				Labour relations
Governance characteristics			→	

Source: adapted from Dicken (2011: figure 14.2), with permission.

in the region capture more value through their connections to global production networks. In terms of *capital flows*, global production networks may bring capital inflows in terms of inward direct investment, portfolio investment, or sales revenues for local firms from exported goods and services. At the same time, capital may leak from the region via the repatriation of profits by transnational corporations or reallocation of profit centres by national firms, the use of internal finance mechanisms such as transfer pricing by multi-location firms, and through the value capture strategies used by powerful extra-regional global production network actors such as lead firms.[24] With respect to the *organizational ecology*, connecting to global production networks may stimulate both firm growth and new firm formation among the region's firm base, often because they offer access to large extra-regional markets. In turn, however, firms will perform highly variable roles with concomitantly variable potential for value capture. As noted above, the key here is to assess the region's organizational ecology in terms of different types of firms that are present, with certain roles generally deriving greater levels of value capture than others.

Global production network enrolment will also have implications in terms of *knowledge and technology* transfer. Again, the implications here may be mixed; access to new forms of technology and more sophisticated knowledge, on the one hand, and the potential for indigenous knowledge and capacity to be leached out of the region through network relations with resultant impacts on value capture trajectories, on the other. Finally, the *employment* effects of plugging in must be evaluated.[25] In some cases, the employment creation benefits of production for global markets will be large and demonstrable (although there may be questions about the quality of jobs created), while in others the displacement effects on local firms and intensification of production may offset such gains or even result in net job losses. Ultimately, the overall balance of each of these four dimensions is an empirical question that will depend on the regional economy in question, and the constituent global production networks and industries involved. Moreover, these balances should be seen in dynamic terms as they will fluctuate over time, and, *contra* to simplistic upgrading accounts, the outcomes in economic development terms may well not be positive on one or more dimensions.

While regional development clearly is a multi-dimensional process that can be profiled by a range of indicators, here our next step is to conceptualize the variety of ways in which regional economies couple with global production networks in overall cumulative terms. As noted above, in some regions there may be little coherence to the aggregation of firm–global production network intersections. In most cases, however, some level of coherence is apparent at the regional level. Put another way, there is often a dominant kind of strategic coupling that can be used to characterize regional development trajectories. Here we make a simple distinction between *modes* and *types* of strategic coupling.[26] In terms of modes, we distinguish between:

- indigenous couplings, which are inside–out in nature—in the sense that regional actors reach outside their home region to construct global production networks—and result in considerable autonomy and value capture;

- functional couplings, in which regional actors productively meet the wider needs of global production networks. These can be instigated in either an inside–out or an outside–in manner and offer the regional economy in question a certain degree of autonomy and value capture; and

- structural couplings, which are outside–in in nature—that is, external actors connect the region into global production networks—and are characterized by dependency.

Table 5.2 provides further elucidation of these threes modes of strategic coupling. It relates the modes to the global production network dynamics

Table 5.2. Three modes of strategic coupling with global production networks

	Indigenous coupling	Functional coupling	Structural coupling
Character of mode	Inside–out, autonomy and control	Either inside–out or outside–in, some degree of autonomy	Outside–in, dependency
Global production network dynamics			
• Organizational fix	Dynamic competition and new firm formation	Vertical specialization and the rise of partnership and alliances	International outsourcing and subcontracting
• Technological fix	New product and process technologies	Modularization and faster time to market	Enabling transport technologies
• Spatial fix	Public subsidies and institutional thickness	Cost-capability efficiency	Lower production costs
Coupling mechanisms			
• Industrial organization	Rise of national champions and new lead firms	Rise of strategic partners and global localization of TNCs	Export processing zones, weakly embedded TNC subsidiaries, and externally owned subcontractors
• States and institutions	Implicit and explicit role: strategic industrial policies	Explicit role and policy led: upgrading of labour, technology, and infrastructure	Explicit role but limited capacity through fiscal and financial incentives
• Transnational communities	Key nodes in transnational knowledge communities and high skill migrant flows	Transactional links, business intelligence, and market knowledge	Managerial competence and intermediaries

Source: adapted from Yeung (2009b: table 2). Copyright © Regional Studies Association, by permission of Taylor & Francis Ltd (<http://www.tandfonline.com>) on behalf of The Regional Studies Association.

discussed in Chapter 3, and also provides details of the coupling mechanisms involved. We identify three such mechanisms, encompassing industrial organization, states and institutions, and transnational communities.

Table 5.3, in turn, exemplifies eight real-world types of regional strategic coupling. The typology is derived by intersecting the three modes of coupling introduced above with an inductive understanding of the on-the-ground geographies of the global economy. It is intended to be comprehensive, but not exhaustive, and it seeks to maintain a productive balance between parsimony and complexity. Moving beyond the more limited typology developed in some macro-regional contexts (for example, industrialization in East Asian regions (see Yeung 2009a, 2010)) has several interrelated advantages. First, it allows us to cover more effectively the types of regional economies that global production networks emanate from as well as those in which they touch down. Second, it allows us to push beyond the simple and mistaken view that developing as a production base is the only way to connect into global production networks. Reflecting our dynamic drivers (Chapter 3), we can move beyond purely productionist logics to look at how market and financial imperatives may present opportunities for certain types of strategic coupling (for example, offshore jurisdictions and market regions). Third, and again chiming with a running theme of this book, it enables us to show how corporate actors hitherto rarely studied in the GVC/GPN literature may actually be at the heart of regional strategic couplings—for instance, in world cities (advanced business service firms) and logistics hubs (transport and logistics operators). Ultimately, constructing any such typology is necessarily an exercise in simplification. We feel, however, that it offers a useful window onto the full range of strategic couplings that can result between regional economies and global production networks, and provides strong coverage of the considerable regional variation that exists within the global economy.

Of course there is no one-to-one correspondence between coupling types and specific regional economies, although for some types—notably offshore jurisdictions and commodity source regions—a singular form of coupling will be the norm. Many regions, however, will experience more than one type of strategic coupling simultaneously. As Table 5.3 suggests, a city region such as Singapore may be thought of as connected to global production networks through the global cities, international partnership, offshore jurisdiction, and logistics hub types of strategic coupling. Except for the first coupling type, however, the rest all conform to the same mode of coupling—namely, functional—suggesting that Singapore has successfully found a range of niches within wider global production networks. Beyond the Singapore case, regions that engage with global production networks through more than one mode of strategic coupling are uncommon. Where examples can be found—such as the electronics industry of Hsinchu-Taipei, which encompasses both functional

Table 5.3. Key types of regional strategic coupling with global production networks

Type	Mode of coupling	Brief description	Regional examples	Relevant sectors	Likelihood of decoupling	Regional trajectories
Innovation hubs	Indigenous	Lead firm regions that initiate formation of, and subsequently drive, global production networks	Seoul Metropolitan Area, Silicon Valley, south-east England, Baden-Württemberg, Stockholm, Paris, Milan	Electronics, automobiles, fashion	Low	Distinctive regional assets and strong autonomy
Global cities	Indigenous	Command and control nodes bringing together HQs of lead firms and strategic partners with specialized service providers	London, New York, Tokyo, Frankfurt, Hong Kong, Shanghai etc.	Headquarters from all advanced business services	Very low	Highly distinctive regional assets and strong autonomy
International partnerships	Functional	Meeting strategic needs of global lead firms and their production networks through balanced partnership of regional and extra-regional actors	Singapore, Taipei-Hsinchu (Taiwan), Ireland, Rotterdam, South Africa	Electronics, petrochemicals, precious metals and gems	Medium	Distinctive regional assets and some regional autonomy
Offshore jurisdictions	Functional	Key nodes of the extraction and circulation of value within global production networks. Either small islands or embedded within larger jurisdictions	Offshore: Cayman Islands, British Virgin Islands, Bahamas; Offshore–onshore: Singapore, Netherlands, Hong Kong	All financial services	Medium	Distinctive regulatory systems and some regional autonomy
Logistics hubs	Functional	Usually airports/ports and their hinterlands. Import, export, or transhipment nodes (or combination thereof)	Singapore, Hong Kong, Shanghai, Dubai, Rotterdam, etc.	Transport and logistics	Medium	Distinctive locational assets and global interdependency

Market regions	Functional	Owing to either strong corporate and/or final customer base, a key region for sales and distribution for a range of global production networks	Growing middle-class city regions of Asia Pacific	All, tourism, retail, education, health	Medium	Generic regional assets and external dependency
Assembly platforms	Structural	Standardized assembly of offshored (and often outsourced) goods and services for export	Penang and Selangor (Malaysia), Greater Bangkok (Thailand), Yangtze and Pearl River Deltas, Bangalore, Manila, Mexican *maquiladoras*, Sofia (Bulgaria) and Bratislava (Slovakia)	Electronics, automobiles, apparel, toys, offshore services	High	Generic regional assets and external dependency
Commodity source regions	Structural	Sources of raw or processed inputs, usually for distant consumption	Russian gas fields, Western Australia, horticulture regions of Africa, Latin America	Mining, oil and gas, agriculture	High	Narrow regional assets and external dependency

and indigenous modes of coupling—they are usually indicative of the dynamic and evolutionary development trajectory of the region in question. In this example, Taiwanese electronics firms have progressed from being strategic partners in global production networks to emerging as innovators and lead firms in their own right.

Hence, as with firm-level value capture trajectories, different modes of strategic coupling are necessarily dynamic in nature. It is entirely possible for regions to progress from structural, through functional, to indigenous modes of coupling. Such trajectories of course will be path dependent, and will depend on the types of coupling in a particular region. Structural coupling based on commodity sourcing, for instance, will be harder to translate into functional coupling (for example, processing of commodities) than structural coupling based on the assembly platform type (for example, from low-cost OEM suppliers to OBM or partnership). Equally, these trajectories will also probably not be smooth journeys; in this regard we can use the same language of coupling, decoupling, and recoupling that we introduced at the firm level to apply to the regional scale.[27] As MacKinnon (2012: 242) argues, 'recoupling and decoupling as a result of regional selection and abandonment processes, respectively, can be seen as key mechanisms of uneven socio-economic development'. In other words, it is important to consider historical periods when links between global production networks and regional economies are broken and remade, and the actors and events shaping such transitions, as well as historical periods when such links are productive.[28] Decoupling and recoupling events may be initiated either by actors within the regional economy—corporate or state—or by global production network actors outside the region (for example, lead firms).[29] From a dynamic perspective, decoupling and subsequent recoupling may actually be beneficial in developmental terms: 'ultimately, if decoupling leads to the building up of firms that are domestically owned and controlled . . . greater value is likely to be captured within the territorial economy' (Horner 2014: 6). In Tables 5.2 and 5.3, the likelihood of decoupling is highest in the structural modes of strategic coupling as compared to functional and indigenous modes. But, of course, there is no guarantee that such decoupling can lead to successful recoupling in a 'better' mode of regional coupling.

Again reprising an argument from earlier in the chapter—that regional strategic coupling with global production networks has a strong and direct influence on regional development, we are not necessarily arguing that the influence is always positive. There may be negative consequences from strategic coupling, and there may also be conflicting logics between global production networks and regional economies. In either scenario it becomes clear that the dynamics of strategic coupling will shift towards decoupling, with the subsequent possibility of recoupling into different and perhaps more appropriate global production networks. In terms of the former, strategic coupling with global production networks may take place, even though it leads to negative consequences for regional economies. For instance, regional actors and institutions may engage with global production networks in order to legitimize their political and economic ambitions. Owing to regional resources dedicated to specific network actors, regional assets may become locked into the competitive imperatives of global lead firms.[30] Moreover, global production network actors may tap into regional dynamics to exploit cost advantages or cheap resources without holding any interest in the longer-term sustainability of the coupling and regional growth trajectory. These dark sides of strategic coupling are perhaps most apparent in the structural mode of coupling with global production networks. In emerging regions such as Penang and Selangor (Malaysia), Greater Bangkok (Thailand), Yangtze and Pearl River Deltas (China), Sofia (Bulgaria), and Bratislava (Slovakia), the lack of indigenous technological capabilities and lead firms has compelled these regions to take the low road to industrialization and strategic coupling. While their coupling as assembly platforms can be considered relatively successful, these regions exhibit a wide range of potential ruptures (for example, divestments, financial risks, and limited local linkages) and frictions (for example, external dependency, labour exploitation, and social and class conflicts).

There may also be downsides to functional modes of incorporation—for instance, when regional institutions devote excessive resources to develop territorialized capabilities among selected local firms so that they can serve as strategic partners of global lead firms. As these local firms emerge to become key partners in different global production networks, they are less likely to be bounded by regional interests and are more likely to be embedded in the competitive logics of these global production networks. The massive relocation of Taiwanese firms in the ICT industry to mainland China during the 2000s, for instance, has often been accused of resulting in the industrial hollowing-out of several ICT-dominant regions in Taiwan.[31] Even in the more developmental indigenous mode of incorporation, stresses and strains may be evident. In South Korea, for example, the enormous state-sanctioned benefits received by leading *chaebol* or conglomerates (for example, Samsung, LG, and Hyundai) and their spatially concentrated production networks within South Korea have created ruptures (for example, political exclusion) and frictions (for example, social and class conflicts) within the national economy. In industries such as automobiles and electronics, the highly spatially selective anchoring of global production networks by these leading *chaebol* in the Seoul Metropolitan Area (for example, Seoul, Incheon, and Gyeonggi) and southeast region (for example, Busan, Ulsan, and Gyeongnam) has been shown to exacerbate seriously pre-existing regional differences and socio-economic inequalities.[32] As these South Korean *chaebol* continue to reorganize and restructure their home region-embedded production networks, the dependency on local suppliers is likely to decrease over time.

While the above points to the possibility of the actually existing strategic coupling with negative consequences, a second scenario arises when major conflicts and struggles between global production network and regional logics emerge over time. In this evolutionary scenario, the strategic imperatives of actors in global production networks and regional economies may diverge as they face new challenges and/or gain new sources of strength and aspirations for future growth. In terms of challenges, existing global production network actors are likely to face significant technological, market, and cost pressures over time. New lead firms may develop in the same or emerging global industries. What used to work for these actors (for example, seeking cost efficiency) may no longer be effective in sustaining their competitiveness (for example, need for technological upgrading and innovation). As these actors look for new technology-based growth dynamics and restructure their operations, the prevailing mode of strategic coupling with regional economies (for example, structural) is likely to break down and disintegrate. On the other hand, regional actors and institutions may develop higher-order developmental goals and consciously seek to break away from the current mode of strategic coupling.[33] In the structural mode, for example, the competitive logics of global production network dynamics (for example, cost efficiency) may become highly incompatible with those of regional dynamics (for example, political pressure to eschew a race to the bottom approach). In China's high-growth coastal regions, regional governments have since the late 2000s adopted various policy instruments to accelerate the industrial restructuring of domestic firms, particularly large state-owned enterprises, and to reduce the technological and market dependency on foreign lead firms and their production networks.[34] What all these issues highlight is that strategic couplings are embedded within wider politics of growth and development in regions that go far beyond direct engagement with global production network actors. We now move on to consider different aspects of these tensions in more detail in the next section.

GLOBAL PRODUCTION NETWORKS AND CONTESTED REGIONAL AND NATIONAL DEVELOPMENT

In this final section we consider some of the wider influences that will also shape the character of regional economic growth (or decline) that results from strategic coupling with global production networks. While we will discuss these influences only briefly here, the purpose is to demonstrate that a theory of strategic coupling can never fully encompass the range of economic development impacts that are associated with such couplings. There are three aspects to this, which will be considered in turn in what follows. First, real-world regional economies are complex, multi-actor, and contested entities. Our GPN approach knowingly prioritizes corporate and institutional actors as key drivers of economic development processes, but others—notably labour and civil society organizations—are also an integral part of such dynamics. Second, aggregate development effects at the level of the regional economy may efface significant intra-regional variation in terms of who benefits from such growth, or who suffers most from decline. There will, therefore, be a wider politics, as noted in the previous section, concerning the general acceptability and sustainability of particular modes and types of strategic coupling. Third, that political context will not be constrained to the regional scale; rather, regions must be placed and understood within different national (and indeed macro-regional) political and regulatory contexts.

For the different regional actors who are directly enrolled into global production networks, the gains and losses of such enrolment will be unevenly distributed. While firm and state organizations are necessarily central to understanding strategic coupling and have been discussed above, we also pay attention to the role of *labour* in conditioning and experiencing such couplings. Although as Cumbers et al. (2008) tellingly point out, global production networks are as much systems of labour as they are systems of value creation and circulation, until recently labour was a chronically neglected dimension of these systems. Research on the labour dimension is now rapidly expanding, however. First, there is growing recognition of how the uneven availability of an 'appropriate' workforce—most notably in terms of the intersecting attributes of skills, productivity, cost, and controllability—across different regional economies is an important factor underpinning strategic coupling and subsequent processes of uncoupling and recoupling. Many accounts remain largely silent, however, on how the workforces that underpin global production network activities are produced and reproduced through the activities of a wide range of organizations, of which the key actors in much research, firms and states, are but two of several (also trade unions, households, etc.).[35] As Werner (2012: 407) observes, the upgrading discourse, 'centers industrial change on the relations of power and dynamics of competition among firms, rendering the social relations that mediate the production of exploitable workers and the conditions of their exploitation marginal to the analysis'.

Second, the multifarious impacts of global production network structures and strategies on different kinds of workers are increasingly being foregrounded.[36] One potentially fertile line of enquiry seeks to apply the language of upgrading (and downgrading) to the working conditions within global production networks. Social upgrading has two principle dimensions—namely, measurable standards (wages, benefits, etc.) and enabling rights (freedom of association, collective bargaining, etc.).[37] Initial investigations suggest that the relationships between social and economic upgrading are complex and far from uni-directional, however. In terms of the language of this chapter, there is no simple relationship between value capture trajectories and social upgrading outcomes at the firm level, and, in many cases, a growing degree of value capture may be underpinned by worsening terms and conditions for workers.[38] This connects to a third strand of research—namely, the extent to which workers are able to contest their relative position within global production networks through exercising agency. The agency potential of workers is highly uneven across global production networks, depending on whether they perform a strategic role, are effectively able to organize collectively, and are supported in their activities by local institutional and regulatory conditions.[39] While some workers will be able to make relative gains through coordinated action targeted at strategic weak points in global production networks (for example, logistics hubs), many others are weakly organized, possess eminently replaceable skills, and are not sufficiently protected by local legislation. Indeed, in some instances such differences may even be manifest within an individual firm.

It is important, then, that the economic impacts of different modes and types of strategic coupling are evaluated in terms of how the value captured from global production networks within a particular region is differentially distributed across the various actors involved. Some kinds of firms will benefit more than others, and the local state may make gains (for example, tax revenues) or losses (for example, through subsidies and institutional capture). Foregrounding labour, however, reminds us that even within firms the value captured will be unevenly shared out, and that positive value capture dynamics at the firm and regional level may or may not lead to improved terms and conditions for those that are labouring to produce that value. Importantly, the three aspects described above—labour availability, impacts, and agency—are all heavily shaped by local institutional and regulatory conditions, and so will vary considerably between regional economies: place matters, to a powerful degree, when it comes to labour.

The next step, after looking at the distribution of value capture across different global production network actors within a region, is to consider the extent to which the benefits of strategic coupling spill over to the region more generally—that is, to those who are not directly plugged in. Again, it is perfectly possible for a region to be on a positive value capture trajectory in aggregate terms, but for there to be no benefit for the majority of the population if, for instance, value is retained within a few highly profitable enterprises and among select groups of highly skilled professionals and the managerial class. This highlights the *distributional* element of regional development; development in a region may, or may not, lead to development of that region in collective terms. Adopting a wider perspective in this way has several implications. Conceptually, it demonstrates the need to grapple with how the economic development outcomes of strategic coupling interact with pre-existing socio-economic and political structures within regions. As Hadjimichalis and Hudson (2006: 869) point out, 'the major problem in dominant conceptions of networks in analyses of economic relations and governance of regional development is that power relations and power hierarchies existed long before these networks came into being. As a result, these networks are unavoidably enmeshed in relations of inequality'.[40] Strategic coupling with global production networks does not just happen at time zero; understanding wider regional development impacts will ultimately depend in part on how the coupling mode aligns with, or even challenges, existing social and political relations within the region.

Analytically, our analysis points to the conceptual necessity to move beyond firms, institutions, and indeed labour organizations to look at the wider distributional impacts of strategic couplings on individual and household livelihoods, for, as Kelly (2013: 83) argues, 'important elements of developmental change are often experienced at some degree of separation from direct connection with the global production network'.[41] This implies a more fine-grained analysis of impact that may consider, for instance, how, in certain places and contexts, employment in a global production network provides just one element of a household's income, or how wider labour markets are distorted by the demand for workers from strategically coupled firms. It also potentially shines light on the domain of social reproduction and the relations of class, gender, ethnicity, and so on that underpin that domain. For regional institutions shaping development policy, a wider perspective means balancing what Christopherson and Clark (2007: 148) call 'investment regionalism' (focused on overall economic growth and value added) with a more 'distributive regionalism' that includes the reduction of intra-regional inequality: 'the search for ways to connect investment regionalism, centered on regional innovation systems, with distributive regionalism, centered on equity, access, and quality of life is a search for a model of sustainable economic development'. The desire to pursue a more equitable mode of growth may, as we saw earlier, ultimately lead to institutional efforts to decouple from (and subsequently recouple to) global production networks.

Finally, it is important that the regional economy is placed within its national and macro-regional context. The importance of this step has already been made explicit in the original conceptualization of strategic coupling (see Figure 1.2) and the notion of the multi-scalar institutional mediation between global production networks and regional assets. In short, the institutional policies and practices that impinge on strategic coupling will not all emanate from within the region; some will reflect national policies and priorities, and some may in turn reflect the wider macro-regional regulatory landscape in which the national economy is embedded. In theoretical terms, it is important that the national state is not relegated to a mere backdrop.[42] Smith (2014: 22) forcefully argues for an understanding of 'states at different spatial scales as agents in the regulation of accumulation strategies and forms of integration into the world market' and 'the state as constituted at different geographical scales and as an institutional and relational actor in the governance of global production arrangements'. One productive way forward is to think of the state as a multi-scalar intermediary that profoundly affects regional-level development outcomes.[43]

More specifically, the importance of the state is evident in several ways. Most basically, many of the policy levers that will affect regional strategic coupling are still pulled at the national level—for instance, in the domains of fiscal policy, education, infrastructure, science and technology policy, engagement with macro-regional trade agreements, and bargaining with inward investors.[44] The nature of the state will, in turn, affect how, and to what extent, these policies impinge on specific regional economies. The political–ideological orientation of the state (for example, neoliberal versus corporatist) will set an important context for the regional debates about the desirability of modes of strategic coupling discussed above, while its internal structure (for example, federal versus centralist) will be significant in terms of the precise level of intervention in regional affairs. The territorial configuration of states will also be influential; in some cases, the regional scale equates to that of the national economy (for example, Singapore, Monaco, British Virgin Islands), in some the national economy is dominated by a primate, dynamic region (for example, Thailand, Ireland), and in others there is a more complex mosaic of dynamic and laggard regions (for example, China, Germany, the United States). The intersection of these three attributes will influence the extent to which states seek to influence the nature of strategic coupling in and across their constituent regions. Potential interventions can take many forms—for instance, regional development policies that try and even out economic activity across the national territory, policies that redistribute the gains of global production network engagement across regions, the imposition of social policies to mitigate intra-regional disparities in wealth, and interventions that seek to manage the potential 'over-heating' effects of strategic coupling (for example, in housing and labour markets).

In sum, this short section has sought to broaden out our analysis to suggest that the economic development outcomes of strategic coupling are always conditioned by the territorial political–economic contexts in which they are embedded (see Figure 5.2). Centrally, this involves looking at the distributional outcomes in terms of (1) all regional actors in the global production network, and in particular labour; (2) other actors and groups within the region but not directly enrolled into global production networks; and (3) the national politics of economic development and the extent to which they lead to inter-regional transfers of wealth. More broadly, the discussion has served as a salient reminder that, despite our primary focus on regional economic development, the national state remains a critically important actor shaping regional-level outcomes.

CONCLUSION

This chapter has completed the analytical arc of the book. While previous chapters have conceptualized the organizational elements and structures of global production networks, identified the dynamic drivers underlying their formation and evolution, and connected those drivers to the various strategies that constituent firms may pursue, here the focus has been on the *developmental implications* for the places that are enrolled into these networks. As noted at the outset of the chapter, it is vital that an integrated GPN approach responds to the challenge of offering more explanatory purchase with respect to patterns and processes of territorial economic development. Conceptually, this requires us to integrate what we have termed the vertical dimensions of global production networks—the primary focus of our analysis in preceding chapters—with the horizontal dimension—namely, the on-the-ground places and territories that constitute the interconnected global economy.

We opened by placing some necessary analytical limits around the notion of development as we mobilize it here. To reiterate, our argument is not that GPN theory can explain all patterns and processes of human development in the broadest sense. Rather, we propose that it can go a significant way towards explaining patterns of *economic* growth and decline within the contemporary global economy. Importantly, we have also argued that the appropriate scale for understanding how global production networks shape economic development dynamics is that of the sub-national region, which is seen as the key functional unit within the global economy.

We have developed two important concepts as a means of connecting causal global production network dynamics and strategies to territorial outcomes. First, in seeking to move beyond some of the limitations of the prevailing upgrading debate, we have conceptualized the myriad *value capture trajectories* that can result when a firm in a particular locality connects into a global production network. The concept frames the multiple possible outcomes—both positive and negative—in dynamic and evolutionary terms, and reflects the multiple roles that a single firm may perform in a wider network. Regional economic development is then thought of as powerfully shaped by the aggregation of these firm-level value capture trajectories. Second, we have further developed the dynamic notion of *strategic coupling* to conceptualize the different modes and types of coupling that characterize the global economy. These modes and types reflect how certain kinds of value capture trajectories and couplings often come to dominate at the regional level. While individual regions may exhibit more than one type of coupling, straddling different modes is much less common. These different modes, in turn, underpin economic development owing to their variable potential for value capture, their different configurations of control and dependency, and their different susceptibilities to decoupling. Importantly, strategic coupling is always framed in dynamic terms (that is, decoupling and recoupling) and as driving both positive and negative economic developmental outcomes.

Finally, the chapter has moved beyond the global production network–territory interface itself to highlight some of the wider political contexts and conflicts that will ultimately shape whether the economic development outcomes of global production network engagement will be socially and politically acceptable within different territories. In the next, concluding, chapter, we step back to consider the wider implications of our analysis in terms of both scholarly value and praxis. We attempt to 'reconnect' to the main social science literatures on the remaking of the global economy in order to highlight the distinctive attributes and contributions of GPN 2.0, before offering some reflections on how it might be productively applied in the interconnected domains of research and policy.

NOTES

1. Moreover, we do not focus here on non-capitalist, or more-than-capitalist modes of economic activity. For more on the possibilities and perils of such modes, see the trio of books by Gibson-Graham (1996, 2006; Gibson-Graham et al. 2013).
2. David Harvey (2003) and Neil Smith (2005) offer *tour de force* accounts of the wider geopolitical context to economic globalization.
3. This a large and sprawling multidisciplinary literature that has mobilized a wide range of terminology to capture the continued or even enhanced salience of agglomeration economies under conditions of economic globalization, including, among others: new industrial spaces, industrial districts, local agglomerations, city regions, regional motors, learning regions, regional innovation systems, and clusters. For some key contributions to these 'new regionalism' debates, see Scott (1988, 1998, 2012), Storper (1997, 2013), Morgan (1997), Amin (1999), and MacLeod (2001). Overall, the metaphor of regional nodes in global networks (cf. Amin and Thrift 1992) provides perhaps the best shorthand description of the contemporary geographies of production, while Veltz's notion (1996) of the archipelago economy also resonates.
4. This focus on the extra-regional relationships underpinning regional development taps into a strand of literature that dates back to the pioneering work of Dicken (1976) and Massey (1979, 1984). For more recent contributions, see Amin (1999), Phelps and Fuller (2000), Coe et al. (2004), and Yeung (2009b, 2015a).
5. For other studies that assert the need to combine both network and territorial perspectives on regions, and regional development, see Yeung (2005a), Hudson (2007), Pike et al. (2007), Kelly (2013), and Pickles and Smith (2015).
6. See Martin (2010) for an excellent exegesis on notions of path dependence in local and regional economic development.

7. For contemporary examples of such reworking of commodity chain thinking and world-system theory, see Bair's special issue (2014) in the *Journal of World-Systems Research*.

8. This is not to deny persistent and broad patterns of uneven development at the global scale. As Brewer (2011: 309, emphasis in original) argues, 'findings from the most relevant measures of world income inequality support the basic world-systems hypothesis that the *structure* of income distribution across the capitalist world-economy remains quite stable over time—even if the positions of individual nations within that hierarchy (can) shift over time'. Rather it is to say that at the regional level, our primary focus here, the ever-changing mosaic of economic growth and decline increasingly defies such broad categorizations.

9. Singapore, for instance, offers a prime example of a model of development predicated on leveraging the inward investments of foreign lead firms. This model has propelled the city state into the ranks of the richest countries in the world. Other well-known examples of FDI-led economic development are China, Ireland, and Mexico.

10. We focus here on regions that have been plugged into global production networks at some point in time, usually for a significant period and with some clear developmental outcomes. Regions that to this point have not yet been connected to global production networks necessarily fall outside the scope of our analysis, although the reasons for non-engagement themselves may be analytically interesting and practically significant.

11. See Coe and Hess (2011) and Yeung (2015a) for more on these potential ruptures and frictions. The work of the anthropologist Anna Tsing (2004) productively develops the metaphor of 'friction' for considering the tensions that inevitably surround the forging of global connections. Pickles and Smith's work (2015) on different regions in Central and Eastern Europe offers in-depth empirical materials on the contingent and variegated effects of such connections to global production networks in the apparel industry.

12. Several references on this topic were provided in Chapter 1. See Kaplinsky (2005: ch. 4) for a particularly clear and concise account of these upgrading processes.

13. See Bazan and Navas-Alemán (2004), Schrank (2004), Gibbon and Ponte (2005), Pickles et al. (2006), Ponte and Ewert (2009), Navas-Alemán (2010), Brewer (2011), Pipkin (2011), Werner (2012), Havice and Campling (2013), Tokatli (2013), and Smith et al. (2014) for key contributions to this critical deconstruction of the notion of economic upgrading.

14. A good example of this silence of the upgrading literature on global lead firms is the changing fortune of lead firms in the global mobile devices industry. The rise of Apple and Samsung and the fall of Nokia and Motorola, as such global lead firms, are instructive examples of how their differential organization of global production networks impact not only directly on their strategic partners and suppliers, but also recursively on their own strategic future in the same industry.

15. See Schrank (2004), Werner (2012), and Horner (2014) for more on this aspect.

16. See Bazan and Navas-Alemán (2004), Pickles et al. (2006), Navas-Alemán (2010), Pipkin (2011), Havice and Campling (2013), and Pickles and Smith (2015) for empirical studies that elucidate this dimension.

17. Importantly, these value capture trajectories can be different from firm growth or decline *per se*. For instance, a firm may be growing in aggregate employment or revenue terms, but may still be experiencing a declining share of value capture from the global production network in which it is enrolled (e.g. if under pressure from a major buyer to reduce unit costs).

18. While firms may sometimes knowingly pursue a strategy of downgrading, as argued by Ponte and Ewert (2009), seeking the highest level of value capture through coupling with global production networks is a common goal across most capitalist enterprises.

19. Upgrading studies in the GVC genre tend to use static categories of governance types (modular, relational, or captive) to describe dynamic value capture trajectories under the guise of upgrading prospects. This, in turn, has lead to numerous descriptive empirical studies of governance types in different industries and localities and their corresponding or consequential upgrading prospects (or the lack of such prospects).

20. One of the more effective attempts to profile value capture dynamics along different types of global value chain is offered by Milberg and Winkler (2013: figure 4.5), who contrast 'vertical competition', 'pressure on subcontractor', 'strong first-tier supplier', and 'strong middleman' scenarios. The assumed linearity of the production process, however, ultimately limits the usefulness of this schematic approach.

21. For similar arguments, see Schrank (2004), Bair (2005), and Tokatli (2013).

22. As noted in Chapter 2, localized clusters of economic activity are often an on-the-ground manifestation of the strategic coupling of global production networks with regional economies. Here our work connects with the huge body of research on economic clustering, although our strongly held belief is that much of this work is limited by its preoccupation with the importance of local connections, often without empirical demonstration of that importance. For some of the most nuanced economic geographical research on clusters, see Bathelt and Glückler (2011) and Storper (2013). For sympathetic yet trenchant critiques of the clustering literature, see Martin and Sunley (2003) and Taylor (2010).

23. For a more thorough discussion and evaluation of these four dimensions, see Dicken (2011: ch. 14).

24. In a thought provoking piece, Seabrooke and Wigan (2014: 257) argue that wealth chains are a little studied corollary of global production networks: 'wealth chains are the yin to the yang of value chains. While actors in value chains share an interest in transparency and coordination, those in wealth chains thrive on rendering movements through the chain opaque. Wealth chains hide, obscure and relocate wealth to the extent that they break loose from the location of value creation and heighten inequality'.

25. We consider this aspect through the lens of social upgrading in the section on 'Global Production Networks and Contested Regional and National Development'.

26. MacKinnon (2012), in his important and constructive critique of our earlier theorization of regional strategic coupling (i.e. Coe et al. 2004; Yeung 2009b), posits the distinction between organic, strategic, and structural 'types' (his terminology) of coupling. The first evokes the co-evolution of regional assets and lead firms in global

production networks, the second a conscious selection and partnership between regional and global production network actors, and the last a simple engagement of regions to meet the wider needs of global production networks. We chose to retain, however, the conception that *all* forms of coupling are inherently strategic, and reflect the conscious and intentional interactions of regional and extra-regional actors, albeit often within a context of uneven power relations (cf. Figure 1.2).

27. In so doing, there are clear echoes to work done on economic restructuring and uneven regional development in economic geography during the 1980s, mainly at the intra-national scale, perhaps best typified by Doreen Massey's magisterial *Spatial Divisions of Labour* (1984) and Michael Storper and Richard Walker's *The Capitalist Imperative* (1989).

28. There may be inter-regional shifts associated with such processes of decoupling and recoupling. See Yang (2013, 2014), for instance, on how Hong Kong and Taiwanese firms in China have sought to decouple from coastal provinces and recouple with inland provinces at the same time as they have sought to reorient from export production to production for China's domestic market. Pickles and Smith (2015) also offer detailed examples of dynamic regional transformations in Central and Eastern Europe.

29. For example, in an illustrative study of India's pharmaceutical industry, Horner (2014) contrasts 'structural' decoupling as a result of shifting global market conditions with 'strategic' decoupling, intentionally managed by domestic state and corporate actors as part of a project to develop indigenous capacity. This distinction is important, but again to us both modes are strategic—the key question is which actors are initiating the decoupling.

30. This phenomenon is known more widely as institutional capture, and reflects the active use of extra-firm strategies by corporate actors. It refers to asymmetrical engagements between local institutions and external firms leading to the direct and indirect subsidization of the activities of inward investors through economic development strategies that prioritize the needs of such firms at the expense of indigenous firms (Phelps 2000). Christopherson and Clark (2007), for instance, argue that the reality of power relations between external investors and regional institutions is that the former are able to co-opt regional growth agendas in their favour, especially in terms of influencing regulatory policy, driving the research agendas of publicly supported research centres, and dominating the regional labour market.

31. For more, see Yang (2009), Yang et al. (2009), and Hsu (2011).

32. For more on the South Korean electronics case, see Park and Koo (2010) and Lee et al. (2014).

33. This is an important reminder of the central role of 'regional' institutions in seeking to mediate and manage strategic coupling mechanisms (see Figure 1.2 and related discussion in Chapter 1). To recap, regional is placed in quotation marks to indicate that, in addition to local institutions, national and even macro-regional institutions may have an influence on regional level strategic coupling. See Dawley (2014: 93) for more on 'the apparent neglect of the multiple roles of the state, quasi-state, and local and regional policy interventions in mediating the creation and unfolding development of paths'.

34. For more, see Zhou et al. (2011), Wei et al. (2012), Sun et al. (2013), and Yang (2014).
35. The role of migration processes in underpinning such labour needs is also underplayed. See Zhu and Pickles (2014) for a study on the role of migrant labour in China's garment industry, and Azmeh's research (2014a) on the same industry in Egypt and Jordan.
36. See Posthuma and Nathan (2011) for an indicative cross section of such work. On the heavy gendering of such processes, see Barrientos (2014).
37. Important early contributions to this literature are Barrientos et al. (2011) and Milberg and Winkler (2011).
38. See Brewer (2011), Pipkin (2011), Rossi et al. (2014), and Smith et al. (2014) for more on this argument.
39. For key contributions to this strand, see Coe and Jordhus-Lier (2011), Riisgaard and Hammer (2011), Rainnie et al. (2011), and Selwyn (2012).
40. Brewer (2011: 319) similarly argues, with specific reference to GCC analysis, that it 'need not remain silent on the issue, for the commodity chain construct is well suited to highlight the interface between the global division of labor and local conditions, social structures and inequalities. As such, it is not difficult to envision how commodity chain analysis could be used to demonstrate why and how firm-level growth has, and has not, improved welfare or well-being in different places, at different times'.
41. Challies (2008) and Hess (2009) expand on the livelihoods dimension. See Goto and Endo (2014) for an empirical study of such livelihood strategies in Thailand's garment industry.
42. Ravenhill (2014) offers a sage reminder of these fundamental aspects of the state's role in driving economic development. See also Hough (2011).
43. We take this notion from Lee et al. (2014), who develop the idea in the context of the South Korean economy.
44. One of the major problems facing many regions, for instance, is the fact that their revenue-raising powers via taxation and their abilities to spend are commonly circumscribed by the policy frameworks of the national state of which they are part. We thank Peter Dicken for this important point.

6

Praxis

This book opened with the premiss that global production has become much more organizationally fragmented and spatially dispersed since the early 1990s. These fragmented and dispersed production systems, in turn, are increasingly controlled and coordinated via an organizational-cum-spatial 'fix' known as the global value chain (GVC) or global production network (GPN). In its *World Investment Report 2013*, for instance, UNCTAD (2013b) estimated that some 80 per cent of international trade was now organized through global value chains/production networks coordinated by lead firms investing in cross-border productive assets and trading inputs and outputs with partners, suppliers, and customers worldwide. Empirically, it seems, there remains little doubt that global value chains or global production networks are the most critical organizational platforms through which production in primary, manufacturing, and service sectors is coordinated and organized on a global basis. Equally, there is no doubt that these chains and networks are now firmly on the agenda of all the leading international organizations involved in the governance of the global economy, in terms of both their policy prognoses and their ongoing data collection efforts.

In theoretical terms, however, significant questions and challenges remain. Arguably, many commentators in the social sciences, including economic geographers, have thus far remained unable to provide a comprehensive and dynamic explanation of *why* these global production structures have emerged and *how* they are actually organized. Since its inception in the early 1990s, GVC/GPN research has gathered significant momentum and achieved wide circulation and analytical adoption. As we saw in Chapter 1, the two strands of research are closely related and connect across the cognate social science fields of economic geography, economic sociology, development studies, regional studies, international political economy, international economics, and international business. These parallel strands of an increasingly vast literature, however, have arguably provided only limited theoretical development beyond the analysis of value chain governance structures, relational network configurations, and industrial upgrading and the strategic coupling of clusters and regions. This book, then, represents an effort in *theory development* that has sought to provide an overarching apparatus for explaining why and how, and with what implications, global production networks—our preferred terminology—have risen to such prominence within the global economy. To be clear, our aim has explicitly not been to provide an empirical mapping of global production networks, sector by sector, and region by region; as noted at the outset, our use of empirical materials in the preceding chapters has been selective and illustrative only, with an emphasis on demonstrating industry, sectoral, firm, and geographical variability. Rather, it is our hope that the theoretical tools offered in these pages serve to stimulate further rounds of GPN research that can 'stress test' those tools in different industrial and geographical contexts.[1]

In developing a more dynamic theory of global production networks, the book has identified three critical competitive dynamics and their risk environments, and connected their structural properties with actor-specific strategies to arrive at the causal mechanisms of global production network formation and operation. Moving beyond the conventional wisdom of the existing GVC framework, and building upon the conceptual groundwork provided by the GPN 1.0 approach, our conceptualization of global production networks has then explained why and how firms adopt diverse strategies to cope with different sets of competitive dynamics and risk environments. By mapping these structural dynamics and risks onto four actor-level strategic choices—namely, intra-firm coordination, inter-firm control, inter-firm partnership, and extra-firm bargaining—we have demonstrated that there are multiple strategic choices and network configurations within and across global industries. A dynamic GPN analysis not only accounts for the origins of these networks, but also specifies their changing configurations over time. In short, competitive dynamics are the independent variables driving firm strategies, as dependent variables, which in turn lead to different network configurations and organizational outcomes. As these competitive dynamics are themselves geographically variegated within and across different global industries—a historical consequence of capitalist restructuring and global transformations—their causal outcomes on actor strategies and network organization are geographically specific.

Coded GPN 2.0, this approach therefore allows for an actor-centred conceptualization of the causal mechanisms shaping the differentiated organization of global production networks in diverse industries and territories. Its theoretical foundations extend beyond both the industry approach commonly found in the existing frameworks of value chain governance and the micro-level analysis of actor practices found in many studies of industrial upgrading and local development. In turn, understanding these variegated strategies allows us to diagnose the various value capture trajectories experienced by different firms within global production networks. We can then 'pivot' the analysis to think about the territorial development outcomes for regional economies that have strategically coupled with global production networks. This requires a nuanced understanding of the inherent territoriality of all global production network activities, and of how that territoriality shapes and reshapes those activities—for instance, through place-specific institutional and regulatory structures. Regional economies are territorial formations that are driven by the aggregation of the value capture trajectories of the myriad firms located within their boundaries. In most cases, dominant modes and types of strategic coupling emerge over time that can then be evaluated in terms of their potential for value capture, stability, and degree of external dependency or control. Integrated in this way, GPN theory can ultimately provide a powerful framework for explaining patterns of uneven development—both between and within countries—in the contemporary global economy. It also provides, we hope, an effective response to Sunley's challenge (2008: 20) that network thinking in economic geography should 'develop theory that is more problem driven and focused on identifying causal economic mechanisms and processes'.

In this final chapter we explore the wider implications of our analysis in two registers. First, we profile the benefits of our approach in relation to other prevailing theories and models of global production. More specifically, we seek to demonstrate the value added of our integrated GPN theory with respect to three fields of work; GVC research in economic sociology and industry/development studies, comparative institutionalism research in political science and cognate social science disciplines, and international economics research on the outsourcing and offshoring of production.[2] A common refrain is that by foregrounding the strategic actions of economic actors and the impulses that drive them, we are able to develop a nuanced and dynamic conceptualization of global production networks that can capture the huge degree of sectoral and geographical variability within the global economy. We eschew simplistic accounts that generalize across actors, industries, and territories, assuming standardized motivations and strategic responses. From our perspective, embracing variability in theoretical terms is a necessary precursor to understanding effectively the development outcomes that result from strategic coupling with global production networks.

Second, we explore the policy implications that stem from our mode of analysis. We firmly believe in making our framework useful to the policy and stakeholder communities so that they can navigate better the complex politics and practice of capturing the gains of economic development in an interconnected world economy organized through the extensive presence of global production networks. In keeping with our line of argument in this book, our focus is mainly on the *regional* economic development challenges and possibilities that are posed by dynamic processes of strategic coupling. Crucially, we argue that the move from a world primarily shaped by the direct investment decisions of transnational corporations (TNCs) to a world dominated by global production networks (though clearly the two are linked) has important policy implications that are only just starting to be thought through by academics and practitioners alike.

CAPTURING THE VALUE OF GPN 2.0

Before engaging in a dialogue with research in comparative institutionalism and international economics, we first consider the implications of our analysis for GVC research. We do so relatively briefly, for, as noted above and in Chapter 1, it is closely related to research in the GPN 1.0 tradition, and there has been an ongoing engagement with the key precepts of GVC work in the previous chapters. Accordingly, here we will simply reprise four key ways in which GPN 2.0 has sought to extend current conceptualization in GVC research.

First, GPN 2.0 has enhanced the explanatory capacity of the theory beyond that currently offered in GVC research. Our conceptualization of the causal role of cost–capability ratios, markets, and finance as key competitive dynamics within the broader risk environment foregrounds dynamic variables that are largely overlooked or at best underdeveloped in the existing GVC framework, which has focused primarily on industry-specific variables such as the complexity and codifiability of inter-firm transactions and knowledge capabilities within the supply base.[3] Second, GPN theory has moved beyond the narrow focus on already existing inter-firm governance structures in the GVC typology. By analyzing the competitive dynamics and risk environments of global production networks and by mapping actor-specific strategies onto these structural imperatives, we offer a coherent conceptualization of causal mechanisms—that is, structural dynamics as causality and firm-specific strategies as mechanisms—that extends beyond the existing GVC typology of industrial governance as inter-firm organizational outcomes. The explanatory power of the two leading and interrelated conceptual frameworks in GVC research—Gereffi's pioneering distinction (1994) between producer-driven and buyer-driven commodity chains and Gereffi et al.'s fivefold inter-firm governance typology (2005)—has been somewhat limited by their dyadic and static conception of industrial governance, their relative neglect of territorial organization, and their inability to interpret competitive dynamics and evolutionary processes in multi-commodity or multi-industry production networks.

Third, GPN 2.0 has redeveloped and refined its conceptual tools, comprising value capture trajectories and modes of strategic coupling, for understanding developmental outcomes in a world of global production networks. As was outlined in some detail in Chapter 5, the crucial GVC concept of industrial upgrading is far from adequate for empirical analysis, and is increasingly being subject to stern critique from both within the GVC community and beyond. In short, it is overly deterministic, simplifies what in reality are complex trajectories of change, effaces the *social* foundations and implications of industrial change, and often confuses the means and ends of firm strategies. It is also ill placed to consider firms that fulfil multiple roles in different global production networks, and shows analytical slippage across firms, industries, and regional/ national economies in terms of what is actually being seen to upgrade. Instead, we have proposed the notion of firm-level value capture trajectories as a way of (re)framing the multiple and dynamic outcomes of firm enrolment in global production networks. This then allows us to 'aggregate up' to profile regional development outcomes by evaluating the organizational ecology of particular territories.

Finally, it is important to note that GPN 2.0 has consciously incorporated geographical variation and multi-scalar institutional contexts into its epistemology. This is not to embrace complexity for complexity's sake, but rather to argue that place-to-place variation *matters* for the nature and operation of the global production networks that interconnect those places. In contrast, in their desire for a parsimonious GVC theory that is 'useful to policymakers', Gereffi et al. (2005: 82, emphasis added) prefer to 'to create the *simplest* framework that generates results relevant to real-world outcomes'. In doing so, they knowingly underplay how 'history, institutions, geographic and social contexts, the evolving rules of the game, and path dependence matter; and many factors will influence how firms and groups of firms are linked in the global economy'.[4] This is a fundamental difference in approach to theory. While this parsimony undoubtedly underpins the uptake of GVC by a wide range of international organizations as highlighted earlier, it runs the risk of creating a blinkered vision of a global economy in which history and geography do not seem to matter and industry value chains operate freely alongside pre-existing socio-economic inequalities. This simplicity both reduces the effectiveness of GVC theory in conceptual terms, and may lead to impoverished policy recommendations if applied uncritically.

Political Economy and Comparative Institutionalism

We introduced the varieties of capitalism (VoC) literature in Chapter 1 as a formative influence on the development of GPN 1.0 theory through its emphasis on the spatial variation in capitalist institutional conditions and the ensuing impacts upon economic actors both emanating from, and investing into, different territories. Here, we revisit this literature from the perspective of GPN 2.0. At the outset, it is worth highlighting that what is often termed the VoC literature for short—and associated with the seminal work of political scientists Hall and Soskice (2001)—is in reality a large and multi-stranded field of work anchored in comparative politics and international political economy, but also incorporating areas of economic sociology, management studies, and, to a lesser extent, economic geography.[5] The various approaches all share a similar grounding in political economy and perhaps more correctly define a field of *comparative institutionalism*. They have in common a concern with how firm behaviour is deeply shaped by national political–economic institutions that serve as self-reinforcing, coordinating systems, encompassing business and labour associations, training regimes, corporate governance, employment relations, and financial systems. Different configurations of these institutions are used to derive different types—or varieties—of national capitalisms, with Hall and Soskice's distinction (2001) between liberal market economies (LMEs; usually exemplified by the United States and the United Kingdom) and coordinated market economies (CMEs; often exemplified by Germany or Japan) often being taken as the archetype of this work.[6] Firms in CMEs are purported to take a long-term view of economic change and develop cooperative relationships with other firms; in LMEs, by contrast, firms supposedly experience low levels of inter-firm trust that reduce incentives for long-term collaboration with other firms.

This work in the field of comparative institutionalism has been vitally important in challenging the homogenizing logics inherent in many globalization discourses. However, since 2000 it has been subject to a broad range of both internal and external critiques. These generally concern some or all of the following: the need to move beyond the binary typology (LME/SME) and/or narrow types that prevail in many versions of the literature; how best to theorize processes of institutional change involving both internal and external actors organized at different spatial scales; conceptualizing systemic trends in more nuanced ways beyond simple processes of divergence or convergence; and recognizing and theorizing the potential for sectoral and sub-national variations within national varieties. It is too easy to critique a straw-person version of what is in reality a highly dynamic and polycentric body of work, and scholars working within comparative institutionalism have sought directly to address these conceptual challenges.[7] At the same time, there is clearly a need for moving further towards the study of what Peck and Theodore (2007) term the 'qualitative variegation' in national modes of capitalism. This would involve 'emphasis on decisive moments of economic transformation and institutional restructuring; real time analysis of regulatory projects and experiments in the organization of production; [and] multi-scalarity' (Peck and Theodore 2007: 763). Here we suggest that GPN 2.0, as presented in this book, can contribute to such a project and help overcome some of the persistent limitations of comparative institutionalist approaches. To be clear, we are not presenting this as an either/or choice—the literatures are, and will continue to be, complementary—but rather assert that a focus on strategic actors embedded in multi-scalar transnational networks must be central to any explanatory theory of the contemporary global economy.

The first observation to make in this regard is that the advent of *global* production networks poses a challenge to the fundamental tenet of comparative institutionalism—namely, that firm actions conform to the broader *national* institutional context in which they are embedded. The development of organizationally fragmented and spatially dispersed global production networks complicates the idea that lead firms (and indeed any other type of firm) will act in a way that reflects deterministically their home institutional environment. As Lane and Probert (2009: 17) describe, global production networks constitute 'a more far-reaching externalization of activities than occurs in [TNCs], involving the surrendering of ownership rights and the transfer of complete segments/functions in the value chain to third-party contractors. Hence important coordination problems, particularly around labour . . . no longer arise and important domestic institutional domains, for these firms, become redundant'. As we have discussed in Chapter 3, for instance, lead firms that have aggressively outsourced and offshored non-core activities may largely be shaped by financial institutions in their home economy. In comparison to TNC-driven modes of growth, Lane and Probert (2009: 17) continue: 'global production networks therefore constitute a more radical process of dis-embedding from the home nation, with a potentially more destructive impact on institutional coherence. This insight has hardly been considered in the comparative capitalisms literature'.[8] This is not to say that lead firms will not bear the traits of their home economy, and that in turn there will be no imprint on how they control and coordinate their global production networks, but rather that the lines of influence may be more partial, more complex, and less coherent than the comparative institutionalism literature tends to suggest.

The focus on strategic actors in GPN 2.0 thus offers a way of breaking out of what Crouch and Farrell (2004: 8) term the 'new determinism' in comparative institutionalism—namely, the 'recent tendency in the social sciences, and in political economy in particular, to emphasize how institutional systems tend to crystallize around coherent logics of ordering'. They diagnose that in many VoC-style accounts, firm behaviour outside these coherent logics is deemed to be 'untheorized empirical "noise" which needs to be disregarded in the interests of an elegant and sharply profiled account'. By placing strategic firm actors squarely in the centre of our analysis, GPN 2.0 avoids reading off actions from the broader institutional context. The national institutional context is considered to be an important but not determining influence on firm action, and the exact strength and nature of that influence are ultimately an empirical question. In many cases, global production network structures and the mode of firm incorporation will be an even more important determinant, overcoming aspects of the home institutional environment. Enrolled firms may experience a relative dis-embedding from their home context and a re-embedding in the transnational relational and governance structures of global production networks.[9] This accords with institutionalist accounts that couch industrial change as a 'bottom-up, socially reflexive process of creative action' and moreover a recompositional process in which 'creative actors rearrange, modify, reconceive, and reposition inherited organizational forms and governance mechanisms as they experiment with solutions to the challenges that they face' (Herrigel 2010: 2). By focusing on firms of different types, and the key organizational structure through which they are interconnected (that is, global production networks), GPN theory offers a powerful means of disentangling the various influences shaping the actions of situated economic actors.

GPN 2.0 also tackles another key limitation of comparative institutionalist accounts diagnosed by Lane and Probert (2009: 17), which is that the 'global influences' deemed to be driving institutional change in particular national contexts are 'conceptually under-specified'. It demonstrates how the actions of firms in particular territories are determined by relationships with global production network actors in other national economies, be they customers, partners, or suppliers. This in turn points to the need for a multi-scalar approach that moves beyond the straitjacket of *methodological nationalism* that still constrains most VoC-style accounts.[10] The spatial imaginary in such work consists of relatively contained national systems whose integrity is increasingly being challenged by transnational influences, usually of a neoliberal nature. In addition to fleshing out the actors underlying these transnational influences, adopting the vertical–organizational and horizontal–territorial dimensions in GPN 2.0 allows for more nuanced readings of the multi-scalarity of global production and institutional change. The vertical dimension (see Figure 2.4) serves to reveal that, beyond simple national–global dichotomies (often foregrounded in GVC studies), the actors enrolled into global production networks will have a wide range of spatial remits ranging from the local, through the regional and national, to the macro-regional and global scales. As we saw in Chapter 5, for instance, sub-national regional institutions play a critical role in processes of strategic coupling, and the actions of those institutions do not simply reflect the wider national context. Instead there will be 'creative incoherences' between institutions organized at different spatial scales (Crouch et al. 2009). In terms of the horizontal dimension, the territorial manifestations of strategic coupling are also many and varied, ranging from, say, a single export processing zone to complex polycentric city regions. GPN theory thus allows for a more sophisticated appreciation of the territoriality of economic systems, in terms of both the networks of actors involved, and the territorial outcomes of their interactions.

Those outcomes will not simply reflect the national origins of the actors involved, or the characteristics of the global production networks in which they operate, but rather a complex and contingent interplay between the two. New, hybrid forms of capitalism will be produced, on an ongoing basis, which reflect this interplay.[11] To reprise the language of Peck and Theodore (2007), the outcomes will be highly *variegated*, both spatially and sectorally. The interaction of actors from different territories through global production networks will both be influenced by, and influence, dynamics of ongoing institutional change within those territories, at both regional and national scales. In short, comparative institutionalism is an important literature that has lots to offer to GPN and GVC analyses. But without incorporating the crucial insights of an enhanced GPN conceptualization, it will continue to struggle to explain effectively on-the-ground processes of economic change, particularly ones that are global in nature.

The Economics of International Outsourcing

In addition to the literature in comparative political economy, GPN 2.0 also seeks to add value to another important strand of social science literature that examines the economics of international sourcing and 'trading tasks'. In this literature, rooted primarily in international economics, the explanatory emphasis is generally placed on decreasing communications and transport costs and trade-related transaction costs that in turn facilitate the trading of tasks across borders through international production fragmentation and outsourcing arrangements.[12] These economic models attempt to modify or extend the conventional trade-in-finished-goods theory in international economics. In their 'simple' theory of offshoring, for example, Grossman and Rossi-Hansberg (2008) model the variable effects of heterogeneous trade costs on the various tradable production tasks to be performed by different firms in an industry. In this model, the extent of offshoring—a dependent variable—is determined by these heterogeneous costs that allow different factors of production abroad (for example, lower wages) to be exploited through offshoring the selective tasks of producing goods. In short, a fall in offshoring costs leads to a growing volume of offshoring and a positive productivity effect on low-skill labour and wages at home. In their view, this simple model improves on earlier economic models of production fragmentation and trade in intermediate inputs because these models 'tend to be complex, incorporating imperfect information and subtle contracting or matching problems, and so the general equilibrium structure has been kept to a bare minimum . . . A useful taxonomy has emerged, with a myriad of interesting possibilities, but general principles have been obscure' (Grossman and Rossi-Hansberg 2008: 1980).

We believe that in at least three important ways, our GPN 2.0 approach adds significant value to the simple and parsimonious equilibrium models of outsourcing commonly found in international economics. First, our analytical focus is clearly on the *actors* and their organizational relationships that constitute global production networks in different industries, with a lead firm being a central and necessary prerequisite, and on the *multiple locations* that are bound together by the economic relations between those actors. This conceptual focus on economic actors—lead firms and their worldwide partners/suppliers—is critical because they are the primary players in the formation and evolution of global production networks. While our focus on these actors and their organizational choices may add complexity to our empirical analysis, we do not accept that this complexity is necessarily 'obscure' and can simply be assumed away in the spirit of constructing parsimonious general equilibrium models. As admitted by Grossman and Rossi-Hansberg (2008: 1981), these organizational choices by firms involved in international outsourcing are important and interesting, 'but we shall neglect them here for the sake of simplicity. Rather, we assume that a firm needs the same amount of a foreign factor whether it performs a given activity in a foreign subsidiary or it outsources the activity to a foreign supplier'. In Chapter 4, by contrast, we point squarely to substantial differences in firm-level strategic responses to the different dynamic causal drivers conceptualized in Chapter 3. Assuming away these fundamental differences in the causal mechanisms of organizing global production tends to generate misleading diagnoses and prognoses of economic outcomes, such as sweeping generalizations that the declining cost of trading tasks 'directly boosts the productivity of the factor whose tasks become easier to move offshore' and '*all* domestic parties can share in the gains from improved opportunities for offshoring' (Grossman and Rossi-Hansberg 2008: 1995, emphasis added).[13]

Second, our conceptualization of the different *dynamic drivers* or independent variables determining the organization of global production networks offers a broader treatment of the causal factors in explaining the globalization of value activity. In neoclassical economic models of international outsourcing, these causal factors tend to be associated almost exclusively with falling costs arising from improvements in communications and transport technologies and/or better specifications of property rights in international contracting.[14] Baldwin and Venables (2013) argue, for example, that production fragmentation depends largely on what they call 'unbundling costs', associated with the underlying engineering process (for example, technology), and international cost differences. These unbundling costs are conceived as a form of trade friction, the lowering of which increases offshoring through either sequential production processes (known as 'snakes') or monotonic assembly processes in no particular order ('spiders'). This technological view of production unbundling is complemented by the property-rights model of firms involved in global production networks. This latter model (e.g. Antràs and Helpman 2004; Antràs and Chor 2013) specifies the optimal allocation of property rights along uniquely sequenced stages of the value chain such that the relative position of suppliers in the chain gives rise to different contracting frictions because of the incomplete specification of property rights and unequal value capture in this sequential ordering. This stage-dependent contracting relationship, in turn, determines the incentive for lead firms to integrate these suppliers into their production.

While these economic models provide a useful approach to account for firm-specific endogeneity in production fragmentation, their narrow focus on trade costs related to technological progress, and on the economization of transaction costs through contract specifications, remains inadequate in explaining the organization of global production networks across *different* industries and national/regional economies. In GPN 2.0, improvements in these trade and transaction costs are conceptualized as important enabling factors that provide general favourable conditions for global production to take place. But the generality of these costs at the industry or national levels in economic models means that they are not peculiar to specific economic actors because the underlying capabilities of, and power relations between, these actors (for example, firms, state institutions, and NGOs) are not taken into account. We believe that economic actors, even in the same industry and national economy, negotiate and respond to these cost differentials and competitive dynamics in drastically different ways so that industry- or national-level generalizations are often hard to sustain in reality. By explicitly conceptualizing the causal role of optimizing cost–capability ratios and the management of risk and uncertainty by firms (Chapter 3) and their strategic responses (Chapter 4), we are able to account better for these differentiated actor-specific capabilities and their causal effects on the organization of global production networks. More importantly, the equal weight given to markets and finance in GPN 2.0 compares well with the constrained focus on production-specific cost considerations in all of these economic models of outsourcing and trading tasks.[15] As argued strongly in Chapters 3 and 4, we believe these market and financial considerations are necessary causal drivers in any complete understanding of global production networks.

Third, the analysis of global production networks and their *multidimensional consequences* for economic development in GPN 2.0 goes beyond the modelling of productivity and distributional effects of production fragmentation, trading tasks, and outsourcing in international economics. In most of these economic models, outsourcing impacts are measured in terms of their productivity effects on domestic factor prices (for example, wages) and economic gains (for example, firm profitability). For instance, Grossman and Rossi-Hansberg (2008: 1984) argue in their simple model that outsourcing can lead to cost savings for domestic firms that are 'much the same as would result from an economy-wide increase in the productivity of low-skilled labor'. They propose that this productivity effect will raise the firm's demand for low-skilled labour and thereby increase their wages. Even though they note that this productivity effect 'may seem counterintuitive, because it works to the benefit of the factor whose tasks are being moved offshore' (Grossman and Rossi-Hansberg 2008: 1985), they remain convinced that this effect is generally applicable in all trading environments. This unqualified generalization on the productivity effect of international outsourcing is clearly a product of the inherent limits to a rather simplistic model with unrealistic specifications and assumptions, such as a small economy producing two goods with two factors. Other economic models of the organizational choices of international outsourcing also tend to focus on its developmental implications for wages and skill levels.[16]

In GPN 2.0, developmental outcomes are not just expressed narrowly as productivity or wage effects arising from the make/buy decisions of lead firms (often conceptualized in international economics as only those based in advanced economies). We have not only highlighted the actor-specific lead firm coordination strategies through which such cross-border production networks are constructed, managed, and reproduced. More crucially, we have also explained the dynamic effects of these strategies on different value capture trajectories of firms and diverse modes and types of strategic coupling in national and regional economies. As recounted in Chapter 5, the GPN approach allows for a much more geographically grounded empirical analysis of economic development in different places and territories. This central focus on the territorial outcomes of the differential organization of global production networks distinguishes sharply GPN thinking from those in international economics that place excessive theoretical premium on production efficiency and distributional optimality of international outsourcing and trading tasks. In these abstract economic models, far too little theoretical weight has been given to the impact of international outsourcing on the diverse developmental trajectories of different territorial economies. This persistent focus on developmental outcomes leads us now to ask the crucial remaining question pertaining to GPN 2.0: what are its real world implications? More specifically, how might the GPN approach inform the politics and practice of economic development in an increasingly interdependent global economy? We will attempt to address this vital issue in the final section below.

POLITICS AND PRACTICE

To ensure the policy relevance of GPN research, it must be mobilized as an analytical tool for tackling a pressing challenge—namely, how can countries and regions create and capture more economic value from an interconnected global economy? In doing so, we intend GPN 2.0 to serve not just as a theory of global production networks, but also to provide normative lessons for policy and action in steering economic development. As argued in previous chapters, the highly strategic nature of the territory–global production networks articulation, mediated through different actors such as firms and extra-firm institutions, necessitates continual interactions among these actors at various geographical scales, and particularly the regional level. Instead of relying exclusively on inherent territorially based assets and advantages for economic development, these interactive effects are indeed the *raison d'être* of (regional) development in an era of economic globalization. They call for a dynamic conception of the strategic coupling of regional economies with global production networks that encompasses its changing nature of articulation (that is, from coupling to decoupling or recoupling) and multidimensional outcomes. This final section first address the politics of strategic coupling before elaborating on various policy recommendations for economic development in a world of global production networks.

The Politics of Strategic Coupling

In development politics and practice, it is crucial for us to specify the kind of regional development policy that can enable regional economies to (re)articulate into, and, if necessary, disarticulate from, the growth dynamics of global production networks. This politics *for* strategic coupling will require not only reconfiguring existing and conventional policy instruments, but also a significant shift in the mindset of policymakers and practitioners towards a dynamic and multi-scalar view of regional development. In reprising the key insights of GPN 2.0, it is vital for us to reiterate their major implications for the politics of strategic coupling with global production networks. First and foremost, our conception of global production networks entails a diverse range of economic and non-economic *actors*. This actor-oriented approach points to the possibility of different models of economic development that go well beyond the lead firm-led manufacturing development model commonly found in the existing literature. In this book, we have consistently argued that development through value capture can take place with or without the significant presence of global lead firms. As such, we envisage strong potential for territorialized value capture by other firms in global production networks, such as strategic partners and specialized suppliers. These non-lead firms can be in manufacturing and service sectors, eschewing the primacy of a manufacturing-led development model. These non-lead firms can also serve as key intermediaries in global production networks across different industries and sectors, providing the critical 'glue' to embed these different networks in regional economies.

In many ways, the collective value activity of these intermediaries (for example, logistics and risk management) can be viewed as industries in their own right, creating growth dynamics dissimilar to a traditional manufacturing-based view of economic development.

Equally critical is the broadening of *causal dynamics* in GPN 2.0 beyond the conventional notion of production and transaction costs.[17] Our conceptualization of the causal importance of markets, finance, and risks in shaping actor-specific strategies of organizing global production networks opens new horizons in the politics of development, away from an obsession with 'race to the bottom' cost reduction policies and market liberalization. As the relative importance of these causal dynamics changes over time in relation to the evolving global economy, a one-size-fits-all approach to economic development is likely to miss the target. Instead, we advocate a form of development politics that takes into proper account the relevance of specific combinations of these causal dynamics for particular cases of territorial economies. In large developing economies, for example, a development approach based primarily on low cost and labour-intensive export orientation might be useful in laying the initial foundation for plugging into the structural mode of assembly platforms. But it is unlikely to be a sustainable approach to longer-term development through value capture that requires more careful policy initiatives to grow home-based lead firms and/or strategic partners through leveraging on the emerging home market. Similarly, finance and risk have clearly become *de facto* features of today's highly financialized global economy. Any development politics in search of successful strategic coupling with global production networks must not overlook these critical dynamics that are deeply embedded in, and transmitted through, such networks. Untimely liberalization of financial markets and trade regimes in the name of plugging in can be as detrimental to national and regional economies as earlier periods of development politics in favour of import substitution-led industrialization. To us, a key lesson from GPN 2.0 is that appropriate institutional and regulatory safeguards must be built into policy initiatives for strategic coupling with global production networks.

Once development politics seriously takes into account the different actors and causal dynamics involved, it will invariably recognize different actor-specific *strategies* in pursuit of value capture in global production networks. In the development literature, it is not uncommon to find advocates of economic development through attracting foreign direct investment (FDI). This FDI-led practice has so far been proven to be quite effective in many developing as well as developed economies around the world. Nevertheless, our GPN approach points not just to intra-firm coordination as the dominant strategy of organizing global production networks. In this strategy, lead firms actively (re)organize their global production through FDI in various locations.

In GPN 2.0, global lead firms can also pursue inter-firm and extra-firm strategies that do not necessarily entail direct equity stakes in foreign locations. In these strategies for value capture, FDI-specific investment incentives and development politics may not be effective in enticing successful strategic coupling. Instead, a new development practice must be envisioned—one that explicitly recognizes the need to develop investment incentives and favourable policy environments for different actors pursuing a variety of strategies for value capture in global production networks.

Last but not least, the politics of development comes full circle when national or regional economies are articulated into different modes of strategic coupling with global production networks. To us, this variegated understanding of *coupling modes* and *types* is absolutely vital for economic development because consistent and continuous policy diagnosis of different coupling possibilities is always required for practising dynamic coupling. In GPN 2.0, we advocate policy thinking that views global production networks and global value chains not just as individual industries or organizational entities, but also as multidimensional intersections of different industries and economic organizations. These intersections in turn raise the significant issues of the (re)distribution of value capture and appropriate policy instruments in economic development. But to avoid the danger of global production networks being mobilized as a neoliberal device for championing ruthless market liberalization and deregulation, we need to appreciate better and more fully the different consequences of strategic coupling for national and regional economies.[18]

Two critical lessons from our analysis in this book are pertinent here. First, modes of coupling do change over time even in the *same* region or sector-specific global production networks. This evolutionary change is often accomplished through the processes of decoupling and recoupling. It can be gradual in some instances (for example, the innovation hubs in Table 5.3) and dramatic and disruptive in other cases (for example, the structural modes in Table 5.3). At any time, a region is likely to be involved in only one dominant mode of strategic coupling with global production networks, even though some traces of the earlier and/or future coupling mode may exist or appear. For example, the functional mode of international partnership remains dominant in the information and communication technologies (ICT) region of Taipei-Hsinchu, but elements of assembly platforms in the structural mode can also be observed among the small and medium enterprises in this high-tech region. Equally importantly, the leading ICT firms in the region are no longer followers of technological innovation developed elsewhere; some of them have become first movers in their respective market segments (for example, Acer and ASUS in computers; HTC and ASUS in mobile devices) and technological platforms (for example, TSMC and UMC in semiconductors). The region is moving towards an indigenous mode of coupling through which an innovation hub emerges.

Second and more significantly, there are *always* potential pitfalls associated with each mode of strategic coupling. While the precise mix of these pitfalls or dark sides varies with each mode, they provide the underlying rationale for regional actors to consider switching or recombining different modes of strategic coupling in their endeavour towards a better and more sustainable form of regional development trajectory in a volatile global economy. In short, a particular mode of strategic coupling with global production networks should never be viewed as a universal panacea or all-inclusive policy instrument to engender successful regional development. This policy caution is necessary because, for such coupling to take place in regional economies, the needs of actors in global production networks must be strategically matched with the aspirations of regional institutions and the existing regional assets. However, this matching does not necessarily, and cannot always, lead to inclusive growth trajectories and successful value capture in regional economies.

Strategic coupling with global production networks is ultimately a deliberate and selective process that incorporates only certain territorial actors and their counterparts in global production networks. It is unrealistic for policymakers and practitioners to expect such global–national–regional coupling processes to be always inclusive; it is even more dangerous for them to rely exclusively on such strategic coupling as the only pathway to successful territorialized value capture and positive development outcomes. There is always a critical role for national or regional institutions and groups of actors to engage in joint decision-making and collective action to mitigate the negative consequences of such coupling with global production networks and to consider a more balanced and equitable form of national/regional development. In large national economies, this role calls for policy consideration of both positive strategic coupling with global production networks and domestic market-oriented forms of economic development.

Policies for Promoting Strategic Coupling

In order to put these development politics into practice, we now move on to engage critically with the policy recommendations of various international organizations in relation to increasing participation in global value chains and global production networks.[19] To date, UNCTAD's *World Investment Report 2013* (UNCTAD 2013b: 175–6) contains the most comprehensive set of policy frameworks for promoting strategic coupling with global production networks (though not using that exact terminology, of course). In particular, it has identified the following key policy challenges for economic development in an interconnected world economy organized through the extensive presence of global production networks:

1. how to gain access and connect local firms to global production networks;
2. how to maximize the development benefits from participation in global production networks;
3. how to ensure that opportunities to industrial and social upgrading in global production networks are realized;
4. how to mitigate the risks involved in participation in global production networks;
5. how to align and synergize trade and investment policies in a world in which the two are inextricably intertwined.

As one might imagine, these fairly major challenges are presented mostly at the *national* level, as if the entire country can be plugged into global production networks, and the existing development policies can be reworked to stimulate such strategic coupling. To this policy effect, UNCTAD (2013b: 175) recommends that

> active promotion of GVCs [global value chains] and GVC-led development strategies imply the encouragement and provision of support to economic activities aimed at generating exports in fragmented and geographically dispersed industry value chains, based on a narrower set of endowments and competitive advantages. And they imply active policies to encourage learning from GVC activities in which a country is present, to support the process of upgrading towards higher value added activities and diversifying into higher value added chains.

This national approach to promoting strategic coupling with global production networks, as recommended in most reports by major international organizations, is problematic on two levels. First, it does not take into account pre-existing spatial differentiation within the national economy. As argued in the previous chapter, regional variations in resource endowments and institutional repertoires can make a very significant difference to ensuring the successful processes and positive outcomes of regional strategic coupling with global production networks. This, in turn, explains why two contrasting regions in the same national economy can experience very different strategic coupling processes and outcomes. We can witness these differences in advanced economies (for example, ICT in Silicon Valley versus sunset industries in America's Midwest), newly industrialized economies (for example, ICT in Taiwan's Taipei-Hsinchu versus traditional manufacturing industries in Tainan), and developing economies (for example, ICT in Malaysia's Penang versus extractive industries in Terengganu). For a long time, these regional differences have been well recognized in the social sciences (for example, economic geography and regional studies); they should therefore not be an afterthought in any serious national policy and practice for benefiting from participation in global production networks. As such, regional policy for strategic coupling with global production networks should be explicitly constructed in order to take advantage of the appropriate combination of regional assets and institutions.

Second, there is a tendency for these global production network-oriented policy recommendations to eschew sector-specific industrial policies in favour of generic policies. This is because industry policy is often misconstrued as 'an industrial development strategy aimed at building domestic productive capacity, including for exports, in all stages of production (extending to the substitution of imported content of exports) to develop a vertically integrated industry that remains relatively independent from the key actors of GVCs for its learning and upgrading processes' (UNCTAD 2013b: 175). In today's globalizing world economy, while it is hard for almost any national economy to develop fully vertically integrated industries that are competitive, there remains significant room for a modified form of industrial policy that taps into the developmental opportunities inherent in the sectoral specificities of global production networks.[20] As argued by Gereffi and Sturgeon (2013: 330), 'companies, localities and entire countries have come to occupy specialized niches within GVCs. For these reasons, today's industrial policies have a different character and generate different outcomes from before. Intentionally or not, governments currently engage in GVC-oriented industrialization when targeting key sectors for growth'. There is no doubt, for example, that strategic coupling in automobile global production networks can be more challenging than in apparel or agro-food global production networks. Interestingly, there is also substantial intra-sectoral differentiation. In the global ICT industry, articulating into global production networks in consumer electronics is relatively more actionable in policy terms than strategic coupling with global production networks in advanced semiconductors or high-end electronics equipment (for example, medical devices or computing servers). Developing industrial policies oriented towards promoting a niche in a particular sector or intra-sectoral segment can therefore make good sense for regional development.

Recognizing such regional and sectoral differences in global production networks-oriented policy recommendations allows us to provide a more appropriate and nuanced understanding of regional policy and practice. In Table 6.1, we summarize such a policy framework for promoting strategic coupling with global production networks *for* regional development. Based on UNCTAD's policy framework for national development (2013b), this global production networks-led regional development policy framework incorporates the following key considerations:

1. moving from developing nationally integrated industries to specialized niches for regions in global production networks;
2. recognizing the need for detailed knowledge and analysis of regional prospects in different global production networks;

3. promoting new domestic capacity and/or foreign investment in value adding segments of global production networks in regional economies; developing a global supply base through a combination of local and foreign firms;

4. facilitating trade in production inputs and intermediate goods and services;

5. leveraging global production networks for international market access and development of regional firms;

6. providing basic prerequisites for economic activity: skills, infrastructure, logistics, tax regimes, and so on.

To operationalize the regional policy framework in Table 6.1, we believe several regional practices are both necessary and vital: (1) engagement with transnational communities; (2) policy credibility and institutional consistency; and (3) pragmatic choices and flexible pathways. With respect to the first aspect, the critical role of transnational communities and social capital in regional development is now well recognized.[21] One such transnational community refers to the business and technology professionals who originate from one regional economy and shuttle constantly around the globe. In *The New Argonauts*, Saxenian (2006) argues that this transnational community has rewritten the concept of international knowledge formation from one of a one-way brain drain to a two-way process of brain circulation. Through their constant movements between different regions of the world economy, these technologists and entrepreneurs originating from home regions have formed a transnational community of informal knowledge networks forged by common social identities and, sometimes, regional sentiments. In East Asian high-growth regions, these transnational business practices have contributed to the formal coupling of firms and institutions in regional economies with lead firms in global production networks through a variety of organizational arrangements.[22]

For the regional coupling policies in Table 6.1 to work, a more systematic engagement with these transnational communities is vital. Regional policymakers should make a conscious effort to identify such actors who have established themselves in different global industries. The technological, managerial, or entrepreneurial instincts of these transnational actors are obviously different from those embedded in the home regions.[23] Because of their international perspectives, these transnational actors are more likely to identify and take advantage of the niche opportunities arising from vertical specialization in global production. Tapping into their knowledge and network repertoires can allow regional planners and policymakers to develop a more thorough understanding of the relevance of their existing regional capabilities and positions for different value segments of global production

Table 6.1. Policy framework for global production networks and regional development

Key elements	Principal policy actions at the national level	Strategic coupling: regional policy and practice
Embedding global production networks in development strategy	• Incorporating global production networks in industrial development policies • Setting policy objectives along global production network development paths	• Understanding current regional capabilities and positions in global industries • Aligning regional endowments with targeted global industries: be realistic of achievable strategic coupling • Mindful of 'race to bottom' or structural mode of strategic coupling • A network and partnership approach to industrial development in regional economies
Enabling participation in global production networks	• Creating and maintaining a conducive environment for trade and investment • Putting in place the infrastructural prerequisites for global production network participation	• Regional policies facilitating international trade and investment • National policy incentives for regional coupling in global production networks, e.g. special tax regimes or financial grants • Importance of regional ties and transnational communities
Building domestic productive capacity	• Supporting enterprise development and enhancing the bargaining power of local firms • Strengthening skills of the workforce	• National and regional institutional support for capability development of domestic firms: technological transfer and equity investment • Regional clustering and linkage development to enhance strategic coupling • Upgrading of skills and knowledge: from industrial to services and managerial skills
Providing a strong environmental, social and governance framework	• Minimizing risks associated with global production network participation through regulation, and public and private standards • Supporting local enterprise in complying with international standards	• Effective regulation, social dialogue, and an active civil society in the region • Deployment of voluntary and regulatory standards, e.g. CSR programmes • Assistance to domestic firms in their adoption of sector-specific international standards (e.g. Fairtrade or organic certification)
Synergizing trade and investment policies and institutions	• Ensuring coherence between trade and investment policies • Synergizing trade and investment promotion and facilitation • Creating 'regional industrial development compacts'	• Credibility and consistency in regional policy and practice • Establishing regional institutions promoting strategic coupling in global production networks, e.g. industry groups, intermediaries, and public-private consortiums • Developing cross-regional linkages and global production network couplings

Note: 'Key elements' and 'Principal policy actions at the national level' adapted from UNCTAD (2013b: table IV.11).

networks. As noted in Table 6.1, this understanding is crucial to embedding global production networks in regional development strategies. In more practical terms, engaging these transnational communities can enable a more direct participation in global production networks through new enterprise formation and developing the capabilities of domestic firms in the regional economy. The classic cases of this successful engagement of transnational communities are in the deepening linkages between Silicon Valley and Taipei-Hsinchu (Taiwan), Bangalore (India), and Shanghai (China) in the global ICT industry.

Such a social capital approach to regional development, however, can be applied beyond high-tech industries. In more traditional industries such as agro-food processing and consumer goods manufacturing, the key intermediaries in global production networks are often quite different and powerful in terms of value capture. Engaging with transnational community members who hold important positions in these intermediaries (for example, international trading companies and sourcing and supply chain firms) is equally critical to the successful coupling of regional economies into respective global production networks. This regional practice of building strong bonds with transnational communities from the same region can be very helpful to the upgrading of skills and knowledge, ranging from industrial to service and managerial skills that might be lacking among domestic firms and regional actors, particularly those from developing economies.

Moreover, a region's strategic coupling with global production networks can never occur in an institutional vacuum. The emergence of global production networks does not in itself diminish the role of state and non-state institutions in 'governing the market'.[24] Development initiatives formulated and implemented by these institutions matter for establishing successful strategic coupling with global production networks. Apart from the successful examples in East Asia described in this book, it is also evident in the incorporation of Tunisia (North Africa) and Bulgaria and Slovakia (Eastern Europe) into apparel global production networks coordinated by lead firms from the European Union.[25] But all these successful cases point to the need for policy credibility and institutional consistency. In many developing regions, it is one thing for policymakers to develop a set of promotional policies in favour of strategic coupling with global production networks. It is quite another for these policies to be bold enough and consistently implemented.

To begin, bold regional policies require these policymakers to think 'out of the box'. For example, instead of following a straitjacket kind of neoliberal economic policy aimed at market liberalization and trade facilitation, a global production networks-led regional development entails a more interventionist role for regional institutions such as state authorities and non-state organizations. This role cannot be accomplished without the appropriate political support at the national level, which in turn demands considerable political entrepreneurship on the part of key regional actors. As Tomaney et al. (2011: 628) conclude in their *Handbook of Local and Regional Development*, 'decentralised and accountable institutions are necessary conditions for the success of this [place-based] approach, but so too is a supportive system of fiscal redistribution and macro-economic management in the context of multi-level governance. Without such a supportive [national] context, there are limits to local to regional and development'. Securing this national support for region-specific policies can ensure a certain degree of institutional consistency necessary for pro-coupling regional industrial policies to be effective in their intended outcomes.[26] But these bold regional policies must also be credible. As noted in Gereffi and Luo (2014: 20), 'government policy makers do not know enough about the intricacies of global industries to spur specific forms of innovation in GVCs. What government policy can do is to facilitate the development of human capital, including collaborations with universities and private firms to ensure demand-responsive forms of workforce development'. Engaging transnational communities in their formulation and implementation is likely to increase such policy credibility. So will securing strong political support for such region-specific policies. Some of these policies can be manifested in the follow arenas:

1. labour markets: developing workforce intermediaries in vocational training and education, productivity enhancement, and collective efficiency (for example, industrial relations);

2. financial markets: recognizing the limited effectiveness of tax incentives and grants owing to the ever-growing costs of such instruments and their lack of sustainability (lower tax revenue over expenditure over time);

3. intangibles in R&D, design, branding, and marketing: maintaining and developing competencies through public R&D institutions and market promotion agencies, and national institutes of standards and technology vital to setting standards and codification schemes;

4. 'glue' for strategic coupling: growing specialized suppliers, business infrastructure, and logistical capabilities;

5. associational capacities: leveraging business associations, civil society and non-governmental organizations, and public-private partnerships.

Finally, promoting strategic coupling with global production networks through regional policies necessitates a fundamental shift in policy practice towards the recognition of more pragmatic choices and flexible pathways. In particular, policymakers would be wise to promote the articulation of regional economies into cooperative global production networks (for example, the inter-firm partnership mode) through providing financial incentives, developing inter-firm complementarities, and implementing policies for promoting information-sharing, supplier capability development, industry-wide associational capacity, and so on. They should also seek a reversal of bargaining (mis) fortunes in extra-firm relations by mobilizing industry-wide associational capacity and communities of knowledge and practice across different institutional domains and organizational platforms. In this respect, building global production networks-oriented institutions (from research to planning for strategy and policy implementation) is essential in understanding existing capabilities and points-of-entry into different global production networks and their different prospects for value creation and capture.

One of the greatest dangers exhibited in the dark sides of regional development through strategic coupling is external path dependency and regional lock-in. This dependency in asymmetrical global production networks (for example, the inter-firm control mode of structural coupling) can be particularly troubling if a region is locked into a 'race to the bottom' pathway to economic development and social upgrading. Unlocking this path dependency through disarticulating from pre-existing global production networks becomes very difficult once regional endowments (for example, land) and relational assets (for example, labour) are fully committed.[27] To anticipate and prevent this debilitating effect of regional lock-in, policymakers and practitioners must remain pragmatic in their policy choices and developmental pathways. More precisely, they must adopt a dynamic view of regional development and avoid following a one-size-fits-all approach to regional development.[28] While pragmatic policy practice is useful in coupling the region with the most immediately available global industry (for example, agro-food, apparel, or electronics), these regional actors must be constantly looking out for new opportunities *beyond* this industry to upgrade the existing regional industrial and social capabilities and to prepare for another pathway towards a higher-value capture mode of strategic coupling with global production networks. This pragmatism and flexibility in regional policy practice may appear to contradict the earlier point about policy credibility and consistency. But we do think the two are not mutually exclusive. It is entirely conceivable for a region to achieve policy credibility and yet remain pragmatic in its choices of pathways for development over time. In East Asia (for example, Singapore's 'growth triangle', Malaysia's Penang, and China's Yangtze River Delta), we have witnessed several such policy successes in adopting a more dynamic approach to practising development strategies in a world economy organized through global production networks.

To sum up, our conceptual effort in this book unravels the causal mechanisms required to bridge the analytical impasse in existing GPN–GVC studies and the adjacent social science literatures on global economic change. It initiates a more dynamic approach to conceptualizing global production networks as a dominant organizational platform through which actors in different regional and national economies compete and cooperate for a greater share of value capture in global production. Our theory attempts to achieve this through examining the evolving firm-specific capabilities, technological trajectories, and market transformations in global industries, which in turn shape and reshape complex intra-, inter-, and extra-firm power relations. Through relevant empirical mobilization and policy practice, it can in turn afford greater clarity and precision as an analytical tool for resolving the pressing challenge of creating and capturing value in an increasingly interdependent global economy. And, yet, such policy and practice should not be seen as a universal panacea for regional decline or path dependency in a highly competitive global economy. They can instead point to possible scenarios for positive collective action by regional actors to 'hold down the global' and to establish a privileged position through strategic coupling with global production networks. Ultimately, we hope GPN 2.0 provides both the theoretical reasoning and a practical approach for uncovering lasting solutions to this challenge.

NOTES

1. Although we both primarily work in the qualitative tradition, we are convinced that this research agenda will need to bring together the strengths of both qualitative and quantitative approaches to studying global production networks (see also Hess and Yeung 2006b, and Coe et al. 2010).

2. This choice of literatures, in keeping with our 'framing' of economic development in Chapter 5, is deliberately limited to those that directly engage with the same empirical phenomenon. We do not, for example, connect at this stage with the vast literatures on innovation and clustering or international business (besides invoking such work, where appropriate, in preceding chapters).

3. In Gereffi et al. (2005), clearly *the* most influential GVC theory paper in terms of citation impact, theory development actually takes up no more than five pages (pp. 84–8). The rest of the paper is devoted to antecedents of their GVC theory (e.g. GCC work and transaction cost theories of industrial organization) and four sectoral case studies (bicycles, apparel, fresh vegetables, and electronics).

4. Here it is important to recognize the internal variety within the GVC approach. If Gereffi et al. (2005) is representative of GVC theory in its self-proclaimed 'narrow' form, there are other GVC accounts that seek to incorporate the geographical and institutional dimensions much more fully. Neilson and Pritchard's (2009) exemplary book on tea and coffee production in South India and Pickles and Smith's (2015) work on the apparel industry in Eastern European regions are two cases in point, incorporating territorial and institutional factors in a sophisticated manner that starts to morph with GPN theory as we advocate it in this book.

5. For instance, beyond the specific line of research associated with Hall, Soskice, and others, 'varieties of capitalism' is often used more generally as an umbrella term for a range of cognate approaches with a mix of different emphases and disciplinary origins, including national business systems (e.g. Whitley 1992, 1999), national systems of innovation (e.g. Lundvall 1992; Nelson 1993), social systems of production (e.g. Crouch and Streeck 1997; Hollingsworth and Boyer 1999), and social systems of innovation and production (e.g. Amable 2003).

6. For contemporary attempts to apply such VoC theories more systematically in the Asian context—a vital domain for many global production networks—see Walter and Zhang (2012), Zhang and Peck (2013), Zhang and Whitley (2013), and Witt and Redding (2014).

7. See, for example, Allen (2004) and Becker (2009) on the limits to typologies, Crouch (2005) and Hall and Thelen (2009) on the theorization of institutional change, Crouch et al. (2009) on sectoral and sub-national variations in varieties of capitalism, and Morgan and Whitley (2012) on how internationalization reshapes national varieties of capitalism.

8. Lane and Probert (2009) offer a detailed examination of the interplay between global production networks and varieties of capitalism in the context of the UK, US, and German clothing industries. See also Lane (2008) for a comparison of the clothing and pharmaceutical industries.

9. See Yeung (2014) for this line of argument in the context of East Asian firms coupled with lead firms in global production networks.

10. Pries (2005) discusses this concept in more depth in the context of global economic flows.

11. See Yeung (2004), for instance, for an account of how globalization processes are significantly transforming the nature and organization of 'Chinese' capitalism in East and South-East Asia. In this account, the system that is emerging is neither distinctively Chinese nor converging towards the Anglo-American form of capitalism, but a hybrid of both.

12. Leading proponents of this approach in international economics have focused on production fragmentation, outsourcing and offshoring, and trading tasks in tradable goods (e.g. Jones and Kierzkowski 1990, 2001; Feenstra and Hanson 1996; Feenstra 1998; Arndt and Kierzkowski 2001; Antràs and Helpman 2004; Antràs 2005; Antràs et al. 2006; Grossman and Rossi-Hansberg 2008; Antràs and Chor 2013; Baldwin 2013; Baldwin and Venables 2013; Milberg and Winkler 2013; Koopman et al. 2014).

13. For related modelling of the productivity effects of offshoring, see Baldwin and Okubo (2014).

14. Examples of these economic models based on incomplete contract specifications are Antràs (2005), Antràs and Chor (2013), and Baldwin and Venables (2013).

15. On finance, the role of international tax differences has been considered in Antràs and Chor (2013: 2187 n. 42). But they found very similar results from their model specification on 'make or buy' decisions by American firms abroad when they restricted their sample to countries whose effective corporate tax rates for these American TNCs were within a 5% range of that for their domestic activity in the USA. As explained in Chapter 3, the role of financial considerations among global lead firms goes well beyond taxation.

16. For example, Antràs and Helpman's model (2004) predicts the widening of the wage gap between the Global North and the Global South. Other models found wage inequality within the Global North (e.g. Feenstra and Hanson 1996) and within the Global South (e.g. Antràs et al. 2006).

17. A 2010 national survey of the international and domestic sourcing practices of US organizations by Brown et al. (2014), for example, shows that most international

sourcing is to high-cost locations and by organizations in the goods-producing and trade industry groupings. Low-cost locations are more likely to be used by non-goods-producing organizations. Production costs are clearly not the only critical causal driver of international outsourcing.

18. For such a critical view of the mobilization of global value chains by international organizations and national governments, see Starosta (2010a, b), Glassman (2011), Fernández (2014), and Neilson (2014). In particular, Fernández (2014: 4) critically argues that, 'capitalizing on the loss of prestige of the neoliberal tools and policies inspired by the WC [Washington Consensus] dogma, the GVC approach has gained increasing presence in the supranational agenda, providing new theoretical inputs for many assistance programs, financial projects, institutional advisers, and institutional workshops that a few years ago were outstandingly committed to self-regulative market theory'.

19. For a selection of these policy documents, see Cattaneo et al. (2010b), Barrientos et al. (2011), IMF (2013), OECD (2011, 2013), WTO and IDE-JETRO (2011), Elms and Low (2013), UNCTAD (2013a, b), and Gereffi and Luo (2014). In this policy discussion, we also draw upon our experience in conducting GPN–GVC conceptual training and capacity building sessions for government policymakers and regulatory practitioners from a range of developing economies in East, South, and South-East Asia. These seminars and workshops were organized by national governments (e.g. the Malaysian Institute for Economic Research) or macro-regional development organizations (e.g. the Asian Development Bank). See Yeung (2015a) for more discussion on regional policy and practice in a world of global production networks.

20. For some post-crisis arguments in favour of industrial policies, see Cimoli et al. (2009), Lin (2012b), and Fine et al. (2013).

21. See Hsu and Saxenian (2000), Phelps and Wood (2006), Rodríguez-Pose and Storper (2006), and Yeung (2009b).

22. For more empirical details, see Coe et al. (2003), Saxenian and Sabel (2008), Yang et al. (2009), Wang and Lin (2013), and Lin and Rasiah (2014).

23. For an expanded argument on such transnational entrepreneurship, see Yeung (2009e).

24. For different interpretations of the role of the state in governing economic development in a world of global production networks, see Smith (2014) and Yeung (2014, 2015b).

25. See Smith et al. (2014) and Pickles and Smith (2015) for more empirical detail.

26. For more arguments in this institutionalist direction, see Amin (1999) and O'Riain (2011).

27. A range of studies of disarticulations from global production networks have clearly shown the severe consequences of this regional lock-in in the apparel and agro-food industries. See Bair and Werner (2011b), Hough (2011), Ramamurthy (2011), Brown (2013), Havice and Campling (2013), B. R. Wilson (2013), Fold (2014), and Pickles and Smith (2015).

28. For a similar argument, see Bristow (2010), MacKinnon (2012), and Dawley (2014).

References

Abernathy, F. H., Dunlop, J. T., Hammond, J. H., and Weil, D. (1999). *A Stitch in Time: Lean Retailing and the Transformation of Manufacturing—Lessons from the Apparel and Textile Industry*. Oxford: Oxford University Press.

Allen, M. (2004). 'The Varieties of Capitalism Paradigm: Not Enough Variety?', *Socio-Economic Review*, 2/1: 87–108.

Amable, B. (2003). *The Diversity of Modern Capitalism*. Oxford: Oxford University Press.

Amin, A. (1999). 'An Institutionalist Perspective on Regional Economic Development', *International Journal of Urban and Regional Research*, 23/2: 365–78.

Amin, A., and Cohendet, P. (2004). *Architectures of Knowledge: Firms, Capabilities and Communities*. Oxford: Oxford University Press.

Amin, A., and Thrift, N. (1992). 'Neo-Marshallian Modes in Global Networks', *International Journal of Urban and Regional Research*, 16/4: 571–87.

Amsden, A. H. (1989). *Asia's Next Giant: South Korea and Late Industrialization*. New York: Oxford University Press.

Amsden, A. H., and Chu, W.-W. (2003). *Beyond Late Development: Taiwan's Upgrading Policies*. Cambridge, MA: MIT Press.

Angel, D. P. (1994). *Restructuring for Innovation: The Remaking of the US Semiconductor Industry*. New York: Guilford.

Antràs, P. (2005). 'Incomplete Contracts and the Product Cycle', *American Economic Review*, 95/4: 1054–73.

Antràs, P., and Chor, D. (2013). 'Organizing the Global Value Chain', *Econometrica*, 81/6: 2127–204.

Antràs, P., and Helpman, E. (2004). 'Global Sourcing', *Journal of Political Economy*, 112/3: 552–80.

Antràs, P., Garicano, L., and Rossi-Hansberg, E. (2006). 'Offshoring in a Knowledge Economy', *Quarterly Journal of Economics*, 121/1: 31–77.

Aoyama, Y. (2007). 'Oligopoly and the Structural Paradox of Retail TNCs: An Assessment of Carrefour and Wal-Mart in Japan', *Journal of Economic Geography*, 7/4: 471–90.

Appelbaum, R. P. (2008). 'Giant Transnational Contractors in East Asia: Emergent Trends in Global Supply Chains', *Competition and Change*, 12/1: 69–87.

Appelbaum., R. P. (2011). 'Transnational Contractors in East Asia', in G. G. Hamilton, M. Petrovic, and B. Senauer (eds), *The Market Makers: How Retailers Are Reshaping the Global Economy*. Oxford: Oxford University Press, 255–68.

Arndt, S. W., and Kierzkowski, H. (2001) (eds). *Fragmentation: New Production Patterns in the World Economy*. Oxford: Oxford University Press.

Asia-Pacific Economic Cooperation (2014). *Quantitative Analysis on Value Chain Risks in the APEC Region*. APEC Policy Support Unit Paper. Singapore: APEC.

Azmeh, S. (2014a). 'Labour in Global Production Networks: Workers in the Qualifying Industrial Zones (QIZs) of Egypt and Jordan', *Global Networks*, 14/4: 495–513.

Azmeh, S. (2014b). 'Trade Regimes and Global Production Networks: The Case of the Qualifying Industrial Zones (QIZs) in Egypt and Jordan', *Geoforum*, 57: 57–66.

Bair, J. (2005). 'Global Capitalism and Commodity Chains: Looking Back, Going Forward', *Competition & Change*, 9/2: 153–80.

Bair, J. (2008). 'Analysing Global Economic Organization: Embedded Networks and Global Chains Compared', *Economy and Society*, 37/3: 339–64.

Bair, J. (2009) (ed.). *Frontiers of Commodity Chain Research*. Stanford, CA: Stanford University Press.

Bair, J. (2014) (ed.). 'Special Issue: The Political Economy of Commodity Chains', *Journal of World-Systems Research*, 20/1: 1–139.

Bair, J., and Gereffi, G. (2001). 'Local Clusters in Global Chains: The Causes and Consequences of Export Dynamism in Torreon's Blue Jeans Industry', *World Development*, 29/11: 1885–903.

Bair, J., and Werner, M. (2011a). 'Commodity Chains and the Uneven Geographies of Global Capitalism: A Disarticulations Perspective', *Environment and Planning A*, 43/5: 988–97.

Bair, J., and Werner, M. (2011b). 'The Place of Disarticulations: Global Commodity Production in La Laguna, Mexico', *Environment and Planning A*, 43/5: 998–1015.

Bair, J., Berndt, C., and Werner, M. (2013) (eds). 'Theme Issue: Critical Perspectives on Commodity Chain Studies', *Environment and Planning A*, 45/11: 2544–699.

Baird, I. G., and Quastel, N. (2011). 'Dolphin-Safe Tuna from California to Thailand: Localisms in Environmental Certification of Global Commodity Networks', *Annals of the Association of American Geographers*, 101/2: 337–55.

Baldwin, C. Y., and Clark, K. B. (2000). *Design Rules: The Power of Modularity*. Cambridge, MA: MIT Press.

Baldwin, R. (2013). 'Global Supply Chains: Why They Emerged, Why They Matter, and Where They are Going', in D. K. Elms and P. Low (eds), *Global Value Chains in a Changing World*. Geneva: World Trade Organization, 13–60.

Baldwin, R., and Okubo, T. (2014). 'International Trade, Offshoring and Heterogeneous Firms', *Review of International Economics*, 22/1: 59–72.

Baldwin, R., and Venables, A. J. (2013). 'Spiders and Snakes: Offshoring and Agglomeration in the Global Economy', *Journal of International Economics*, 90/2: 245–54.

Barnett, C., Cloke, P., Clarke, N., and Malpass, A. (2011). *Globalizing Responsibility: The Political Rationalities of Ethical Consumption*. Oxford: Wiley-Blackwell.

Barney, J. B. (1991). 'Firm Resources and Sustained Competitive Advantage', *Journal of Management*, 17/1: 99–120.

Barney, J. B. (2001). 'Resource-Based Theories of Competitive Advantage: A Ten-Year Retrospective on the Resource-Based View', *Journal of Management*, 27/6: 643–50.

Barrientos, S. (2014). 'Gendered Global Production Networks: Analysis of Cocoa–Chocolate Sourcing', *Regional Studies*, 48/5: 791–803.

Barrientos, S., and Dolan, C. (2006) (eds). *Ethical Sourcing in the Global Food System*. London: Earthscan.

Barrientos, S., Gereffi, G., and Rossi, A. (2011). 'Economic and Social Upgrading in Global Production Networks: A New Paradigm for a Changing World', *International Labour Review*, 150/3–4: 319–40.

Bathelt, H. (2006). Geographies of Production: Growth Regimes in Spatial Perspective 3: Toward a Relational View of Economic Action and Policy', *Progress in Human Geography*, 30/2: 223–36.

Bathelt, H., and Glückler, J. (2011). *The Relational Economy: Geographies of Knowing and Learning*. Oxford: Oxford University Press.

Baud, C., and Durand, C. (2012). 'Financialization, Globalization and the Making of Profits by Leading Retailers', *Socio-Economic Review*, 10/2: 241–66.

Bazan, L., and Navas-Alemán, L. (2004). 'The Underground Revolution in the Sinos Valley: A Comparison of Upgrading in Global and National Value Chains', in H. Schmitz (ed.), *Local Enterprises in the Global Economy: Issues of Governance and Upgrading*. Cheltenham: Edward Elgar, 110–39.

Becker, U. (2009). *Open Varieties of Capitalism: Continuity, Change and Performances*. Basingstoke: Palgrave Macmillan.

Berger, S., and Dore, R. (1996) (eds). *National Diversity and Global Capitalism*, Ithaca, NY: Cornell University Press.

Berger, S., and Lester, R. K. (2005) (eds). *Global Taiwan: Building Competitive Strengths in a New International Economy*. Armonk, NY: East Gate.

Best, M. H. (1990). *The New Competition: Institutions of Industrial Restructuring*. Cambridge, MA: Harvard University Press.

Beugelsdijk, S., and Mudambi, R. (2013). 'MNEs as Border-Crossing Multi-Location Enterprises: The Role of Discontinuities in Geographic Space', *Journal of International Business Studies*, 44/5: 413–26.

Bhaskar, R. (1979). *The Possibility of Naturalism: A Philosophical Critique of the Contemporary Human Sciences*. Brighton: Harvester.

Bhaskar, R. (1997). *A Realist Theory of Science*. London: Verso.

Birch, K. (2008). 'Alliance-Driven Governance: Applying a Global Commodity Chains Approach to the UK Biotechnology Industry', *Economic Geography*, 84/1: 83–103.

Block, F., and Keller, M. R. (2011) (eds). *State of Innovation: The US Government's Role in Technology Development*. Boulder, CO: Paradigm.

Blowfield, M. (2000). 'Ethical Sourcing: A Contribution to Sustainability or a Diversion?', *Sustainable Development*, 8/4: 191–200.

Bonacich, E., and Hamilton, G. G. (2011). 'Global Logistics, Global Labor', in G. G. Hamilton, M. Petrovic, and B. Senauer (eds), *The Market Makers: How Retailers Are Reshaping the Global Economy*. Oxford: Oxford University Press, 211–30.

Bonacich, E., and Wilson, J. B. (2008). *Getting the Goods: Ports, Labor and the Logistics Revolution*. Ithaca, NY: Cornell University Press.

Bonacich, E., Cheng, L., Chinchilla, N., Hamilton, N., and Ong, P. (1994) (eds). *Global Production: The Apparel Industry in the Pacific Rim*. Philadelphia, PA: Temple University Press.

Brenner, N., Jessop, B., Jones, M., and MacLeod, G. (2003) (eds). *State/Space*. Oxford: Blackwell.

Brewer, B. D. (2011). 'Global Commodity Chains and World Income Inequalities: The Missing Link of Inequality and the "Upgrading" Paradox', *Journal of World-Systems Research*, 17/2: 308–27.

Breznitz, D. (2007). *Innovation and the State: Political Choice and Strategies for Growth in Israel, Taiwan, and Ireland*. New Haven, CT: Yale University Press.

Bridge, G. (2008). 'Global Production Networks and the Extractive Sector: Governing Resource-Based Development', *Journal of Economic Geography*, 8/3: 389–419.

Bristow, G. (2010). *Critical Reflections on Regional Competitiveness: Theory, Policy and Practice*. London: Routledge.

Brown, C., Sturgeon, T., and Cole, C. (2014). 'The 2010 National Organizations Survey: Examining the Relationships between Job Quality and the Domestic and International Sourcing of Business Functions by United States Organizations'. Working Papers 14-001. Cambridge, MA: MIT Industrial Performance Center.

Brown, E., Derudder, B., Parnreiter, C., Pelupessy, W., Taylor, P. J., and Witloz, F. (2010) (eds). 'World City Networks and Global Commodity Chains: Towards a World-Systems' Integration', *Global Networks*, 10/1: 12–34.

Brown, S. (2013). 'One Hundred Years of Labor Control: Violence, Militancy, and the Fairtrade Banana Commodity Chain in Colombia', *Environment and Planning A*, 45/11: 2572–91.

Brunn, S. D. (2006) (ed.). *Wal-Mart World: The World's Biggest Corporation in the Global Economy*. New York: Routledge.

Buckley, P. J. (2009). 'The Impact of the Global Factory on Economic Development', *Journal of World Business*, 44/2: 131–43.

Buckley, P. J. (2011) (ed.). *Globalization and the Global Factory*. Cheltenham: Edward Elgar.

Buckley, P. J., and Ghauri, P. (2004). 'Globalisation, Economic Geography and the Strategy of Multinational Enterprises', *Journal of International Business Studies*, 35/2: 81–98.

Burgelman, R. A., and Grove, A. S. (2002). *Strategy is Destiny: How Strategy-Making Shapes a Company's Future*. New York: Free Press.

Burt, R. S. (1982). *Towards a Structural Theory of Action: Network Models of Social Structure, Perception, and Action*. New York: Academic Press.

Burt, R. S. (1992). *Structural Holes*. Cambridge, MA: Harvard University Press.

Burt, R. S. (2005). *Brokerage and Closure: An Introduction to Social Capital*. Oxford: Oxford University Press.

Burt, R. S. (2010). *Neighbor Networks: Competitive Advantage Local and Personal*. Oxford: Oxford University Press.

Büthe, T., and Mattli, W. (2011). *The New Global Rulers: The Privatization of Regulation in the World Economy*, Princeton: Princeton University Press.

Cammet, M. (2006). 'Development and the Changing Dynamics of Global Production: Global Value Chains and Local Clusters in Apparel Manufacturing', *Competition and Change*, 10/1: 23–48.

Cattaneo, O., Gereffi, G., and Staritz, C. (2010a). 'Global Value Chains in a Postcrisis World: Resilience, Consolidation, and Shifting End Markets', in O. Cattaneo, G. Gereffi, and C. Staritz (eds), *Global Value Chains in a Postcrisis World: A Development Perspective*. Washington: World Bank, 3–20.

Cattaneo, O., Gereffi, G., and Staritz, C. (2010b) (eds). *Global Value Chains in a Postcrisis World: A Development Perspective*. Washington: World Bank.

Challies, E. R. T. (2008). 'Commodity Chains, Rural Development and the Global Agri-Food System', *Geography Compass*, 2/2: 375–94.

Chandler, A. D. (1962). *Strategy and Structure: Chapters in the History of Industrial Enterprise.* Cambridge, MA: MIT Press.

Chandler, A. D. (1977). *The Visible Hand: The Managerial Revolution in American Business,* Cambridge, MA: Harvard University Press.

Chandler, A. D. (1990). *Scale and Scope: The Dynamics of Industrial Capitalism.* Cambridge, MA: Harvard University Press.

Chang, H.-J. (2002). *Kicking Away the Ladder? Economic Development in Historical Perspective.* London: Anthem.

Chang, S.-J. (2008). *Sony versus Samsung: The Inside Story of Electronics Giants' Battle for Global Supremacy.* Singapore: Wiley.

Christensen, C. M. (1997). *The Innovator's Dilemma: When New Technologies Cause Great Firms to Fail.* Boston: Harvard Business School Press.

Christensen, C. M., and Raynor, M. E. (2003). *The Innovator's Solution: Creating and Sustaining Successful Growth.* Boston: Harvard Business School Press.

Christensen, C. M., Anthony, S. D., and Roth, E. A. (2004). *Seeing What's Next: Using the Theories of Innovation to Predict Industry Change.* Boston: Harvard Business School Press.

Christian, M., and Nathan, D. (2013). 'Tourism Overview: Changing End Markets and Hyper Competition', Capturing the Gains Working Paper 26 <http://www. capturingthegains.org/> (accessed November 2014).

Christopherson, S. (2007). 'Barriers to "US Style" Lean Retailing: The Case of Wal-Mart's Failure in Germany', *Journal of Economic Geography,* 7/4: 451–70.

Christopherson, S., and Clark, J. (2007). *Remaking Regional Economies: Power, Labor and Firm Strategies in the Knowledge Economy.* New York: Routledge.

Cimoli, M., Dosi, G., and Stiglitz, J. E. (2009) (eds). *Industrial Policy and Development: The Political Economy of Capabilities Accumulation.* Oxford: Oxford University Press.

Clancy, M. (1998). 'Commodity Chains, Services and Development: Theory and Preliminary Evidence from the Tourism Industry', *Review of International Political Economy,* 5/1: 122–48.

Clark, G. L., and Wojcik, D. (2007). *The Geography of Finance: Corporate Governance in a Global Marketplace.* Oxford: Oxford University Press.

Coe, N. M. (2004). 'The Internationalisation/Globalisation of Retailing: Towards an Economic–Geographical Research Agenda', *Environment & Planning A,* 36(9), 1571–94.

Coe, N. M. (2009). 'Global Production Networks', in R. Kitchin and N. Thrift (eds), *The International Encyclopedia of Human Geography.* 12 vols. Oxford: Elsevier, iv. 556–62.

Coe, N. M. (2012). 'Geographies of Production II: A Global Production Networks A–Z', *Progress in Human Geography,* 36/3: 389–402.

Coe, N. M. (2014). 'Missing Links: Logistics, Governance and Upgrading in a Shifting Global Economy', *Review of International Political Economy,* 21/1: 224–56.

Coe, N. M., and Hess, M. (2005). 'The Internationalization of Retailing: Implications for Supply Network Restructuring in East Asia and Eastern Europe', *Journal of Economic Geography,* 5/4: 449–73.

Coe, N. M., and Hess, M. (2011). 'Local and Regional Development: A Global Production Network Approach', in A. Pike, A. Rodriguez-Pose, and J. Tomaney (eds). *The Handbook of Local and Regional Development*. London: Routledge, 128–38.

Coe, N. M., and Hess, M. (2013) (eds). 'Theme Issue on Global Production Networks, Labour and Development', *Geoforum*, 44: 4–92.

Coe, N. M., and Jordhus-Lier, D. (2011). 'Constrained Agency? Re-Evaluating the Geographies of Labour', *Progress in Human Geography*, 35/2: 211–33.

Coe, N. M., and Lee, Y.-S. (2006). 'The Strategic Localization of Transnational Retailers: The Case of Samsung-Tesco in South Korea', *Economic Geography*, 82/1: 61–88.

Coe, N. M., and Lee, Y.-S. (2013). '"We've learnt how to be local": The Deepening Territorial Embeddedness of Samsung–Tesco in South Korea', *Journal of Economic Geography*, 13/2: 327–56.

Coe, N. M., and Wrigley, N. (2007). 'Host Economy Impacts of Transnational Retail: The Research Agenda', *Journal of Economic Geography*, 7/4: 341–71.

Coe, N. M., and Wrigley, N. (2009) (eds). *The Globalization of Retailing*. 2 vols. Cheltenham: Edward Elgar.

Coe, N. M., Kelly, P. F., and Olds, K. (2003). 'Globalization, Transnationalism, and the Asia-Pacific', in J. Peck and H. W.-C. Yeung (eds), *Remaking the Global Economy: Economic–Geographical Perspectives*. London: Sage, 45–60.

Coe, N. M., Hess, M., Yeung, H. W.-C, Dicken, P., and Henderson, J. (2004). '"Globalizing" Regional Development: A Global Production Networks Perspective', *Transactions of the Institute of British Geographers*, NS 29/4: 468–84.

Coe, N. M., Dicken, P., and Hess, M. (2008a) (eds.). 'Theme Issue on Global Production Networks: Debates and Challenges', *Journal of Economic Geography*, 8/3: 267–440.

Coe, N. M., Dicken, P., and Hess, M. (2008b). 'Global Production Networks: Realizing the Potential', *Journal of Economic Geography*, 8/3: 271–95.

Coe, N. M., Dicken, P., Hess, M., and Yeung, H.W.-C. (2010). 'Making Connections: Global Production Networks and World City Networks', *Global Networks*, 10/1: 138–49.

Coe, N. M., Lai, K., and Wójcik, D. (2014). 'Integrating Finance into Global Production Networks', *Regional Studies*, 48/5: 761–77.

Cohen, B. J. (1996). 'Phoenix Risen: The Resurrection of Global Finance', *World Politics*, 48/2: 268–96.

Colpan, A. M., Hikino, T., and Lincoln, J. R. (2010) (eds). *The Oxford Handbook of Business Groups*. Oxford: Oxford University Press.

Crescenzi, R., Pietrobelli, C., and Rabellotti, R. (2014). 'Innovation Drivers, Value Chains and the Geography of Multinational Corporations in Europe', *Journal of Economic Geography*, 14/6: 1053–86.

Crouch, C. (2005). *Capitalist Diversity and Change: Recombinant Governance and Institutional Entrepreneurs*. Oxford: Oxford University Press.

Crouch, C., and Farrell, H. (2004). 'Breaking the Path of Institutional Development? Alternatives to the New Determinism', *Rationality and Society*, 16/1: 5–43.

Crouch, C., and Streeck, W. (1997) (eds). *Political Economy of Modern Capitalism: Mapping Convergence and Diversity*. London: Sage.

Crouch, C., Schröder, M., and Voelzkow, H. (2009). 'Regional and Sectoral Varieties of Capitalism', *Economy and Society*, 38/4: 654–78.

Cumbers, A., Nativel, C., and Routledge, P. (2008). 'Labour Agency and Union Positionalities in Global Production Networks', *Journal of Economic Geography*, 8/3: 369–87.

Dacin, M. Tina, Ventresca, Marc J., and Beal, Brent D. (1999). 'The Embeddedness of Organizations: Dialogue and Directions', *Journal of Management*, 25/3: 317–56.

Davis, G. F. (2009). *Managed by the Markets: How Finance Reshaped America*. New York: Oxford University Press.

Dawley, S. (2014). 'Creating New Paths? Offshore Wind, Policy Activism and Peripheral Region Development', *Economic Geography*, 90/1: 91–112.

Dawson, J., and Mukoyama, M. (2014) (eds). *Global Strategies in Retailing: Asian and European Experiences*. London: Routledge.

De Marchi, V., Di Maria, E., and Ponte, S. (2014). 'Multinational Firms and the Management of Global Networks: Insights from Global Value Chain Studies', in T. Pedersen, M. Venzin, T. M. Devinney, and L. Tihanyi (eds), *Orchestration of the Global Network Organization*. Advances in International Management, Volume 27. Bingley: Emerald, 463–86.

Dedrick, J., and Kraemer, K. L. (1998). *Asia's Computer Challenge: Threat or Opportunity for the United States and the World?* New York: Oxford University Press.

Dedrick, J., and Kraemer, K. L. (2011). 'Marketing Making in the Personal Computer Industry', in G. G. Hamilton, M. Petrovic, and B. Senauer (eds), *The Market Makers: How Retailers Are Reshaping the Global Economy*. Oxford: Oxford University Press, 291–310.

Dicken, P. (1976). 'The Multiplant Business Enterprise and Geographical Space: Some Issues in the Study of External Control and Regional Development', *Regional Studies*, 10/4: 401–12.

Dicken, P. (1994). 'Global–Local Tensions: Firms and States in the Global Space-Economy', *Economic Geography*, 70/2: 101–28.

Dicken, P. (2004). 'Geographers and "Globalization": (Yet) Another Missed Boat?', *Transactions of the Institute of British Geographers*, 29/1: 5–26.

Dicken, P. (2011). *Global Shift: Mapping the Changing Contours of the World Economy*. 6th edn. London: Sage.

Dicken, P. (2015). *Global Shift: Mapping the Changing Contours of the World Economy*. 7th edn. London: Sage.

Dicken, P., and Lloyd, P. E. (1976). 'Geographical Perspectives on United States Investment in the United Kingdom', *Environment and Planning A*, 8/6: 685–705.

Dicken, P., Kelly, P., Olds, K., and Yeung, H. W.-C. (2001). 'Chains and Networks, Territories and Scales: Towards an Analytical Framework for the Global Economy', *Global Networks*, 1/2: 89–112.

DiMaggio, P. J. (2001) (ed.). *The Twenty-First-Century Firm: Changing Economic Organization in International Perspective*, Princeton: Princeton University Press.

Doremus, P. N., Keller, W. W., Pauly, L. W., and Reich, S. (1998). *The Myth of the Global Corporation*. Princeton: Princeton University Press.

Dörry, S. (2008). 'Business Relations in the Design of Package Tours in a Changing Environment: The Case of Tourism from Germany to Jordan', in P. Burns and

M. Novelli (eds), *Tourism and Mobilities: Local–Global Connections*. Wallingford: CABI, 204–18.

Dossani, R. (2013). 'A Decade after the Y2K Problem: Has Indian IT Emerged?', in D. Breznitz and J. Zysman (eds), *The Third Globalization*. Oxford: Oxford University Press, 158–77.

Doz, Y. L., and Hamel, G. (1998). *Alliance Advantage: The Art of Creating Value through Partnering*. Boston: Harvard Business School Press.

Duhigg, C., and Barboza, D. (2012). 'In China, Human Costs are Built into an iPad', *New York Times*, 25 January.

Dunaway, W. (2014) (ed.). *Gendered Commodity Chains: Seeing Women and Households in 21st Century Global Production*. Stanford, CA: Stanford University Press.

Dunning, J. H. (1958). *American Investment in British Manufacturing Industry*. London: Allen and Unwin.

Dunning, J. H. (1998). 'Location and the Multinational Enterprise: A Neglected Factor?', *Journal of International Business Studies*, 29/1: 45–66.

Dunning, J. H. (2009). 'Location and the Multinational Enterprise: John Dunning's Thoughts on Receiving the *Journal of International Business Studies* 2008 Decade Award', *Journal of International Business Studies*, 40/1: 20–34.

Dunning, J. H., and Lundan, S. M. (2008). *Multinational Enterprises and the Global Economy*. 2nd edn. Cheltenham: Edward Elgar.

Dussel Peters, E. (2008). 'GCCs and Development: A Conceptual and Empirical Review', *Competition and Change*, 12/1: 11–27.

Elms, D. K., and Low, P. (2013) (eds). *Global Value Chains in a Changing World*. Geneva: World Trade Organization.

Epstein, G. A. (2005) (ed.). *Financialization and the World Economy*. Cheltenham: Edward Elgar.

Ernst, D. (2005). 'Complexity and Internationalisation of Innovation: Why Is Chip Design Moving to Asia?', *International Journal of Innovation Management*, 9/1: 47–73.

Ernst, D. (2009). 'A New Geography of Knowledge in the Electronics Industry? Asia's Role in Global Innovation Networks', *Policy Studies*, 54: 1–65 (Honolulu: East–West Center).

Ernst, D., and Kim, L. (2002). 'Global Production Networks, Knowledge Diffusion and Local Capability Formation', *Research Policy*, 31/6: 1417–29.

Evans, P. (1995). *Embedded Autonomy: States and Industrial Transformation*. Princeton: Princeton University Press.

Faulconbridge, J., and Muzio, D. (2009). 'The Financialization of Large Law Firms: Situated Discourses and Practices of Reorganization', *Journal of Economic Geography*, 9/5: 641–61.

Feenstra, R. C. (1998). 'Integration of Trade and Disintegration of Production in the Global Economy', *Journal of Economic Perspectives*, 12/4: 31–50.

Feenstra, R. C., and Hamilton, G. G. (2006). *Emergent Economies, Divergent Paths: Economic Organization and International Trade in South Korea and Taiwan*. Cambridge: Cambridge University Press.

Feenstra, R. C., and Hanson, G. H. (1996). 'Globalization, Outsourcing, and Wage Inequality', *American Economic Review: Papers and Proceedings*, 86/2: 240–5.

Fernández, V. R. (2014). 'Global Value Chains in Global Political Networks: Tool for Development or Neoliberal Device?', *Review of Radical Political Economics* <doi: 10.1177/0486613414532769> (accessed November 2014).

Fernandez-Stark, K., Bamber, P., and Gereffi, G. (2011). 'The Offshore Services Value Chain: Upgrading Trajectories in Developing Countries', *International Journal of Technological Learning, Innovation and Development*, 4/1–3: 206–34.

Ferrarini, B., and Hummels, D. (2014) (eds). *Asia and Global Production Networks Implications for Trade, Incomes and Economic Vulnerability.* Cheltenham: Edward Elgar.

Fine, B., Saraswati, J., and Tavasci, D. (2013) (eds). *Beyond the Developmental State: Industrial Policy into the 21st Century.* London: Pluto Press.

Fine, C. H. (1998). *Clockspeed: Winning Industry Control in the Age of Temporary Advantage,* Reading, MA: Perseus Publishing.

Fligstein, N. (2001). *The Architecture of Markets: An Economic Sociology of Twenty-First-Century Capitalist Societies.* Princeton: Princeton University Press.

Fold, N. (2002). 'Lead Firms and Competition in "Bi-polar" Commodity Chains: Grinders and Branders in the Global Cocoa-Chocolate Industry', *Journal of Agrarian Change*, 2/2: 228–47.

Fold, N. (2014). 'Value Chain Dynamics, Settlement Trajectories and Regional Development', *Regional Studies*, 48/5: 778–90.

Frederick, S., and Gereffi, G. (2011). 'Upgrading and Restructuring in the Global Apparel Value Chain: Why China and Asia Are Outperforming Mexico and Central America', *International Journal of Technological Learning, Innovation and Development*, 4/1–3: 67–95.

Freidberg, S. (2004). *French Beans and Food Scares: Culture and Commerce in an Anxious Age.* New York: Oxford University Press.

Frieden, J. (1991). 'Invested Interests: The Politics of National Economic Policies in a World of Global Finance', *International Organization*, 45/4: 425–51.

Fröbel, F., Heinrichs, J., and Kreye, O. (1980). *The New International Division of Labour.* Cambridge: Cambridge University Press.

Froud, J., Haslam, C., Johal, S., and Williams, K. (2002). 'Cars after Financialisation: A Case Study in Financial Under-Performance, Constraints and Consequences', *Competition and Change*, 6/1: 13–41.

Froud, J., Johal, S., Leaver, A., and Williams, K. (2012). 'Financialization across the Pacific: Manufacturing Cost Ratios, Supply Chains and Power', *Critical Perspectives on Accounting*, 25/1: 46–57.

Fung, Victor K. (2013). 'Preface: Governance through Partnership in a Changing World', in D. K. Elms and P. Low (eds), *Global Value Chains in a Changing World.* Geneva: World Trade Organization, pp. xix–xxiii.

Gattorna, J. (2010). *Dynamic Supply Chains: Delivering Value through People*, 2nd edn. Harlow: FT Prentice Hall.

Gattorna, J. (2013). 'The Influence of Customer Buying Behaviour on Product Flow Patterns between Trading Countries, and the Implications for Regulatory Policy', in D. K. Elms and P. Low (eds), *Global Value Chains in a Changing World.* Geneva: World Trade Organization, 221–44.

Gawer, A. (2010) (ed.). *Platforms, Markets and Innovation*. Cheltenham: Edward Elgar.

Gawer, A., and Cusumano, M. (2002). *Platform Leadership: How Intel, Microsoft, and Cisco Drive Industry Innovation*. Boston: Harvard Business School Press.

Gellert, P. K. (2003). 'Renegotiating a Timber Commodity Chain: Lessons from Indonesia on the Political Construction of Global Commodity Chains', *Sociological Forum*, 18/1: 53–84.

Gereffi, G. (1994). 'The Organization of Buyer-Driven Global Commodity Chains: How US Retailers Shape Overseas Production Networks', in G. Gereffi and M. Korzeniewicz (eds), *Commodity Chains and Global Capitalism*, Westport, CT: Praeger, 95–122.

Gereffi, G. (1995). 'Global Production Systems and Third World Development', in B. Stallings (ed.), *Global Change, Regional Response*. New York: Cambridge University Press, 100–42.

Gereffi, G. (1996). 'Global Commodity Chains: New Forms of Coordination and Control among Nations and Firms in International Industries', *Competition and Change*, 1/4: 427–39.

Gereffi, G. (1999). 'International Trade and Industrial Upgrading in the Apparel Commodity Chain', *Journal of International Economics*, 48/1: 37–70.

Gereffi, G. (2005). 'The Global Economy: Organization, Governance, and Development', in N. J. Smelser and R. Swedberg (eds), *The Handbook of Economic Sociology*. 2nd edn. Princeton: Princeton University Press, 160–82.

Gereffi, G. (2014). 'Global Value Chains in a Post-Washington Consensus World', *Review of International Political Economy*, 21/1: 9–37.

Gereffi, G., and Fernandez-Stark, K. (2010). 'The Offshore Services Value Chain: Developing Countries and the Crisis', in O. Cattaneo, G. Gereffi, and C. Staritz (eds), *Global Value Chains in a Postcrisis World: A Development Perspective*. Washington: World Bank, 335–72.

Gereffi, G., and Frederick, S. (2010). 'The Global Apparel Value Chain, Trade, and the Crisis: Challenges and Opportunities for Developing Countries', in O. Cattaneo, G. Gereffi, and C. Staritz (eds), *Global Value Chains in a Postcrisis World: A Development Perspective*. Washington: World Bank, 157–208.

Gereffi, G., and Korzeniewicz, M. (1990). 'Commodity Chains and Footwear Exports in the Semiperiphery', in W. G. Martin (ed.), *Semiperipheral States in the World-Economy*. Westport, CT: Greenwood Press, 45–68.

Gereffi, G., and Korzeniewicz, M. (1994) (eds). *Commodity Chains and Global Capitalism*. Westport, CT: Praeger.

Gereffi, G., and Luo, X. (2014). 'Risk and Opportunities of Participation in Global Value Chains'. Background Paper to the 2014 World Development Report, Policy Research Working Paper 6847. Washington: World Bank.

Gereffi, G., and Sturgeon, T. (2013). 'Global Value Chain-Oriented Industrial Policy: The Role of Emerging Economies', in D. K. Elms and P. Low (eds), *Global Value Chains in a Changing World*. Geneva: World Trade Organization, 329–60.

Gereffi, G., Korzeniewicz, M., and Korzeniewicz, R. P. (1994). 'Introduction: Global Commodity Chains', in G. Gereffi and M. Korzeniewicz (eds), *Commodity Chains and Global Capitalism*. Westport, CT: Praeger, 1–14.

Gereffi, G., Humphrey, J., and Sturgeon, T. (2005). 'The Governance of Global Value Chains', *Review of International Political Economy*, 12/1: 78–104.

Gibbon, P. (2002). 'At the Cutting Edge? Financialisation and UK Clothing Retailers' Sourcing Patterns and Practices', *Competition and Change*, 6/3: 289–308.

Gibbon, P. (2008). 'Governance, Entry Barriers, Upgrading: A Re-Interpretation of Some GVC Concepts from the Experience of African Clothing Exports', *Competition & Change*, 12/1: 29–48.

Gibbon, P., and Ponte, S. (2005). *Trading down: Africa, Value Chains, and the Global Economy*. Philadelphia: Temple University Press.

Gibbon, P., and Ponte, S. (2008). 'Global Value Chains: From Governance to Governmentality?', *Economy and Society*, 37/3: 365–92.

Gibbon, P., Bair, J., and Ponte, S. (2008). 'Governing Global Value Chains: An Introduction', *Economy and Society*, 37: 315–38.

Gibson-Graham, J. K (1996). *The End of Capitalism (as we Knew it): A Feminist Critique of Political Economy*. Oxford: Blackwell.

Gibson-Graham, J. K. (2006). *A Postcapitalist Politics*. Minneapolis: University of Minnesota Press.

Gibson-Graham, J. K., Cameron, J., and Healy, S. (2013). *Take Back the Economy: An Ethical Guide for Transforming our Communities*. Minneapolis: University of Minnesota Press.

Giddens, A. (1979). *Central Problems in Social Theory: Action, Structure and Contradiction in Social Analysis*. Basingstoke: Macmillan.

Giddens, A. (1984). *The Constitution of Society: Outline of the Theory of Structuration*. Cambridge: Polity Press.

Glassman, J. (2011). 'The Geo-Political Economy of Global Production Networks', *Geography Compass*, 5/4: 154–64.

Glyn, A. (2006). *Capitalism Unleashed: Finance, Globalization, and Welfare*. Oxford: Oxford University Press.

Goto, K., and Endo, T. (2014). 'Upgrading, Relocating, Informalising? Local Strategies in the Era of Globalisation: The Thai Garment Industry', *Journal of Contemporary Asia*, 44/1: 1–18.

Gourevitch, P., Bohn, R., and McKendrick, D. (2000). 'Globalization of Production: Insights from the Hard Disk Drive Industry', *World Development*, 28/2: 301–17.

Grabher, G. (2006). 'Trading Routes, Bypasses, and Risky Intersections: Mapping the Travels of "Networks" between Economic Sociology and Economic Geography', *Progress in Human Geography*, 30/2: 163–89.

Granovetter, M. (1985). 'Economic Action and Social Structure: The Problem of Embeddedness', *American Journal of Sociology*, 91/3: 481–510.

Grossman, G., and Helpman, E. (2002). 'Integration versus Outsourcing in Industry Equilibrium', *Quarterly Journal of Economics*, 117/1: 85–120.

Grossman, G., and Rossi-Hansberg, E. (2008). 'Trading Tasks: A Simple Theory of Offshoring', *American Economic Review*, 98/5: 1978–97.

Guillén, M. F., Collins, R., England, P., and Meyer, M. (2003) (eds). *The New Economic Sociology: Developments in an Emerging Field*. New York: Russell Sage.

Gulati, R. (2007). *Managing Network Resources: Alliances, Affiliations, and Other Relational Assets*. Oxford: Oxford University Press.

Gwynne, R. N. (1999). 'Globalisation, Commodity Chains and Fruit Exporting Regions in Chile', *Tijdschrift voor Economische en Sociale Geografie*, 90/2: 211–25.

Hadjimichalis, C., and Hudson, R. (2006). 'Networks, Regional Development and Democratic Control', *International Journal of Urban and Regional Research*, 30/4: 858–72.

Hall, P., and Soskice, D. (2001). *Varieties of Capitalism: The Institutional Foundations of Comparative Advantage*. Oxford: Oxford University Press.

Hall, P., and Thelen, K. (2009). 'Institutional Change in Varieties of Capitalism', *Socio-Economic Review*, 7/1: 7–34.

Hamilton, G. G. (2005). 'Remaking the Global Economy: US Retailers and Asian Manufacturers'. Presentation at the US–China Economic and Security Review Commission's Hearing on 'China and the Future of Globalization', 19–20 May 2005.

Hamilton, G. G., and Feenstra, R. C. (2006). *Emergent Economies, Divergent Paths: Economic Organization and International Trade in South Korea and Taiwan*. New York: Cambridge University Press.

Hamilton, G., and Gereffi, G. (2009). 'Global Commodity Chains, Market-Makers, and the Rise of Demand-Responsive Economies', in J. Bair (ed.), *Frontiers of Commodity Chain Research*. Palo Alto, CA: Stanford University Press, 136–61.

Hamilton, G. G., and Kao, C.-S. (2011). 'The Asian Miracle and the Rise of Demand-Responsive Economies', in G. G. Hamilton, M. Petrovic, and B. Senauer (eds), *The Market Makers: How Retailers Are Reshaping the Global Economy*. Oxford: Oxford University Press, 181–210.

Hamilton, G. G., and Petrovic, M. (2011). 'Introduction', in G. G. Hamilton, M. Petrovic, and B. Senauer (eds), *The Market Makers: How Retailers Are Reshaping the Global Economy*. Oxford: Oxford University Press, 1–30.

Hamilton, G. G., Petrovic, M., and Senauer, B. (2011) (eds). *The Market Makers: How Retailers Are Reshaping the Global Economy*. Oxford: Oxford University Press.

Hancké, B. (2009) (ed.). *Debating Varieties of Capitalism: A Reader*. Oxford: Oxford University Press.

Hancké, B., Rhodes, M., and Thatcher, M. (2007) (eds). *Beyond Varieties of Capitalism: Conflict, Contradictions and Complementarities in the European Economy*. Oxford: Oxford University Press.

Hart, G. (2001). 'Development Critiques in the 1990s: *Culs de sac* and Promising Paths', *Progress in Human Geography*, 25/4: 649–58.

Harvey, D. (1989). *The Condition of Postmodernity: An Enquiry into the Origins of Cultural Change*. Oxford: Blackwell.

Harvey, D. (2003). *The New Imperialism*. Oxford: Oxford University Press.

Haslam, C., Tsitsianis, N., Andersson, T., and Yin, Y. P. (2013). 'Apple's Financial Success: The Precariousness of Power Exercised in Global Value Chains', *Accounting Forum*, 37/4: 268–79.

Hassler, M. (2004). 'Raw Material Procurement, Industrial Upgrading and Labor Recruitment: Intermediaries in Indonesia's Clothing Industry', *Geoforum*, 35/4: 441–51.

Havice, E., and Campling, L. (2013). 'Articulating Upgrading: Island Developing States and Canned Tuna Production', *Environment and Planning A*, 45/11: 2610–27.

Helleiner, E. (1994). *States and the Reemergence of Global Finance: From Bretton Woods to the 1990s*. Ithaca, NY: Cornell University Press.

Henderson, J. (1989). *The Globalisation of High Technology Production.* London: Routledge.

Henderson, J., Dicken, P., Hess, M., Coe, N. M., and Yeung, H. W-C. (2002). 'Global Production Networks and the Analysis of Economic Development', *Review of International Political Economy,* 9/3: 436–64.

Herrigel, G. (1996). *Industrial Constructions: The Sources of German Industrial Power.* Cambridge: Cambridge University Press.

Herrigel, G. (2010). *Manufacturing Possibilities: Creative Action and Industrial Recomposition in the United States, Germany, and Japan.* Oxford: Oxford University Press.

Hess, M. (2004). ' "Spatial" Relationships? Towards a Reconceptualization of Embeddedness', *Progress in Human Geography,* 28/2: 165–86.

Hess, M. (2008). 'Governance, Value Chains and Networks: An Afterword', *Economy and Society,* 37/3: 452–9.

Hess, M. (2009). 'Investigating the Archipelago Economy: Chains, Networks and the Study of Uneven Development', *Journal fuer Entwicklungspolitik,* 2: 20–37.

Hess, M., and Coe, N. M. (2006). 'Making Connections: Global Production Networks, Standards, and Embeddedness in the Mobile Telecommunications Industry', *Environment and Planning A,* 38/7: 1205–27.

Hess, M., and Yeung, H. W-C. (2006a) (eds). 'Theme Issue on Global Production Networks', *Environment and Planning A,* 38/7: 1193–305.

Hess, M., and Yeung, H. W-C. (2006b). 'Whither Global Production Networks in Economic Geography? Past, Present and Future', *Environment and Planning A,* 38/7: 1193–204.

Hetherington, K., and Law J. (2000). 'After Networks', *Environment and Planning D: Society and Space,* 18/2: 127–32.

Hirst, P., and Zeitlin, J. (1996). *Governing Flexibility: Flexible Specialisation, Industrial Districts and Economic Governance.* London: Routledge.

Hobday, M. (1995). *Innovation in East Asia: The Challenge to Japan.* Cheltenham: Edward Elgar.

Hobday, M. (2001). 'The Electronics Industries of the Asia–Pacific: Exploiting International Production Networks for Economic Development', *Asian–Pacific Economic Literature,* 15/1: 13–29.

Hollingsworth, J. Rogers, and Boyer, R. (1999) (eds). *Contemporary Capitalism: The Embeddedness of Institutions.* Cambridge: Cambridge University Press.

Hopkins, T., and Wallerstein, I. (1986). 'Commodity Chains in the World Economy prior to 1800', *Review,* 10/1: 157–70.

Horner, R. (2014). 'Strategic Decoupling, Recoupling and Global Production Networks: India's Pharmaceutical Industry', *Journal of Economic Geography,* 14/6: 1117–40.

Hough P. A (2011). 'Disarticulations and Commodity Chains: Cattle, Coca, and Capital Accumulation along Colombia's Agricultural Frontier', *Environment and Planning A,* 43/5: 1016–34.

Hsu, J.-Y. (2011). 'State Transformation and Regional Development in Taiwan: From Developmentalist Strategy to Populist Subsidy', *International Journal of Urban and Regional Research,* 35/3: 600–19.

Hsu, J.-Y., and Saxenian, A. (2000). 'The Limits of Guanxi Capitalism: Transnational Collaboration between Taiwan and the USA', *Environment and Planning A*, 32/11: 1991–2005.

Hudson, R. (2007). 'Regions and Regional Uneven Development Forever? Some Reflective Comments upon Theory and Practice', *Regional Studies*, 41/9: 1149–60.

Hudson, R. (2008). 'Cultural Political Economy Meets Global Production Networks: A Productive Meeting?', *Journal of Economic Geography*, 8/3: 421–40.

Hughes, A. (2001). 'Global Commodity Networks, Ethical Trade and Governmentality: Organizing Business Responsibility in the Kenyan Cut Flower Industry', *Transactions of the Institute of British Geographers*, 26/4: 390–406.

Hughes, A. (2012). 'Corporate Ethical Trading in an Economic Downturn: Recession-ary Pressures and Refracted Responsibilities', *Journal of Economic Geography*, 12/1: 33–45.

Hughes, A., Wrigley, N., and Buttle, M. (2008). 'Global Production Networks, Ethical Campaigning, and the Embeddedness of Responsible Governance', *Journal of Economic Geography*, 8/3: 345–68.

Humphrey, J., and Schmitz, H. (2002a). 'How Does Insertion in Global Value Chains Affect Upgrading in Industrial Clusters?', *Regional Studies*, 36/9: 1017–27.

Humphrey, J., and Schmitz, H. (2002b). 'Developing Country Firms in the World Economy: Governance and Upgrading in Global Value Chains'. IDS-INEF Report No. 61. Institut für Entwicklung und Frieden der Gerhard-Mercator-Universität Duisburg.

Hymer, S. H. (1976). *The International Operations of National Firms: A Study of Foreign Direct Investment*. Cambridge, MA: MIT Press.

IMF (2013). *Trade Interconnectness: The World with Global Value Chains*, 26 August 2013. Washington: IMF <http://www.imf.org/external/np/pp/eng/2013/082613.pdf> (accessed July 2014).

Johal, S., and Leaver, A. (2007). 'Is the Stock Market a Disciplinary Institution? French Giant Firms and the Regime of Accumulation', *New Political Economy*, 12/3: 349–67.

Jones, R. W., and Kierzkowski, H. (1990). 'The Role of Services in Production and International Trade: A Theoretical Framework', in R. W. Jones and A. O. Krueger (eds), *The Political Economy of International Trade*. Oxford: Blackwell, 31–48.

Jones, R. W., and Kierzkowski, H. (2001). 'Globalization and the Consequences of International Fragmentation', in G. A. Calvo, R. Dornbusch, and M. Obstfeld (eds), *Money, Capital Mobility and Trade: Essays in Honor of Robert A. Mundell*. Cambridge, MA: MIT Press, 365–83.

Kaplinsky, R. (1998). 'Globalisation, Industrialisation and Sustainable Growth: The Pursuit of the Nth Rent'. IDS Discussion Paper 365. Sussex: Institute of Development Studies.

Kaplinsky, R. (2005). *Globalization, Poverty and Inequality*. Cambridge: Polity.

Kaplinsky, R. (2010). 'The Role of Standards in Global Value Chains'. Policy Research Working Paper 5396. Washington: World Bank.

Kaplinsky, R., and Farooki, M. (2010). 'Global Value Chains, the Crisis, and the Shift of Markets from North to South', in O. Cattaneo, G. Gereffi, and C. Staritz (eds), *Global Value Chains in a Postcrisis World: A Development Perspective*. Washington: World Bank, 125–54.

Kaplinsky, R., and Farooki, M. (2011). 'What are the Implications for Global Value Chains when the Market Shifts from the North to the South?', *International Journal of Technological Learning, Innovation and Development*, 4/1–3: 13–38.

Kaplinsky, R., and Morris, M. (2001). *A Handbook for Value Chain Research*. Prepared for the IDRC <http://asiandrivers.open.ac.uk/documents/Value_chain_Handbook_RKMM_Nov_2001.pdf> (accessed November 2014).

Kapner, S. (2009). 'The Unstoppable Fung Brothers', *CNN Money*, 8 December <http://money.cnn.com> (accessed November 2013).

Keck, M. E., and Sikkink, K. (1998). *Activists beyond Borders: Advocacy Networks in International Politics*. Ithaca, NY: Cornell University Press.

Keil, R., and Mahon, R. (2009) (eds). *Leviathan Undone: Towards a Political Economy of Scale?* Vancouver: UBC Press.

Kelly, P. F. (2013). 'Production Networks, Place and Development: Thinking through Global Production Networks in Cavite, Philippines', *Geoforum*, 44: 82–92.

Kenney, M. (2004). 'Introduction', in M. Kenney and R. Florida (eds), *Locating Global Advantage: Industry Dynamics in the International Economy*. Stanford, CA: Stanford University Press, 1–20.

Kenney, M., and Florida, R. (2004) (eds). *Locating Global Advantage: Industry Dynamics in the International Economy*, Stanford, CA: Stanford University Press.

Khanna, T., and Palepu, K. (1997). 'Why Focused Strategies may be Wrong for Emerging Markets', *Harvard Business Review* (July–August), 41–51.

Khanna, T., and Yafeh, Y. (2007). 'Business Groups in Emerging Markets: Paragons or Parasites?', *Journal of Economic Literature*, 45/2: 331–72.

Khanna, T., and Yafeh, Y. (2010). 'Business Groups in Emerging Markets: Paragons or Parasites?', in Asli M. Colpan, Takashi Hikino, and James R. Lincoln (eds), *The Oxford Handbook of Business Groups*. Oxford: Oxford University Press, 575–601. (Update of their 2007 paper in *JEL* with new references.)

Kharas, H. (2010). 'The Emerging Middle Class in Developing Countries'. OECD Development Centre Working Paper No. 285. Paris: OECD.

Kilduff, M., and Tsai, W. (2003). *Social Networks and Organizations*. London: Sage.

King, I., Cuplan, T., and Satariano, A. (2012). 'Apple, Qualcomm Bids Spurned for Exclusive TSMC Supplies', 30 August <http://www.Bloomberg.com> (accessed November 2013).

Kleibert, J. M. (2014). 'Strategic Coupling in "Next Wave Cities": Local Institutional Actors and the Offshore Service Sector in the Philippines', *Singapore Journal of Tropical Geography*, 35/2: 245–60.

Knickerbocker, F. T. (1973). *Oligopolistic Reaction and Multinational Enterprises*. Boston: Harvard Business School Press.

Knight, F. H. (1921). *Risk, Uncertainty, and Profit*. Boston: Hart, Schaffner & Marx.

Kogut, B. (1985). 'Designing Global Strategies: Comparative and Competitive Value-added Chains', *Sloan Management Review*, 26/4: 15–28.

Koopman, R., Wang, Z., and Wei, S.-J. (2014). 'Tracing Value-Added and Double Counting in Gross Exports', *American Economic Review*, 104/2: 459–94.

Krippner, G. R. (2011). *Capitalizing on Crisis: The Political Origins of the Rise of Finance*. Cambridge, MA: Harvard University Press.

Krippner, G. R., and Alvarez, A. S. (2007). 'Embeddedness and the Intellectual Projects of Economic Sociology', *Annual Review of Sociology*, 33: 219–40.

Lane, C. (2008). 'National Capitalisms and Global Production Networks: An Analysis of their Interaction in Two Global Industries', *Socio-Economic Review*, 6/2: 227–60.

Lane, C., and Probert, J. (2009). *National Capitalisms, Global Production Networks: Fashioning the Value Chain in the UK, US, and Germany*. Oxford: Oxford University Press.

Langley, P. (2008). *The Everyday Life of Global Finance: Saving and Borrowing in Anglo-America*. Oxford: Oxford University Press.

Latour, B. (2005). *Reassembling the Social*. Oxford: Blackwell.

Law, J. (2004). *After Method: Mess in Social Science Research*. London: Routledge.

Lazonick, W., and O'Sullivan, M. (2000). 'Maximizing Shareholder Value: A New Ideology for Corporate Governance', *Economy and Society*, 29/1: 13–35.

Lee, H. L., Padmanabhan, V., and Whang, S. (1997a). 'Information Distortion in a Supply Chain: The Bullwhip Effect', *Management Science*, 43/4: 546–58.

Lee, H. L., Padmanabhan, V., and Whang, Seungjin (1997b). 'The Bullwhip Effect in Supply Chains', *Sloan Management Review*, 38/3: 93–102.

Lee, J., Gereffi, G., and Beauvais, J. (2012). 'Global Value Chains and Agrifood Standards: Challenges and Possibilities for Smallholders in Developing Countries', *Proceedings of the National Academy of Sciences of the United States of America*, 109/31: 12326–31.

Lee, Y.-S., Heo, I., and Kim, H. (2014). 'The Role of the State as an Interscalar Mediator in Globalizing Liquid Crystal Display Industry Development in South Korea', *Review of International Political Economy*, 21/1: 109–29.

Lessard, D. (2013). 'Uncertainty and Risk in Global Supply Chains', in D. K. Elms and P. Low (eds), *Global Value Chains in a Changing World*. Geneva: World Trade Organization, 195–220.

Levy, D. L. (2008). 'Political Contestation in Global Production Networks', *Academy of Management Review*, 33/4: 943–63.

Lichtenstein, N. (2006) (ed.). *Wal-Mart: The Face of Twenty-First-Century Capitalism*. New York: New Press.

Lin, J. Y. (2012a). *New Structural Economics: A Framework for Rethinking Development*. Washington: The World Bank.

Lin, J. Y. (2012b). *The Quest for Prosperity: How Developing Economies Can Take Off*. Princeton: Princeton University Press.

Lin, Y., and Rasiah, R. (2014). 'Human Capital Flows in Taiwan's Technological Catch Up in Integrated Circuit Manufacturing', *Journal of Contemporary Asia*, 44/1: 64–83.

Liu, W., and Dicken, P. (2006). 'Transnational Corporations and "Obligated Embeddedness": Foreign Direct Investment in China's Automobile Industry', *Environment and Planning A*, 38/7: 1229–47.

Locke, R. M., Qin, F., and Brause, A. (2007). 'Does Monitoring Improve Labor Standards: Lessons from Nike', *Industrial and Labor Relations Review*, 61/3: 3–31.

Low, P. (2013). 'The Role of Services in Global Value Chains', in D. K. Elms and P. Low (eds), *Global Value Chains in a Changing World*. Geneva: World Trade Organization, 61–81.

Lundvall, B. (1992) (ed.), *National Systems of Innovation: Towards a Theory of Innovation and Interactive Learning*. London: Pinter.

Lung, Y., Van Tulder, R., and Carillo, J. (2004) (eds). *Cars, Carriers of Regionalism?* New York: Palgrave Macmillan.

Lüthje, B. (2002). 'Electronics Contract Manufacturing: Global Production and the International Division of Labor in the Age of the Internet', *Industry and Innovation*, 9/3: 227–47.

Lüthje, B., Hürtgen, S., Pawlicki, P., and Sproll, M. (2013). *From Silicon Valley to Shenzhen: Global Production and Work in the IT Industry*. Lanham, MD: Rowman & Littlefield.

McGrath-Champ, S. (1999). 'Strategy and Industrial Restructuring', *Progress in Human Geography*, 23/2: 236–52.

Macher, J. T., Mowery, D. C., and Simcoe, T. S. (2002). 'E-Business and Disintegration of the Semiconductor Industry Value Chain', *Industry and Innovation*, 9/3: 155–81.

MacKinnon, D. (2012). 'Beyond Strategic Coupling: Reassessing the Firm–Region Nexus in Global Production Networks', *Journal of Economic Geography*, 12/1: 227–45.

MacLeod, G. (2001). 'New Regionalism Reconsidered: Globalization and the Remaking of Political Economic Space', *International Journal of Urban and Regional Research*, 25/4, 804–29.

Mahutga, M. C. (2012). 'When Do Value Chains Go Global? A Theory of the Spatialization of Global Value Chains', *Global Networks*, 12/1: 1–21.

Mahutga, M. C. (2014). 'Global Models of Networked Organization, the Positional Power of Nations and Economic Development', *Review of International Political Economy*, 21/1: 157–94.

Martin, R. (2010). 'Roepke Lecture in Economic Geography—Rethinking Path Dependency: Beyond Lock-in to Evolution', *Economic Geography*, 86/1: 1–27.

Martin, R., and Sunley, P. J. (2003). 'Deconstructing Clusters: Chaotic Concept or Policy Panacea?', *Journal of Economic Geography*, 3/1: 5–35.

Massey, D. (1979). 'In what Sense a Regional Problem?', *Regional Studies*, 13/2: 233–43.

Massey, D. (1984). *Spatial Divisions of Labour: Social Structures and the Geography of Production*. London: Methuen.

Mathews, J. A. (2005). 'Strategy and the Crystal Cycle', *California Management Review*, 47/2: 6–32.

Mathews, J. A. (2006). *Strategizing, Disequilibrium and Profit*. Stanford, CA: Stanford University Press.

Mathews, J. A., and Cho, D.-S. (2000). *Tiger Technology: The Creation of a Semiconductor Industry in East Asia*. Cambridge: Cambridge University Press.

Meyer, K. E., Mudambi, R., and Narula, R. (2011). 'Multinational Enterprises and Local Contexts: The Opportunities and Challenges of Multiple Embeddedness', *Journal of Management Studies*, 48/2: 235–52.

Milberg, W. (2008). 'Shifting Sources and Uses of Profits: Sustaining US Financialization with Global Value Chains', *Economy and Society*, 37/3: 420–51.

Milberg, W., and Winkler, D. (2010). 'Financialisation and the Dynamics of Offshoring in the USA', *Cambridge Journal of Economics*, 34/2: 275–93.

Milberg, W., and Winkler, D. (2011). 'Economic and Social Upgrading in Global Production Networks: Problems of Theory and Measurement', *International Labour Review*, 150/3–4: 341–65.

Milberg, W., and Winkler, D. (2013). *Outsourcing Economics: Global Value Chains in Capitalist Development*. Cambridge: Cambridge University Press.

Morgan, G., and Whitley, R. (2012) (eds). *Capitalisms and Capitalism in the 21st Century*. Oxford: Oxford University Press.

Morgan, K. (1997). 'The Learning Region: Institutions, Innovation and Regional Renewal', *Regional Studies*, 31/5: 491–503.

Morgan, K., and Sayer, A. (1988). *Microcircuits of Capital*. Oxford: Polity Press.

Morgan, K., Marsden, T., and Murdoch, J. (2006). *Worlds of Food: Place, Power and Provenance in the Food Chain*. Oxford: Oxford University Press.

Mudambi, R. (2008). 'Location, Control and Innovation in Knowledge-Intensive Industries', *Journal of Economic Geography*, 8/5: 699–725.

Murdoch, J. (1998). 'The Spaces of Actor–Network Theory', *Geoforum*, 29/4: 357–74.

Murphy, J. T. (2012). 'Global Production Networks, Relational Proximity, and the Socio-Spatial Dynamics of Market Internationalization in Bolivia's Wood Products Sector', *Annals of the Association of American Geographers*, 102/1: 208–33.

Murphy, J. T., and Schindler, S. (2011). 'Globalizing Development in Bolivia? Alternative Networks and Value-Capture Challenges in the Wood Products Industry', *Journal of Economic Geography*, 11/1: 61–85.

Mutersbaugh, T. (2005). 'Fighting Standards with Standards: Harmonization, Rents, and Social Accountability in Certified Agrofood Networks', *Environment and Planning A*, 37/11: 2033–51.

Nadvi, K. (2008). 'Global Standards, Global Governance and the Organization of Global Value Chains', *Journal of Economic Geography*, 8/3: 323–44.

Nadvi, K., and Waltring, F. (2004). 'Making Sense of Global Standards', in H. Schmitz (ed.), *Local Enterprises in the Global Economy: Issues of Governance and Upgrading*. Cheltenham: Edward Elgar, 53–94.

Navas-Alemán, L. (2010). 'The Impact of Operating in Multiple Value Chains for Upgrading: The Case of the Brazilian Furniture and Footwear Industries', *World Development*, 39/8: 1386–97.

Neilson, J. (2014). 'Value Chains, Neoliberalism and Development Practice: The Indonesian Experience', *Review of International Political Economy*, 21/1: 38–69.

Neilson, J., and Pritchard, B. (2009). *Value Chain Struggles: Institutions and Governance in the Plantation Districts of South India*. Oxford: Wiley-Blackwell.

Neilson, J., Pritchard, B., and Yeung, H. W.-C. (2014) (eds). 'Special Issue on Global Value Chains and Global Production Networks in the Changing International Political Economy', *Review of International Political Economy*, 21/1: 1–274.

Nelson, R. R. (1993) (ed.). *National Systems of Innovation*. Oxford: Oxford University Press.

Nohria, N., and Eccles, R. G. (1992) (eds). *Networks and Organizations: Structure, Form, and Action*. Boston: Harvard Business School Press.

Nohria, N., and Ghoshal, S. (1997). *The Differentiated Network: Organizing Multinational Corporations for Value Creation*. San Francisco, CA: Jossey-Bass.

O'Neill, P., and Gibson-Graham, J. K. (1999). 'Enterprise Discourse and Executive Talk: Stories that Destabilize the Company', *Transactions of the Institute of British Geographers*, 24/1: 11–22.

O'Riain, S. (2011). 'Globalization and Regional Development', in A. Pike, A. Rodríguez-Pose, and J. Tomaney (eds), *Handbook of Local and Regional Development*. London: Routledge, 17–29.

O'Sullivan, M. (2000). *Contests for Corporate Control: Corporate Governance and Economic Performance in the United States and Germany*. Oxford: Oxford University Press.

OECD (2011). *Global Value Chains: Preliminary Evidence and Policy Issues*. Paris: Organization for Economic Cooperation and Development, DSTI/IND(2011)3 <http://www.oecd.org/dataoecd/18/43/47945400.pdf> (accessed September 2012).

OECD (2013). *Interconnected Economies: Benefiting from Global Value Chains* <http://www.oecd.org/sti/ind/global-value-chains.htm> (accessed November 2014).

OECD–WTO–UNCTAD (2013). 'Implications of Global Value Chains for Trade, Investment, Development and Jobs'. Report Prepared for the G-20 Leaders Summit, September 2013 <http://unctad.org/en/PublicationsLibrary/unctad_oecd_wto_2013d1_en.pdf> (accessed September 2013).

Ouma, S. (2010). 'Global Standards, Local Realities: Private Agrifood Governance and the Restructuring of the Kenyan Horticulture Industry', *Economic Geography*, 86/2: 197–222.

Ouma, S. (2015). *Assembling Export Markets: The Making and Unmaking of Global Market Connections in West Africa*. Chichester: Wiley.

Palpacuer, F. (2008). 'Bringing the Social Context back in: Governance and Wealth Distribution in Global Commodity Chains', *Economy and Society*, 37/3: 393–419.

Palpacuer, F., Gibbon, P., and Thomsen, L. (2005). 'New Challenges for Developing Country Suppliers in Global Clothing Chains: A Comparative European Perspective', *World Development*, 33/3: 409–30.

Park, S. O., and Koo, Y. (2010). 'Evolution of New Spatial Division of Labour and Spatial Dynamics in Korea', *Regional Science Policy & Practice*, 2/1: 21–39.

Parrilli, M. D., Nadvi, K., and Yeung, H. W.-C. (2013). 'Local and Regional Development in Global Value Chains, Production Networks and Innovation Networks: A Comparative Review and the Challenges for Future Research', *European Planning Studies*, 21/7: 967–88.

Parthasarathy, B. (2013). 'The Changing Character of Indian ICT Offshore Services Provision, 1985–2010', in A. Bardhan, D. M. Jaffee, and C. A. Kroll (eds), *The Oxford Handbook of Offshoring and Global Employment*. Oxford: Oxford University Press, 380–404.

Peck, J., and Theodore, N. (2007). 'Variegated Capitalism', *Progress in Human Geography*, 31/6: 731–72.

Petrovic, M. (2011). 'US Retailing and its Global Diffusion', in G. G. Hamilton, M. Petrovic, and B. Senauer (eds), *The Market Makers: How Retailers Are Reshaping the Global Economy*. Oxford: Oxford University Press, 79–116.

Petrovic, M., and Hamilton, G. G. (2011). 'Retailers as Market Makers', in G. G. Hamilton, M. Petrovic, and B. Senauer (eds), *The Market Makers: How Retailers Are Reshaping the Global Economy*. Oxford: Oxford University Press, 31–49.

Phelps, N. A. (2000). 'The Locally Embedded Multinational and Institutional Capture', *Area*, 32/2: 169–78.

Phelps, N. A., and Fuller, C. (2000). 'Multinationals, Intracorporate Competition, and Regional Development *Economic Geography*, 76/3: 224–43.

Phelps, N. A., and Wood, A. (2006). 'Lost in Translation? Local Interests, Global Actors and Inward Investment Regimes', *Journal of Economic Geography*, 6/4: 493–515.

Pickles, J. (2006) (ed). 'Theme Issue on Trade Liberalization, Industrial Upgrading, and Regionalization in the Global Apparel Industry', *Environment and Planning A*, 38/12: 2201–344.

Pickles, J. (2007) (ed). *State and Society in Post-Socialist Economies*. New York: Palgrave.

Pickles, J. (2008) (ed). *Globalization and Regionalization in Socialist and Post-Socialist Economies: Common Economic Spaces of Europe*. New York: Palgrave.

Pickles, J., and Smith, A. (2011). 'Delocalization and Persistence in the European Clothing Industry: The Reconfiguration of Trade and Production Networks', *Regional Studies*, 45/2: 167–85.

Pickles, J., and Smith, A. (2015). *Articulations of Capital: Global Production Networks and Regional Transformations*. Oxford: Wiley-Blackwell.

Pickles, J., Smith, A., Buček, M., Roukova, P., and Begg, R. (2006). 'Upgrading, Changing Competitive Pressures, and Diverse Practices in the East and Central European Apparel Industry', *Environment and Planning A*, 38/12: 2305–24.

Pietrobelli, C., and Rabellotti, R. (2007) (eds). *Upgrading to Compete: SMEs, Clusters and Value Chains in Latin America*. Cambridge, MA: Harvard University Press.

Pietrobelli, C., and Rabellotti, R. (2011). 'Global Value Chains Meet Innovation Systems: Are There Learning Opportunities for Developing Countries?', *World Development*, 39/7: 1204–12.

Pike, A., Rodríguez-Pose, A., and Tomaney, J. (2007). 'What Kind of Local and Regional Development and for Whom?', *Regional Studies*, 41/9: 1253–69.

Piore, M., and Sabel, C. (1984). *The Second Industrial Divide*. New York: Basic Books.

Pipkin, S. (2011). 'Local Means in Value Chain Ends: Dynamics of Product and Social Upgrading in Apparel Manufacturing in Guatemala and Colombia', *World Development*, 39/12: 2119–31.

Polanyi, K. (1944). *The Great Transformation*. New York: Holt, Rinehart.

Ponte, S., and Ewert, J. (2009). 'Which Way is "Up" in Upgrading? Trajectories of Change in the Value Chain for South African Wine', *World Development*, 37/10: 1637–50.

Ponte, S., and Gibbon, P. (2005). 'Quality Standards, Conventions and the Governance of Global Value Chains', *Economy and Society*, 34/1, 1–31.

Ponte, S., and Sturgeon, T. (2014). 'Explaining Governance in Global Value Chains: A Modular Theory-Building Effort', *Review of International Political Economy*, 21/1: 195–223.

Ponte, S., Gibbon, P., and Vestergaard, J. (2011a) (eds). *Governing through Standards: Origins, Drivers and Limitations*. Basingstoke: Palgrave Macmillan.

Ponte, S., Gibbon, P., and Vestergaard, J. (2011b). 'Governing through Standards: An Introduction', in S. Ponte, P. Gibbon, and J. Vestergaard (eds), *Governing through Standards: Origins, Drivers and Limitations*. Basingstoke: Palgrave Macmillan, 1–24.

Porter, M. E. (1980). *Competitive Strategy: Techniques for Analyzing Industries and Competitors*. New York: Free Press.

Porter, M. E. (1985). *Competitive Advantage: Creating and Sustaining Performance.* New York: Free Press.

Porter, M. E. (1990). *The Competitive Advantage of Nations.* London, Macmillan.

Porter, M. E. (2000). 'Locations, Clusters, and Company Strategy', in G. L. Clark, M. A. Feldman, and M. S. Gertler (eds), *The Oxford Handbook of Economic Geography.* Oxford: Oxford University Press, 253–74.

Posthuma, A., and Nathan, D. (2011). (eds) *Labour in Global Production Networks in India.* Oxford: Oxford University Press.

Power, D., and Hallencreutz, D. (2007). 'Competitiveness, Local Production Systems and Global Commodity Chains in the Music Industry: Entering the US market', *Regional Studies*, 41/3: 377–89.

Power, M. (2009). *Organized Uncertainty: Designing a World of Risk Management.* Oxford: Oxford University Press.

Prahalad, C. K. (2005). *The Fortune at the Bottom of the Pyramid: Eradicating Poverty through Profits*, Upper Saddle River, NJ: Pearson.

Pries, L. (2005). 'Configurations of Geographic and Societal Spaces: A Sociological Proposal between 'Methodological Nationalism' and the 'Spaces of Flows', *Global Networks*, 5/2: 167–90.

Pun, N. (2005). 'Global Production and Corporate Business Ethics: Company Codes of Conduct Implementation and its Implication on Labour Rights in China', *China Journal*, 54: 101–13.

Quark, A. A. (2013). *Global Rivalries: Standards Wars and the Transnational Cotton Trade.* Chicago: University of Chicago Press.

Rabach, E., and Kim, E. M. (1994). 'Where is the Chain in Commodity Chains? The Service Sector Nexus', in G. Gereffi and M. Korzeniewicz (eds), *Commodity Chains and Global Capitalism.* Westport, CT: Praeger, 123–41.

Rainnie, A., Herod, A., and McGrath-Champ, S. (2011). 'Review and Positions: Global Production Networks and Labour', *Competition and Change*, 15/2: 155–69.

Ramamurthy, P. (2011). 'Rearticulating Caste: The Global Cottonseed Commodity Chain and the Paradox of Smallholder Capitalism in South India', *Environment and Planning A*, 43/5: 1035–56.

Ravenhill, J. (2014). 'Global Value Chains and Development', *Review of International Political Economy*, 12/1: 264–74.

Reardon, T., Timmer, C. P., Barrett, C. B., and Berdegué, J. (2003). 'The Rise of Supermarkets in Africa, Asia, and Latin America', *American Journal of Agricultural Economics*, 85/5: 1140–6.

Reardon, T., Berdegué, J. A., and Timmer, C. P. (2005). 'Supermarketization of the Emerging Markets of the Pacific Rim: Development and Trade Implications', *Journal of Food Distribution Research*, 36/1: 3–12.

Reardon, T., Henson, S., and Berdegué, J. A. (2007). 'Proactive Fast-Tracking Diffusion of Supermarkets in Developing Countries: Implications for Market Institutions and Trade', *Journal of Economic Geography*, 7/4: 399–431.

Riisgaard, L., and Hammer, N. (2011). 'Prospects for Labour in Global Value Chains: Labour Standards in the Cut Flower and Banana Industries', *British Journal of Industrial Relations*, 49/1: 168–90.

Rodríguez-Pose, A., and Storper, M. (2006). 'Better Rules or Stronger Communities? On the Social Foundations of Institutional Change and its Economic Effects', *Economic Geography*, 82/1: 1–25.

Ros, J. (2013). *Rethinking Economic Development, Growth, and Institutions*. Oxford: Oxford University Press.

Rossi, A., Luinstra, A., and Pickles, J. (2014) (eds). *Towards Better Work: Understanding Labour in Apparel Global Value Chains*. Geneva: International Labour Organization and Palgrave Macmillan.

Rugman, A. M. (2005). *The Regional Multinationals: MNEs and 'Global' Strategic Management*. Cambridge: Cambridge University Press.

Saxenian, A. (1994). *Regional Advantage: Culture and Competition in Silicon Valley and Route 128*. Cambridge, MA: Harvard University Press.

Saxenian, A. (2006). *The New Argonauts: Regional Advantage in a Global Economy*. Cambridge, MA: Harvard University Press.

Saxenian, A., and Sabel, C. (2008). 'Roepke Lecture in Economic Geography: Venture Capital in the "Periphery": The New Argonauts, Global Search, and Local Institution Building', *Economic Geography*, 84/4: 379–94.

Sayer, A. (1992). *Method in Social Science: A Realist Approach*. 2nd edn. London: Routledge.

Sayer, A. (2000). *Realism and Social Science*. London: Sage.

Sayer, A., and Walker, R. (1992). *The New Social Economy: Reworking the Division of Labor*. Cambridge, MA: Basil Blackwell.

Schoenberger, E. (1994). 'Competition, Time, and Space in Industrial Change', in G. Gereffi and M. Korzeniewicz (eds, *Commodity Chains and Global Capitalism*. Westport, CT: Praeger, 51–66.

Schoenberger, E. (1997). *The Cultural Crisis of the Firm*. Oxford: Basil Blackwell.

Schoenberger, E. (1999). 'The Firm in the Region and the Region in the Firm', in T. J. Barnes and M. S. Gertler (eds), *The New Industrial Geography: Regions, Regulation and Institutions*. London: Routledge, 205–24.

Schmitz, H. (2004) (ed.). *Local Enterprises in the Global Economy: Issues of Governance and Upgrading*. Cheltenham: Edward Elgar.

Schrank, A. (2004). 'Ready-to-Wear Development? Foreign Investment, Technology Transfer, and Learning by Watching in the Apparel Trade', *Social Forces*, 83/1: 123–56.

Schumpeter, J. A. (1934). *The Theory of Economic Development: An Inquiry into Profits, Capital, Credit, Interest and the Business Cycle*. Cambridge, MA: Harvard University Press.

Scott, A. J. (1988). *New Industrial Spaces: Flexible Production Organization and Regional Development in North America and Western Europe*. London: Pion.

Scott, A. J. (1998). *Regions and the World Economy: The Coming Shape of Global Production, Competition and Political Order*. Oxford: Oxford University Press.

Scott, A. J. (2006a). 'The Changing Global Geography of Low-Technology, Labor-Intensive Industry: Clothing, Footwear, and Furniture', *World Development*, 34/9: 1517–36.

Scott, A. J. (2006b). *Geography and Economy*. Oxford: Oxford University Press.

Scott, A. J. (2008). *Social Economy of the Metropolis: Cognitive–Cultural Capitalism and the Global Resurgence of Cities*. Oxford: Oxford University Press.

Scott, A. J. (2012). *A World in Emergence: Cities and Regions in the 21st Century*. Cheltenham: Edward Elgar.

Seabrooke, L., and Wigan, D. (2014). 'Global Wealth Chains in the International Political Economy', *Review of International Political Economy*, 21/1: 257–63.

Selwyn, B. (2012). 'Beyond Firm-Centrism: Re-Integrating Labour and Capitalism into Global Commodity Chain Analysis', *Journal of Economic Geography*, 12/2: 205–26.

Shackleton, R. (1998). 'Exploring Corporate Culture and Strategy: Sainsbury at Home and Abroad', *Environment and Planning A*, 30/5: 921–40.

Sheffi, Y. (2005). *The Resilient Enterprise: Overcoming Vulnerability for Competitive Advantage*. Cambridge, MA: MIT Press.

Simchi-Levi, D. (2010). *Operations Rules: Delivering Value through Flexible Operations*. Cambridge, MA: MIT Press.

Smelser, N., and Swedberg, R. (2005) (eds). *The Handbook of Economic Sociology*, 2nd edn. Princeton: Princeton University Press.

Smith, A. (2014). 'The State, Institutional Frameworks and the Dynamics of Capital in Global Production Networks', *Progress in Human Geography* <doi: 10.1177/0309132513518292> (accessed November 2014).

Smith, A., Pickles, J., Bucek, M., Pastor, R., and Begg, B. (2014). 'The Political Economy of Global Production Networks: Regional Industrial Change and Differential Upgrading in the East European Clothing Industry', *Journal of Economic Geography*, 14/6: 1023–51.

Smith, N. (2005). *The Endgame of Globalization*. New York: Routledge.

Sovacool, B. K. (2012). 'Reconfiguring Territoriality and Energy Security: Global Production Networks and the Baku–Tbilisi–Ceyhan (BTC) Pipeline', *Journal of Cleaner Production*, 32: 210–18.

Spender, J.-C. (2014). *Business Strategy: Managing Uncertainty, Opportunity, and Enterprise*. Oxford: Oxford University Press.

Stalk, G. R. (1988). 'Time—the Next Source of Competitive Advantage', *Harvard Business Review*, 66 (July–August), 41–51.

Stalk, G. R., and Hout, T. (1990). *Competing against Time: How Time-Based Competition is Reshaping Global Markets*. New York: Free Press.

Staritz, C., Gereffi, G., and Cattaneo, O. (2011a). 'Special Issue on "Shifting End Markets and Upgrading Prospects in Global Value Chains"', *International Journal of Technological Learning, Innovation and Development*, 4/1–3: 1–259.

Staritz, C., Gereffi, G., and Cattaneo, O. (2011b). 'Editorial', *International Journal of Technological Learning, Innovation and Development*, 4/1–3: 1–12.

Starosta, G. (2010a). 'Global Commodity Chains and the Marxian Law of Value', *Antipode*, 42/2: 433–65.

Starosta, G. (2010b). 'The Outsourcing of Manufacturing and the Rise of Giant Global Contractors: A Marxian Approach to some Recent Transformations of Global Value Chains', *New Political Economy*, 15/4: 543–63.

Stopford, J., and Strange, S. (1991). *Rival States, Rival Firms: Competition for World Market Shares*. Cambridge: Cambridge University Press.

Storper, M. (1997). *The Regional World: Territorial Development in a Global Economy*. New York: Guilford Press.

Storper, M. (2013). *Keys to the City: How Economics, Institutions, Social Interaction, and Politics Shape Development*. Princeton: Princeton University Press.

Storper, M., and Salais, R. (1997). *Worlds of Production: The Action Frameworks of the Economy*. Cambridge, MA: Harvard University Press.

Storper, M., and Walker, R. (1989). *The Capitalist Imperative: Territory, Technology and Industrial Growth*. Oxford: Blackwell.

Stringer, C. (2006). 'Forest Certification and Changing Global Commodity Chains', *Journal of Economic Geography*, 6/5: 701–22.

Sturgeon, T.J. (2002). 'Modular Production Networks: A New American Model of Industrial Organization', *Industrial and Corporate Change*, 11/3: 451–96.

Sturgeon, T. J. (2003). 'What Really Goes on in Silicon Valley? Spatial Clustering and Dispersal in Modular Production Networks', *Journal of Economic Geography*, 3/2: 199–225.

Sturgeon, T. J. (2009). 'From Commodity Chains to Value Chains: Interdisciplinary Theory Building in an Age of Globalization', in J. Bair (ed.), *Frontiers of Commodity Chains Research*. Stanford, CA: Stanford University Press, 110–35.

Sturgeon, T. (2013). 'Global Value Chains and Economic Globalisation—Towards a Measurement Framework: A Report to Eurostat'. May 2013, MIT IPC <http://epp.eurostat.ec.europa.eu/portal/page/portal/european_business/documents/Sturgeon_report_Eurostat.pdf> (accessed November 2014).

Sturgeon, T. J., and Kawakami, M. (2010). 'Global Value Chains in the Electronics Industry: Was the Crisis a Window of Opportunity for Developing Countries?', in O. Cattaneo, G. Gereffi, and C. Staritz (eds), *Global Value Chains in a Postcrisis World: A Development Perspective*. Washington: World Bank, 245–302.

Sturgeon, T. J., and Kawakami, M. (2011a). 'Global Value Chains in the Electronics Industry: Characteristics, Crisis, and Upgrading Opportunities for Firms from Developing Countries', *International Journal of Technological Learning, Innovation and Development*, 4/1–3: 120–49.

Sturgeon, T. J., and Kawakami, M. (2011b) (eds). *Local Learning in Global Value Chains: Experiences from East Asia*. Basingstoke: Palgrave Macmillan.

Sturgeon, T. J., and Lester, R. K. (2004). 'The New Global Supply Base: New Challenges for Local Suppliers in East Asia', in S. Yusuf, M. A. Altaf, and K. Nabeshima (eds). *Global Production Networking and Technological Change in East Asia*. Washington: Oxford University Press, 35–87.

Sturgeon, T., and Memedovic, O. (2011). 'Mapping Global Value Chains: Intermediate Goods Trade and Structural Change in the World Economy'. UNIDO Working Paper 05/2011. Vienna: United National Industrial Development Organization.

Sturgeon, T. J., and Van Biesebroeck, J. (2011). 'Global Value Chains in the Automotive Industry: An Enhanced Role for Developing Countries?', *International Journal of Technological Learning, Innovation and Development*, 4/1–3: 181–205.

Sturgeon, T. J., Van Biesebroeck, J., and Gereffi, G. (2008). 'Value Chains, Networks and Clusters: Reframing the Global Automobile Industry', *Journal of Economic Geography*, 8/3: 297–321.

Sturgeon, T., Humphrey, J., and Gereffi, G. (2011). 'Making the Global Supply Base', in G. G. Hamilton, M. Petrovic, and B. Senauer (eds), *The Market Makers: How Retailers Are Reshaping the Global Economy*. Oxford: Oxford University Press, 231–54.

Sun, Y., Zhou, Y., Lin, G. C. S., and Wei, Y. H. D. (2013). 'Subcontracting and Supplier Innovativeness in a Developing Economy: Evidence from China's Information and Communication Technology Industry', *Regional Studies*, 47/10: 1766–84.

Sunley, P. (2008). 'Relational Economic Geography: A Partial Understanding or a New Paradigm?', *Economic Geography*, 84/1: 1–26.

Sunley, P., Pinch, S., and Reimer, S. (2011). 'Design Capital: Practice and Situated Learning in London Design Agencies', *Transactions of the Institute of British Geographers*, 36/3: 377–92.

Swyngedouw, E. (2004). 'Globalisation or "Glocalisation"? Networks, Territories and Rescaling', *Cambridge Review of International Affairs*, 17/1: 25–48.

Taylor, M. (2010). 'Clusters: A Mesmerising Mantra', *Tijdschrift voor Economische en Sociale Geografie*, 101/3: 276–86.

Teece, D. J. (2009). *Dynamic Capabilities and Strategic Management: Organizing for Innovation and Growth*. Oxford: Oxford University Press.

Teece, D., and Pisano, G. (1994). 'The Dynamic Capabilities of Firms: An Introduction', *Industrial and Corporate Change*, 3/3: 537–56.

Tokatli, N. (2011). 'Creative Individuals, Creative Places: Marc Jacobs, New York and Paris', *International Journal of Urban and Regional Research*, 35/6: 1256–71.

Tokatli, N. (2013). 'Toward a Better Understanding of the Apparel Industry: A Critique of the Upgrading Literature', *Journal of Economic Geography*, 13/6: 993–1011.

Tomaney, J., Pike, A., and Rodríguez-Pose, A. (2011). 'Local and Regional Development: Reflections and Futures', in A. Pike, A. Rodríguez-Pose, and J. Tomaney (eds), *Handbook of Local and Regional Development*. London: Routledge, 618–30.

Topik, S. (2009). 'Historicizing Commodity Chains: Five Hundred Years of the Global Coffee Commodity Chain', in J. Bair (ed.), *Frontiers of Commodity Chain Research*. Stanford, CA: Stanford University Press, 37–62.

Tsing, A. (2004). *Friction: An Ethnography of Global Connection*. Princeton: Princeton University Press.

UNCTAD (2013a). *Global Value Chains and Development: Investment and Value Added Trade in the Global Economy*. New York: United Nations.

UNCTAD (2013b). *World Investment Report 2013: Global Value Chains: Investment and Trade for Development*. New York: United Nations.

Van Biesebroeck, J., and Sturgeon, T. J. (2010). 'Effects of the 2008–09 Crisis on the Automotive Industry in Developing Countries: A Global Value Chain Perspective', in O. Cattaneo, G. Gereffi, and C. Staritz (eds), *Global Value Chains in a Postcrisis World: A Development Perspective*. Washington: World Bank, 209–44.

Van Tulder, R., van Wijk, J., and Kolk, A. (2009). 'From Chain Liability to Chain Responsibility', *Journal of Business Ethics*, 85/2: 399–412.

Veltz, P. (1996). *Mondialisation, villes et territoires: L'Économie d'Archipel*. Paris: Presses Universitaires de France.

Vitols, S. (2002). 'Shareholder Value, Management Culture and Production Regimes in the Transformation of the German Chemical-Pharmaceutical Industry', *Competition and Change*, 6/3: 309–25.

Wade, R. (1990). *Governing the Market: Economic Theory and the Role of Government in East Asian Industrialization*. Princeton: Princeton University Press.

Wallerstein, I. (1974). 'The Rise and Future Demise of the World Capitalist System: Concepts for Comparative Analysi's, *Comparative Studies in Society and History*, 16/4: 387–415.

Walter, A., and Zhang, X. (2012) (eds). *East Asian Capitalism: Diversity, Continuity, and Change*. Oxford: Oxford University Press.

Wang, C. C., and Lin, G. C. S. (2013). 'Dynamics of innovation in a Globalizing China: Regional Environment, Inter-Firm Relations and Firm Attributes', *Journal of Economic Geography*, 13/3: 397–418.

Wei, Y. H. D., Zhou, Y., Sun, Y., and Lin, G. C. S. (2012). 'Production and R&D Networks of Foreign Ventures in China: Implications for Technological Dynamism and Regional Development', *Applied Geography*, 32/1: 106–18.

Weiss, L. (2014). *America Inc.? Innovation and Enterprise in the National Security State*. Ithaca, NY: Cornell University Press.

Werner, M. (2012). 'Beyond Upgrading: Gendered Labor and the Restructuring of Firms in the Dominican Republic', *Economic Geography*, 88/4: 403–22.

Whatmore, S., and Thorne, L. (1997). 'Nourishing Networks: Alternative Geographies of Food', in D. J. Goodman and M. J. Watts (eds), *Globalizing Food: Agrarian Questions and Global Restructuring*. London, Routledge, 287–304.

White, H. C. (1992). *Identity and Control: A Structural Theory of Social Action*, Princeton: Princeton University Press.

White, H. C. (2002). *Markets from Networks: Socioeconomic Models of Production*. Princeton: Princeton University Press.

Whitford, J. (2005). *The New Old Economy: Networks, Institutions, and the Organizational Transformation of American Manufacturing*. Oxford University Press: Oxford.

Whitley, R. (1992). *Business Systems in East Asia*. London: Sage.

Whitley, R. (1999). *Divergent Capitalisms*. New York: Oxford University Press.

Whitley, R. (2007). *Business Systems and Organizational Capabilities: The Institutional Structuring of Competitive Competences*. Oxford: Oxford University Press.

Whitley, R., and Kristensen P. H. (1996) (eds). *The Changing European Firm: Limits to Convergence*. Routledge: London.

Whitley, R., and Kristensen, P. H. (1997) (eds). *Governance at Work: The Social Regulation of Economic Relations in Europe*. Oxford University Press: Oxford.

Whittaker, D. H., Zhu, T., Sturgeon, T., Tsai, M. H., and Okita, T. (2010). 'Compressed Development', *Studies in Comparative International Development*, 45/4: 439–67.

Williamson, O. E. (1975). *Markets and Hierarchies: Analysis and Antitrust Implications*. New York: Free Press.

Williamson, O. E. (1985). *The Economic Institution of Capitalism*. New York: Free Press.

Wilson, B. R. (2013). 'Breaking the Chains: Coffee, Crisis, and Farmworker Struggle in Nicaragua', *Environment and Planning A*, 45/11: 2592–609.

Wilson, J. D. (2013). *Governing Global Production: Resource Networks in the Asia-Pacific Steel Industry*, New York: Palgrave.

Winter, S. G. (2008). 'Dynamic Capability as a Source of Change', in Alexander Ebner and Nikolaus Beck (eds), *The Institutions of the Market: Organizations, Social Systems, and Governance*. Oxford: Oxford University Press, 40–65.

Witt, M. A., and Redding, G. (2014) (eds). *The Oxford Handbook of Asian Business Systems*. Oxford: Oxford University Press.

Wong, J. (2011). *Betting on Biotech: Innovation and the Limits of Asia's Development State*. Ithaca, NY: Cornell University Press.

World Bank (1993). *The East Asian Miracle*. Oxford: Oxford University Press.

Wrigley, N., Coe, N. M., and Currah, A. (2005). 'Globalizing Retail: Conceptualizing the Distribution-Based TNC', *Progress in Human Geography*, 29/4: 437–57.

WTO and IDE-JETRO (2011). *Trade Patterns and Global Value Chains in East Asia: From Trade in Goods to Trade in Tasks*. Geneva and Tokyo: World Trade Organization and Institute of Developing Economies.

Yang, C. (2009). 'Strategic Coupling of Regional Development in Global Production Networks: Redistribution of Taiwanese Personal Computer Investment from the Pearl River Delta to the Yangtze River Delta, China', *Regional Studies*, 43/3: 385–408.

Yang, C. (2013). 'From Strategic Coupling to Recoupling and Decoupling: Restructuring Global Production Networks and Regional Evolution in China', *European Planning Studies*, 21/7: 1046–63.

Yang, C. (2014). 'Market Rebalancing of Global Production Networks in the Post-Washington Consensus Globalizing Era: Transformation of Export-Oriented Development in China', *Review of International Political Economy*, 21/1: 130–56.

Yang, D., and Coe, N. M. (2009). 'The Governance of Global Production Networks and Regional Development: A Case Study of Taiwanese Production Networks', *Growth and Change*, 40/1: 30–53.

Yang, D. Y., Hsu, J.-Y., and Ching, C.-H. (2009). 'Revisiting the Silicon Island: The Geographically Varied "Strategic Coupling" in the Development of High-Technology Parks, Taiwan', *Regional Studies*, 43/3: 369–84.

Yeung, H. W.-C. (1994). 'Critical Reviews of Geographical Perspectives on Business Organizations and the Organization of Production: Towards a Network Approach', *Progress in Human Geography*, 18/4: 460–90.

Yeung, H. W.-C. (1998). *Transnational Corporations and Business Networks: Hong Kong Firms in the ASEAN Region*. Routledge Advances in Asia Pacific Business 9. London: Routledge.

Yeung, H. W.-C. (2004). *Chinese Capitalism in a Global Era: Towards Hybrid Capitalism*. London: Routledge.

Yeung, H. W.-C. (2005a). 'Rethinking Relational Economic Geography', *Transactions of the Institute of British Geographers*, NS 30/1: 37–51.

Yeung, H. W.-C. (2005b). 'The Firm as Social Networks: An Organizational Perspective', *Growth and Change*, 36/3: 307–28.

Yeung, H. W.-C. (2007a). 'From Followers to Market Leaders: Asian Electronics Firms in the Global Economy', *Asia Pacific Viewpoint*, 48/1: 1–25.

Yeung, H. W.-C. (2007b) (ed.), *Handbook of Research on Asian Business*. Cheltenham: Edward Elgar.

Yeung, H. W.-C. (2008). 'Perspectives on Inter-Organizational Relations in Economic Geography', in S. Cropper, M. Ebers, C. Huxham, and P. Smith Ring (eds), *The Oxford Handbook of Inter-Organizational Relations*. Oxford: Oxford University Press, 473–501.

Yeung, H. W.-C. (2009a) (ed.). 'Special Issue on "Local and Regional Development in Asia"', *Regional Studies*, 43/3: 325–512.

Yeung, H. W.-C. (2009b). 'Regional Development and the Competitive Dynamics of Global Production Networks: An East Asian Perspective', *Regional Studies*, 43/3: 325–51.

Yeung, H. W.-C. (2009c). 'Transnational Corporations, Global Production Networks, and Urban and Regional Development', *Growth and Change*, 40/2: 197–226.

Yeung, H. W.-C. (2009d). 'The Rise of East Asia: An Emerging Challenge to the Study of International Political Economy', in Mark Blyth (ed.), *Routledge Handbook of International Political Economy*. London: Routledge, 201–15.

Yeung, H. W.-C. (2009e). 'Transnationalizing Entrepreneurship: A Critical Agenda for Economic Geography', *Progress in Human Geography*, 33/2: 210–35.

Yeung, H. W.-C. (2010) (ed.). *Globalizing Regional Development in East Asia: Production Networks, Clusters, and Entrepreneurship*. London: Routledge.

Yeung, H. W.-C. (2013). 'Globalizing Competition in Asia: An Evolutionary Perspective', in M. W. Dowdle, J. S. Gillespie, and I. Maher (eds), *Asian Capitalism and the Regulation of Competition: Towards a Regulatory Geography of Global Competition Law*, Cambridge: Cambridge University Press, 265–82.

Yeung, H. W.-C. (2014). 'Governing the Market in a Globalizing Era: Developmental States, Global Production Networks, and Inter-Firm Dynamics in East Asia', *Review of International Political Economy*, 21/1: 70–101.

Yeung, H. W.-C. (2015a). 'Regional Development in the Global Economy: A Dynamic Perspective of Strategic Coupling in Global Production Networks', *Regional Science Policy & Practice*, 7/1.

Yeung, H. W.-C. (2015b). 'Production Networks: Global and Local', in G. L. Clark, M. P. Feldman, M. S. Gertler, and D. Wójcik (eds), *The New Oxford Handbook of Economic Geography*. Oxford: Oxford University Press.

Yeung, H. W.-C., and Coe, N. M. (2015). 'Toward a Dynamic Theory of Global Production Networks', *Economic Geography*, 91/1: 29–58.

Yeung, H. W.-C., and Lin, G. C. S. (2003). 'Theorizing Economic Geographies of Asia', *Economic Geography*, 79/2: 107–28.

Zhang, J., and Peck, J. (2013). 'A Variety of Capitalism . . . with Chinese Characteristics?', *Journal of Economic Geography*, 13/3: 357–96.

Zhang, X., and Whitley, R. (2013). 'Changing Macro-Structural Varieties of East Asian capitalism', *Socio-Economic Review*, 11/2: 301–36.

Zhou, Y., Sun, Y., Wei, Y. H. D., and Lin, G. C. S. (2011). 'De-Centering "Spatial Fix": Patterns of Territorialization and Regional Technological Dynamism of ICT Hubs In China', *Journal of Economic Geography*, 11/1: 119–50.

Zhu, S., and Pickles, J. (2014). 'Bring in, Go up, Go West, Go out: Upgrading, Regionalization, and Delocalization in China's Apparel Production Networks', *Journal of Contemporary Asia*, 44/1: 36–63.

Author Index

Subject Index